W9-CMR-210

Reading to Learn and Writing to Teach

LITERACY STRATEGIES FOR ONLINE WRITING INSTRUCTION

Beth L. Hewett

Past Chair, CCCC Committee for Effective Practices in Online Writing Instruction

President & Educational Consultant, Defend & Publish, LLC

Bedford/St. Martin's   BOSTON ◆ NEW YORK

For Bedford/St. Martin's
Vice President, Editorial, Macmillan Higher Education Humanities: Edwin Hill
Editorial Director for English and Music: Karen S. Henry
Publisher for Composition: Leasa Burton
Executive Editor for Professional Development: Karita France dos Santos
Developmental Editor: Rachel C. Childs
Publishing Services Manager: Andrea Cava
Production Manager: Joe Ford
Project Management: DeMasi Design and Publishing Services
Senior Art Director: Anna Palchik
Text Design: Ewing Systems; DeMasi Design and Publishing Services
Cover Design: William Boardman
Composition: Achorn International, Inc.
Printing and Binding: RR Donnelley and Sons

Copyright © 2015 by Bedford/St. Martin's

All rights reserved. No part of this book may be reproduced, stored in a retrieval system, or transmitted in any form or by any means, electronic, mechanical, photocopying, recording, or otherwise, except as may be expressly permitted by the applicable copyright statutes or in writing by the Publisher.

0   9   8   7   6   5
f   e   d   c   b   a

For information, write: Bedford/St. Martin's, 75 Arlington Street, Boston, MA 02116   (617-399-4000)

ISBN 978-1-4576-6399-4

Acknowledgments
De Zengotita, Thomas, "Why we worship 'American Idol,'" from the *Los Angeles Times*, February 12, 2006. Copyright © 2006 by Thomas de Zengotita. Reprinted by permission of the author.

From *Comprehension Connections: Bridges to Strategic Reading* by Tanny McGregor. Copyright © 2007 by Tanny McGregor. Published by Heinemann, Portsmouth, NH. Reprinted by permission of the publisher.

Preface

Digital tools have changed the writing game. Any of us—teachers and students alike—may read and write more often and in greater quantity than in years past as we use instant message (IM) chat, send text and e-mail messages, blog public arguments and personal memoirs, prepare reports, write letters, post random thoughts on Facebook, review products on websites, respond to others' comments in a number of social networking venues, and generally live lives constructed in text. We need to be able to read and write flexibly among home, work, school, and community environments in this digitally influenced world (Cleary 2013, 661).

Online writing instruction (OWI)—whether it occurs fully online or in hybrid (often called "blended") settings—takes advantage of digital tools for teaching reading and writing. Its intense focus on using writing to teach writing renders OWI as traditional writing instruction on steroids.

Both student and instructor literacy needs are high in OWI environments because student preparation for reading to learn and instructor preparation for writing to teach is too low. Text-based challenges in reading and writing may account for some of the frustration that educators express about online learning, particularly expressions that compare the traditional setting with the online venue and find OWI distinctly lacking. Because focus has been on time flexibility and affect via body/face/voice—leading some people to avoid text and to add audio/video to online courses—it seems that the cognitive components of reading and writing have been overlooked generally. However, when the instructional venue is primarily text-based, reading and writing skills become more crucial and require stronger and even different literacy muscles. This book provides a series of strategies that can aid in pumping up students' reading-to-learn skills and power and in filling out instructors' writing-to-teach skills and strength.

Although some educators might see these text-rich challenges as a reason to avoid OWI—or at least to circumvent its inherently text-based nature—it cannot be denied that OWI, particularly in the asynchronous text-based modality, is commonplace. Each year, more students opt for online writing courses (OWCs) over onsite courses for a variety of reasons (e.g., finances, geographical limitations, and/or access to a particular institution). It is our job as researchers and educators to find ways to help OWI work well for the wide variety of students who find that online instruction is their best way into higher education.

The reading comprehension themes of metacognition, schema, inference, questioning, relevance, visualizing, analyzing, and synthesizing, outlined in Part Two of this book, are central to strong reading skills at every step—from elementary school through college and into the workplace. Students benefit from conscious reminders and reinforcement of these concepts especially in the still unfamiliar online educational environment. Certainly, reading and writing problems are not encountered only in an online setting. Students' reading problems in OWI most likely occur in any setting, but they are exacerbated and exaggerated online because of the high literacy load and because oral/aural/visual access to the teacher or tutor is limited by the environment.

The concepts of instructional writing strategies that include writing with semantic integrity to develop helpful instructional feedback, clear assignments, and comprehensible interpersonal communications, outlined in Part Three of this book, also are central writing skills for instructors. Although teachers' and tutors' instructional writing problems also occur in traditional, onsite settings, they, too, are exacerbated in the text-heavy—nay, text-rich—digital setting. Nonetheless, educators in both settings would benefit from the kinds of literacy strategies that this book recommends.

Audience for the Book

Frankly, although the subject of this book is OWI and the more robust literacy needs of online writing students and teachers, almost everything discussed is applicable to strong onsite writing instruction, too. Many instructors, for example, teach primarily onsite yet also use online platforms to post instructional materials and resources. The explanations and exercises in Parts Two and Three certainly can be applied usefully in those and other onsite classes. If OWI is like traditional, onsite writing instruction on steroids, as I indicated at the beginning of this Preface, then all teachers of writing can benefit from being reminded of their students' needs to transfer and build up their reading skills for postsecondary writing course purposes and of their own needs to continually develop their writing skills for teaching purposes.

The use of the term *OWI* is not meant to suggest only first-year writing (FYW) courses although I certainly do mean those. Writing-intensive disciplinary courses, business and technical writing courses, and upper-level writing courses also are held in online settings. In my experience, it is not unusual to work with even third- or fourth-year-level students who have suboptimal reading and writing skills. Much of what this book addresses can be applied to OWI at all of those levels and for a wide variety of genres.

This book is a resource for writing teachers to use—to pick and choose exercises and activities from—rather than a textbook for undergraduate students. At the graduate student level, especially where teacher preparation includes studying OWI or literacy in general, this book would operate more as a textbook for discussion and practice. That said, secondary school teachers who teach writing online may find some of these literacy strategies useful for their own students' reading needs and their writing instructional purposes.

Regarding terminology with respect to educational professionals, I typically use both *teachers* and *instructors* interchangeably; however, there are occasions — particularly in Part Three — where the advice also applies to tutors. For the greatest benefit to readers, therefore, at times I specifically use *teacher* or *tutor* to delineate these two roles regarding the special needs of each.

Organization of the Book

One goal of this book is to provide a first step in what I hope will become an ongoing collaboration among educators regarding the foundational roles of reading and writing in OWI. To this end, the book's organization addresses a brief theoretical background in Part One. Chapter 1 considers first the nontraditional nature and digital needs of OWI students. Then, Chapter 2 examines how and why both students and educators have literacy problems that must be addressed for effective OWI to occur. Chapter 3 offers practical considerations for teaching literacy strategies, with access issues chief among them.

In Part Two, Chapters 4 through 11 introduce eight literacy comprehension strategies to use with students, including reminders of the many reading skills that they learned as young children. These strategies are treated in the order in which they are introduced: metacognition, schema, inference, questioning, relevance, visualizing, analyzing, and synthesizing. I envision a teacher evaluating students' reading (and writing) needs in a particular course and then choosing among the comprehension strategies to find a few that might help students to transfer the needed skills or develop their weaker literacy muscles. The example strategies are available for use as they are presented or for adaptation and change to suit an individual teacher's needs. Such use naturally is dependent on the length of the course and a given teacher's autonomy in adding to the course material.

Part Two also provides approaches for improving literacy skills at the transition point into higher education where the convergence of new educational opportunities and technology in the course setting can helpfully disrupt old habits and thinking. These approaches are scaffolded such that teachers can address literacy skills chapter by chapter or they can skip around to consider only those skills that their students most seem to need.

Part Three (Chapters 12 through 15) provides instructors with specific strategies for writing to teach students in the online setting. Given the writing-intensive nature of OWI from an instructional perspective, teachers and tutors benefit from explicit strategies for improving their written communications.

Despite the separation of Parts Two and Three as focused on students and teachers respectively, both reading and writing strategies are interwoven in these parts of the book.

Acknowledgments

I am grateful to Denise Wydra, Leasa Burton, and Karita France dos Santos, who believed in this book enough to bring it into the Bedford/St. Martin's professional development family. Every writer needs an editor, so I give profound thanks to Rachel Childs, who found the pearls and helped to showcase them in a straightforward and reader-friendly manner. Any errors that remain are the result of my own stubbornness.

This book would not have been possible without the generous advice of many colleagues. I especially appreciate the willingness of neuroscientist Maryanne Wolf and reading specialist Tanny McGregor, both of whom offered their rare time and spoke with me about how their thinking and practices translated into digital reading concerns and for OWI specifically. Andrew Cavanaugh and David Taylor, colleagues from University of Maryland University College, provided example teaching scenarios for the book, and Andy graciously reviewed a draft, offering critical assessment that surely has improved the book. Others whose reviews sharpened my thinking and have made this book more accessible are Susan Dominguez, Letizia Guglielmo, Emily Nye, and Scott Warnock. My undying appreciation goes to Scott, who has been co-chair of the CCCC Committee for Effective Practices in OWI with me; we have had many developmental meetings about OWI, and I respect his special knowledge. My appreciation, too, to the entire OWI Committee, all of whom have helped me to grow and deepen my understanding of OWI student and teacher needs and as I have considered and theorized about OWI. Others who specifically have offered advice about this book include Cheryl Ball, Linda Adler-Kassner, Kevin Eric DePew, and Jarrod Brown. My colleague Allison Warner, particularly, taught me about the cognitive leaps that students need to make in OWI courses.

Finally, I want to thank my mother, Daryl Lengyel, and my husband, Paul, for taking up the slack as I worked on this book for days on end. My son, Russ, and daughter-in-law, Tara, listened to and commented on my sometimes unformed ideas, which gave me the space to let ideas develop. Special appreciation to my dearest friend, Sue, and her husband, Rick, for their humor and caring when writing simply stumped me.

Beth L. Hewett

Contents

Introduction

Consider this analogy. A gardener who is experienced with tomatoes knows how to use a trowel; he knows how to plant, stake, prune, weed, and water the tomatoes — caring for them to get beautiful, ripe fruit. When this gardener decides he wants to grow peach trees, he uses the same skills to plant, stake, prune, weed, and water them. While the necessary skills are similar, however, the tools must change for this more rigorous job: a shovel instead of a trowel for deeper holes; thicker, longer stakes for the taller plants; pruning shears instead of clippers for tougher fibers; and a more sophisticated irrigation plan for the larger plot of land in which the peach trees are to grow. In addition to different tools, the gardener needs to be physically stronger to plant and care for those peach trees. He needs to develop amped-up muscles — bigger biceps and more powerful shoulders.

In a comparable way, teaching writing in a traditional, face-to-face (or *onsite*) setting and in an online setting uses the same basic skills but requires different tools and muscles. Both venues for writing instruction require that the teachers be familiar with composition theories and be able to engage effective instructional strategies. For instance, in either setting, teachers still need to instruct students in how to analyze and write to an audience; they still need to teach students how to find a subject that is meaningful and content that addresses the purpose of the writing. Fundamentally, online writing instruction (OWI) is about teaching writing. Whether the teaching occurs in the asynchronous (conducted and delivered with time delays) or the synchronous (conducted and delivered in real time) modality, it is about using effective instructional strategies to help students see their writing as process-based, argumentative or expository, audience-focused, responsible, and creative prose. To be a good composition teacher in online settings, one first has to be an effective writing instructor — period. Despite differences

1

inflected by technology, good composition instruction defines OWI as much as it does in any traditional setting.

Whether onsite or online, teachers are still teaching reading and writing and students are still learning these skills. But the generally higher literacy load (i.e., how much a student or teacher must read or write, see Griffin and Minter 2013) requires different tools, theoretical approaches, and working styles. In particular, students will need to strengthen their reading muscles and teachers will need to train different writing muscles. Students, for instance, will read and write thousands of words per class if they are writing and responding to online discussion posts and essays (Warnock 2009, 71)[1]; this is more writing than occurs in most onsite classes. And the teacher who produces a one-page syllabus for an onsite writing course can add to or take away from it when necessary and explain the need orally, but from the start in an OWI setting, the syllabus must be a more complete, specific, and clear contract because students will be scheduling their family and work lives with course completion in mind, leading to a somewhat more independent course schedule than in most onsite classes.[2] These situations are anchored in the digital nature of OWI, of course, but even more so in its uniquely reading- and writing-centric nature.

This book reflects my belief that the increased literacy load of reading and writing is the most crucial difference between OWI and onsite writing instruction. The key to success in OWI is traditional literacy instruction with a digital twist that acknowledges the various challenges of reading and writing online. Students especially must read better to understand what they are being taught while teachers must write better—with semantic integrity—to convey clearly what they are teaching about writing. Hence, reading and writing well requires amped-up muscles like those of the peach tree gardener.

[handwritten margin notes: AT the SAME TIME, mail these skills are declining; need for mor online supports!]

WORRIES ABOUT OWI

For the past eight years, I have been a leader of the Conference on College Composition and Communication's (CCCC) Committee for Effective

---

[1]Indeed, in a study of student discussion posts, Scott Warnock, Kenneth Bingham, Dan Driscoll, Jennifer Fromal, and Nicholas Rouse (2012) find that students who posted discussion comments the earliest and with the most words also tended to be more self-motivated throughout the course and earned the highest grades.

[2]See Warnock (2009, 38-47) for a helpful description of an OWI syllabus's crucial components. For OWI, often, teachers not only need to produce the syllabus as a downloadable document but they also need to post it a second time in separate components with clickable hyperlinks that make accessing it online easier for students.

Practices[3] in OWI. I have helped to set the agenda, shape the focus, and conduct seminal research into OWI. From this work, I have learned that educators typically recognize that OWI benefits students by forcing them to use writing to communicate with each other and the teacher, which naturally increases the amount of (hopefully) thoughtful writing they do. However, there remain some concerns regarding the perceived deficits of OWI when it is contrasted with teaching and learning in onsite settings. Sometimes, online writing courses (OWCs) are conducted through synchronous technology that enables interpersonally sensitive and real-time interactions, but more often they are conducted through asynchronous technology that is less interpersonally connected and less time-immediate. Without the in-person connections produced by body/face/voice interactions in traditional teaching settings, we may worry that online teaching and learning are dehumanized. In fact, to accommodate the desire for positive affect in OWI, many educators have experimented with technology for simulating face-to-face interaction — from using simple emoticons to assigning asynchronous peer group discussions to adding real-time voice or audio/video components (for example, see Warnock 2008).

The more critical difference in writing instruction that happens online, of course, is that when the body/face/voice connections are removed from the instructional environment, most of the work needs to be accomplished textually through the common literacy skills of reading and writing. Perhaps this difference seems so obvious as to not merit discussion, but even more than time shifts and affective relationships, cognition may be altered when body/face/voice connections are removed from the learning setting if one's reading skills are poorly developed or the written instruction is unclear.

While educators know that reading is necessary for developing writing skill, reading and writing become more closely linked in OWI than in other learning environments. Particularly in asynchronous text-based and synchronous chat-based learning environments, reading is crucial to writing instruction because the instruction both *is written* and *is written about the act of writing*. As such, students must read and interpret the reading to make use of it in their discussions, written drafts, and revisions.

Without body/face/voice intervention (including that of audio/video recordings), instructional technology necessarily relies on alphabetic text to convey the writing instruction. Even though synchronous audio-/video-based technologies can be used online, much of what is taught continues to be done through text. Furthermore, despite students' potential preference for the visual (Jukes, McCain, and Crockett 2010), text is not going away — particularly when the skill to be learned is writing. Although multiple modalities and media are encouraged in some college-level writing

---

[3] The CCCC Committee for Effective Practices in OWI hereafter is called the CCCC OWI Committee in this book.

courses (DePew 2015; Blair 2015), alphabetic text currently remains the linchpin for writing instruction. While digital visual and aural media have important rhetorical qualities for twenty-first-century communication and they should be taught, traditional text-based activities are far from passé. Reading and writing are deeply embedded in school and work experiences. Without a full awareness of text's place in OWI and the explicit teaching it invites, many OWI students will struggle with their reading and writing.

THE PERILS OF LEARNING ONLINE

In *Going the Distance: Online Education in the United States, 2011*, Elaine Allen and Jeff Seaman state that "over 6.1 million students were taking at least one online course during the fall 2010 term; an increase of 560,000 students over the number reported the previous year" (2011, 4). Proportionately speaking, that is an increase "from fewer than 1 in 10 in 2002 to nearly one-third by 2010, with the number of online students growing from 1.6 million to over 6.1 million over the same period — an 18.3 percent compound annual growth rate" (Allen, Seamen, Lederman, and Jaschik 2012, 3). Although they do not indicate success or failure rates, these statistics point to an abundance of online students who want to take advantage of digital education as anytime and anywhere learning.

Learning online is hard for many students, however. Too many students struggle with the basic literacy skills, self-engagement, and discipline necessary to learn in the digital environment. According to researchers Alan Sapp and James Simon (2005), there is a disproportionate failure and attrition rate in online classes in comparison to more traditional onsite learning environments:

> In addition to high student attrition (i.e., students who do not complete courses do not earn passing grades), students in online courses often report higher levels of dissatisfaction than students enrolled in equivalent face-to-face courses (Shermis, Mzumara, Olson, & Harrington, 2001). Other researchers add that online courses tend to leave students with higher instances of unfinished learning goals, a sense of decreased importance of teacher feedback, and a lack of engagement in the learning process (Allgood, 2001; Monroe, 2002). . . . Our study indicates that students are consistently less likely to earn passing grades due to drop out, failure to complete, or faculty evaluation in online sections of two writing courses compared to face-to-face sections of the same courses. (472)

There are other reasons that student persistence, success, and satisfaction may be low for some students. In a study that analyzed other research into online student attrition and success, Hannah Street (2010) finds that personal (i.e., self-efficacy, self-determination, autonomy, and time management), environmental (i.e., family support, organizational support, and technical support), and course-related factors (i.e., relevance and design) all affect students' decisions to drop out or persist in their online classes. In another study of online student satisfaction, Yu-Chun Kuo, Andrew E. Walker, Brian R. Belland, and Kerstin E. E. Schroder (2013) report that the most significant predictors of student satisfaction in online learning are learner-instructor interaction, learner-content interaction, and Internet self-efficacy, while learner-learner interaction (i.e., peer group and/or collaborative learning) and self-regulated learning are not predictive indicators.[7] Sapp and Simon's (2005) literature review certainly suggests difficulties for some students in connecting with the intended learning (learner-content interaction) and with their teachers (learner-instructor interaction), who traditionally have been their guides through learning but have been rendered somewhat invisible online. Indeed, Chia-Ling Kuo, Hongbo Song, Renee Smith, and Teresa Franklin theorize from a study of online student satisfaction that "even in online learning, face-to-face meetings with instructors and learners are imperative to facilitate both social and academic interactions between student-instructor, student-student, student-content, and student-outside resources" (2007, 93). Their belief that face-to-face interaction is necessary sheds light on why some students may need extra preparation for online learning and why teachers may need to learn other ways to reach out to students such as by phone or such voice-over-the-Internet software as Skype.

Some of the student populations with troubled histories in online courses include "males, Black students, and students with lower levels of academic preparation" (Xu and Jaggars 2013, 23). These difficulties may be connected to the access issues — especially socioeconomic challenges — discussed in Part One of this book. Di Xu and Shanna Smith Jaggars (2013) research and report on student adaptability in online settings in "Adaptability to Online Learning: Differences across Types of Students and Academic Subject Areas." Although they studied only community college students in Washington state (and completely failed to address students with physical and learning challenges, multilingual students, and students with socioeconomic disadvantages), their research supports "the notion that students are not homogeneous in their adaptability to the online delivery format and may therefore have substantially different outcomes for online learning" (27). In fact:

> These patterns also suggest that performance gaps between key demographic groups already observed in face-to-face classrooms (e.g., gaps between male and female students, and gaps between White and ethnic minority students) are exacerbated in online courses. This is troubling from an equity perspective: If this pattern holds true across other states and educational sectors, it would imply that the continued expansion of online learning could strengthen, rather than ameliorate, educational inequity. (27)

Of course, it is likely that some students who enroll in online courses might not have been accepted in various institutions for comparable onsite courses, which potentially skews some of these data. For example, some open enrollment, onsite institutions with online components and online institutions, such as those developed particularly with working adult learners in mind, do not ask for SAT or ACT scores or other indicators of academic potential beyond a high school diploma.

Another likely reason that students struggle in online courses, according to Arthur Levine and Diane Dean who wrote *Generation on a Tightrope: A Portrait of Today's College Student*, is that "digital natives are being taught by digital immigrants in analog universities" (2012, 49). Such reasoning, explained in Chapters 1 and 2, contends that contemporary students of all ages—but especially those in their midtwenties and younger—may find college and university, as currently conceived, to be anachronistic. Indeed, according to Levine and Dean's 2009 undergraduate survey:

> Four out of five say undergraduate education would be improved if their classes made greater use of technology (78 percent) and if their professors knew more about how to use it (78 percent). A majority (52 percent) want more blended instruction, combining online and in-person classes. A third (33 percent) go even further, asking for more courses to be completely online. (2012, 47)

It is ironic that students ask for more online course offerings in light of the data that they struggle with them. One reason for this paradox is the myth or illusion that online courses offer an easier learning experience as evidenced by advertising from such popular online institutions as the University of Maryland University College, DeVry University, and University of Phoenix. Nonetheless, many students want more technology use in their classrooms from a desire to replicate some of the features of their intense use of digital tools in other parts of their lives.

While it may be true that contemporary higher education is somewhat anachronistic, particularly given the astonishingly rapid advance of technologies that are constructing a new digital world, "analog" universities certainly still have useful knowledge and skills to teach—among them, how to use the new technologies critically through good, old-fashioned reading and writing skills. Rather than looking to scrap the analog for the digital, educators need to consider the values of each and begin to build universities that symbiotically take advantage of these strengths in light of students' current and future needs.

THE NEEDS OF ONLINE WRITING STUDENTS

Online learning is not the same across disciplines. One thing that makes OWI different from most online approaches to disciplinary material is that composition is about both content (i.e., what writing is and why) and skill (i.e., how to write well). Thus, students cannot merely read disciplinary material and take tests. A lecture or other content-based pedagogy, while occasionally helpful for providing information, is an insufficient approach for an OWC. One cannot learn to write better or differently without actually practicing writing. Instead, writing instruction philosophy acknowledges social construction theory in that students are presumed to be able to teach each other, need frequent practice and revision that receives feedback, and need to write for meaningful purposes and real audiences. All of these approaches can be enacted in an OWI setting.

According to Xu and Jaggars (2013), different academic subjects appear to attract students with similar online adaptability levels. Additionally:

> regardless of a particular student's own adaptability to the online environment, her performance in an online course may suffer if her classmates adapt poorly. English and social science were two academic subjects that seemed to attract a high proportion of less-adaptable students, thereby introducing negative peer effects. Perhaps in online courses with a high proportion of less-adaptable students, interpersonal interactions and group projects are more challenging and less effective, which then negatively impacts everyone's course performance; or perhaps instructors devote more attention to students who are struggling most to adapt, leaving the remaining students with less support in their own efforts to adapt. (24)

This finding may help to explain why students in so many OWI classes do not perform to the levels educators would like to see. A strong peer effect — particularly in OWI where interpersonal and group-based interactions are required and the failure of some peers affects the whole class — might explain somewhat high attrition and failure rates. Chapter 1's discussion of the challenges that digital-era undergraduates — both adolescent and adult — experience in using educational technology may help to explain Xu and Jaggars' findings with respect to OWI. Additionally, although social construction posits a positive peer effect for writing instruction, both the nature of online reading and writing (see Chapter 2) and of unrealistic expectations for collaboration (see Chapter 3) may help in understanding why students struggle in online settings.

In the CCCC OWI Committee's report, *The State of the Art of OWI* (2011), national survey respondents reported attrition rates for OWI community college students as higher than students from four-year universities. The CCCC OWI Committee attributes these findings to the community college's generally higher at-risk population, the economics of the community college student, and the mission of open enrollment (20). Although the most commonly reported rates of student attrition were in the 1–10 percent and 11–20 percent ranges for fully online students, up to 25 percent of respondents reported attrition rates of more than 20 percent (17). The highest attrition rates were reported for community college and four-year university students. These self-reported numbers may be low, however. In one respondent's reply to an open-ended question about hybrid courses, he reported an attrition rate of 50 percent statewide in OWCs (45). Anecdotally, in my own OWCs at both the first-year writing (FYW) and higher levels, I have found a 30–40 percent attrition rate to be common among both adolescent and adult students. Additionally, some students either fail to complete the work by the end of the term or do so at a suboptimal level; their failure typically is not included in official attrition rates. We might presume that these attrition and failure rates are at least partially affected by open enrollment policies that encourage underprepared students who otherwise might not attempt college work.

June Griffin and Deborah Minter (2013) recently studied *literacy load*, which is their term for the amount of reading and writing that both teacher and student must handle in writing courses. They compare the required reading of only the students in fully online and traditional onsite writing courses "governed by the same course guidelines (albeit with different instructors and different syllabi)." Griffin and Minter find that "the reading load of the online classes was more than 2.75 times greater than the face-to-face classes" (14). These numbers for student reading alone make sense when one considers that all communication—outside the rare phone call—usually occurs textually. Add the teacher's reading load to the student's reading load and consider the writing both must do. In *Teaching Writing Online: How and Why*, Scott Warnock (2009) estimates that he writes more than 30,000 words per class per term (6). Because of OWI's higher amount of reading and writing in comparison to other disciplinary subjects, both students and teachers spend far more time involved in text than in a comparable onsite course.

What kinds of reading and writing scenarios require student attention in any composition course? Writing students read nonfiction and fiction content as source material for writing. They must attend to instructional content about writing itself, some written by the instructor and others provided by the writing program or textbook authors. Further, writing students must read assignments and directions. All writing students have such writing tasks as essay and report drafts, typically revised in response to feedback. They often write or orally provide responses to peer writing and/or discussion questions provided by the teacher.

However, in addition to these common tasks, OWI students in both fully online and hybrid settings regularly are asked to read:

- written peer discussions (also called *conferences*) and feedback;
- written instructional response (sometimes called *conferences*) to essay drafts and final assignments; and
- interpersonal communications with instructors and peers (e.g., e-mail[4] and IM chat, as well as typed annotations, marginal comments, social media posts, and journal entries).

---

[4]According to Allen et al. (2012), in a survey of 4,564 faculty members, almost 60 percent of those who taught hybrid and fully online courses reported receiving more than ten student

OWI students also must write:

- responses to peer writing, including abstracts of peer writing and marginal comments that pinpoint specific sentences or paragraphs;
- responses to discussion questions provided by the teacher or peers, including responsive discussion about these readings; and
- interpersonal communications with instructors and peers to include e-mails, IM chat, marginal comments, social media posts, and journal entries.

Furthermore, students must read any written clarifications on assignments and other instructions; these run the risk of becoming lengthy or repetitive text-based dialogues when both students and their instructors are confined to written communication.

What kinds of writing scenarios require instructor attention? For both an onsite and online class, most writing teachers need to write instructional content about writing, assignments, directions, and instructional response to essay drafts and final assignments. Sometimes the written feedback is supplemented or substituted by onsite conferences and/or audio/video feedback. Similarly, most instructors must read essay drafts and revisions — sometimes multiple times for each student for each assignment as required or allowed by various writing programs. Additionally, instructors regularly choose nonfiction and fiction content as source material for student writing. Their choices of this material and oral or written explanations about the reading necessary to use it can set students up for success or failure.

However, OWI instructors in both fully online and hybrid settings also must write:

- instructive guidance to and feedback for written peer discussions;
- interpersonal communications with students to include e-mails, IM chat, marginal comments, social media posts, and journal entries; and
- clarifications on written assignments/instructions.

They typically also must read (and respond to):

- written and posted student responses to peer writing and/or discussion questions, and
- interpersonal communications with individual students and groups.

Indeed, whatever would be communicated orally to onsite students typically is communicated online using text — except for those cases where teachers

---

e-mails daily while only about 28 percent of those who taught onsite reported that many (30). Adding to their literacy load was the perceived or required need of 90 percent of the surveyed faculty to respond to such e-mail within twenty-four hours (29).

use audio/video media. Any course with a textbook or required readings will involve similar reading amounts whether the course is conducted onsite or online. When online instructors provide additional reading material designed to mitigate questions they might have answered orally in an onsite setting, however, they might need to write or rewrite those materials and students must read them. Of course, if there is no additional instructional material, that aspect of the literacy load is lessened. And when teachers in an onsite setting provide only written feedback to writing, avoiding face-to-face conferencing, for example, their literacy load is increased by this choice. Nonetheless, the overall higher literacy load in OWI is thought- and time-intensive, and it calls for students and teachers to have strong literacy skills to advance the goals of the course.

In most fully online OWCs (as opposed to hybrid OWCs), students typically do not have any body/face/voice connections to their instructors. And instructors typically do not have such cues as questions or blank expressions that would reveal lack of clarity or understanding to prompt them to rephrase and reframe their content, instructions, assignments, advice, and critique. (Here, affect cues would be beneficial because they can suggest lack of knowledge or understanding.) Hence, in the fully online setting, without an oral/aural/visual signal of student comprehension, instructors do not necessarily know what it is that particular students do not or will not understand no matter how many times they read it — if they read it at all. In such a setting, teachers might discern a problem when the writing fails to reflect a deep understanding of a topic (Warnock 2009, 65), when resource patchwriting[5] occurs, or when no revision happens. At any of those points, however, it may be too late to help the student for that particular assignment or term.

Complicating this picture is the reality of an increasingly digital world that not only requires people to become technologically literate but also introduces even infants to technology. The technology that many educators currently are learning to use in instructional settings is ordinary — even old-fashioned — to many students who have grown up with it. Digital media are exciting, fast-paced, and natural — even necessary — to students' lives. However, while many students may have learned to use technology for communication, social interaction, games, information seeking, and even writing,

---

[5]Patchwriting occurs when a source is copied closely with some words changed; sometimes words are merely exchanged with synonyms, and the paraphrase is too close to the original. Sentences alone may be lifted from the original with little attention to the entire text's meaning. Although often used by inexperienced writers, conveying that the writer has not read or does not fully understand the text, patchwriting may or may not be treated as plagiarism when it clearly demonstrates that the student is at an early stage of learning source use and citation. See Rebecca Moore Howard, Tricia Serviss, and Tanya K. Rodrigue (2010).

few have used it deliberately in fully online and hybrid instructional settings to improve a literacy skill. In essence, their uses of technology are relatively unconnected to formal education. Making this connection requires consciousness about transferring one's skills as well as increased flexibility and endurance when writing longer and deeper texts.

Ian Jukes, Ted McCain, and Lee Crockett (2010), authors of *Understanding the Digital Generation: Teaching and Learning in the New Digital Landscape*, claim that twenty-first-century students still are being taught in nineteenth-century classrooms with twentieth-century methods, and their claim seems apt in some ways. Onsite writing classes sometimes still engage lecture rather than workshop and they may not be led by the writing that students do. A walk down almost any English department hallway will bear out this observation. It remains all too easy to teach in a centralized manner onsite. Even though OWI naturally encourages a decentralized setting because of its call for interactive and student-involved instruction, some teachers still manage to make OWCs lecture-like. To the degree that Jukes et al. are correct about the nature of our students — if not of our teaching practices — the college students commonly called "traditional" because of their younger chronological ages when they begin college really are not traditional in terms of their experiences with various technologies. They are the new digital-era students who often expect to use digital tools in their classes but may not have the necessary skills to do so well. And the students commonly called "nontraditional" because of their older chronological ages and different life experiences have different challenges per their own introduction to digital technologies for educational and workplace purposes. In fact, some chronologically younger students who we might suppose to be steeped in digital technology are remarkably deficient in their technology experiences and some older students who have learned to use digital technology through practice or hit-and-miss opportunities are far more comfortable with educational technology.

I take the position in this book that all of these students are *nontraditional* in that their experiences with digital technology make them different from the students instructors once knew and that may still inhabit the imagination. As described in Chapter 1, all students now have qualities relative to a digital world that are nontraditional to traditional college expectations. One day — perhaps very soon — students and educators will recognize educational uses of digital technology as standard, regular, and common. Until then, however, the varied yet inherently digital experiences of OWI students truly make them nontraditional to educators.

PART ONE

OWI and Literacy Needs

1

The Nontraditional, Digital-Era Student Remixed

WHO ARE CONTEMPORARY OWI STUDENTS?

OWI students are adolescents entering college from high school, young adult students with a few years of work between high school and college, mature adults who tried college earlier and — for a wide range of reasons — stopped and decided to return later in life, and other adults for whom college is a brand-new opportunity. Additionally, as the Americans with Disabilities Act (ADA) rightly insists on providing accessibility, OWI students are people with physical and mental challenges and learning differences as well as students with diverse linguistic backgrounds and from varied socioeconomic lifestyles.

Students often are categorized as either traditional (ages seventeen to twenty-four), comprising approximately 60 percent of the student population, or nontraditional (ages twenty-five and up), comprising approximately 40 percent of the student population, with different purposes for their education at obviously different times of their lives (Jacobs and Hundley 2010, 3).

We sometimes hear writing instructors saying that their current students are somehow different from past years, less present, or oddly deficient in certain communication skills. They seem more entitled and more fearful of failure. Although many students work very hard in their classes, others suddenly disappear, dropping out without indicating there was a problem, leaving teachers wondering what happened. These observations are common because research suggests that contemporary students truly are different from any group that college teachers have taught in the past.

The Traditional Student

One reason instructors struggle with understanding how to reach their younger, traditionally aged students is that these students are not traditional in their overall orientation to college. Different from even ten years ago, many of today's young undergraduates take longer to complete what once was a four-year degree; some take more than five years and others never finish. Many young students work twenty to forty hours per week while taking fifteen or more credits, which not only stifles their ability to take advantage of campus life but dramatically cramps study time.

The younger students are nontraditional precisely because they do not meet the preconceptions that some educators still have for what constitutes a traditional student. For experienced professors, the notion of *traditional* students still may consist primarily of those who use SAT and ACT scores to compete for the best residential colleges their money can buy; who enter college right out of high school; who are full-time students who finish a four-year degree in four years; who spend the thirty-plus hours a week on schoolwork deemed necessary to succeed[1]; who join fraternal organizations, participate in clubs, and attend sports events; and who do not need to work more than a few hours a week to have sufficient spending money. While these measures for a traditional college student once were common and expected — and some students still fit them — many fewer students finish degrees within the traditional four- or two-year goals. In 2011, for example, 59 percent of full-time, first-time students at a four-year institution finished their degrees within six years, while 31 percent of students at two-year, degree-granting institutions finished their degree work within three years (U.S. Dept. of Education 2013). Nevertheless, some students still finish undergraduate studies in four or fewer years and achieve graduate degrees — enough to shape or confirm many instructors' views of what a traditional young student's experiences should be.

Increasingly, however, this young student cohort is focused on new goals as they literally work their way through college. Rebekah Nathan (2005), an anthropology professor who spent a year as an adult freshman living in the dorms with her fellow (but much younger) first-year students, states that, statistically speaking, the students she studied spent about ten hours per week preparing for schoolwork and about twenty hours on outside, paid work (32–33). If we generously double the ten-hour estimate that Nathan says students spent on schoolwork, that time frame still would be minimal for many students' study needs.

The students Nathan studied spent approximately two hours per day on all schoolwork, including "studying, reading, doing research, and writing

---

[1]One version of the study-to-credit hour formula is to spend two study hours outside of class per every one hour in class. Therefore, for fifteen credit hours spent in class, students would study an additional thirty hours each week.

papers, as well as watching class videos and meeting with project groups" (33). These numbers are disappointing for educators who would like students to prepare well for their courses. Although Nathan's sample is small and local to the school she attended, as mentioned earlier, she finds that many students spend most of their time working for pay both within the school and outside of it. Such work hours often are compelled by the rising costs of higher education — even in community colleges — and open enrollment policies that encourage students from a wider range of socioeconomic backgrounds to try college as a way to a better life. For some students, these work-study scenarios are less financially motivated than for resume building as students seek improved employment opportunities both during and after college. Certainly, Nathan's subjects spent more time working for pay than on their school assignments. Other activities that filled their time were professional clubs, hobbies, and volunteer commitments that connected them to their future careers. Play, of course, also had some attention. In all, students' time management decisions were about deciding where to put their energies and when. Their choices were not necessarily the choices that educators would have them make, but Nathan believes they were made in response to the fact that as students, one "serve[s] many masters [professors, in particular], each with his or her own quirks, schedules, and predilections" (112; see also Stapleton, Wen, Starrett, and Kilburn 2007, 100).

Regardless of how hard they work in and out of school, these students currently face an incredibly poor economy with a tough job market while having what Levine and Dean (2012) indicate to be "unrealistic aspirations for the future" (xiii). The researchers believe young undergraduates are "a pragmatic, career-oriented generation" with a practical focus on "jobs and money" (37), gravitating toward material goods and away from nonmaterial goals (38). However, their success in achieving those material goods is at risk because, in contrast to previous college student cohorts, the authors find contemporary students to be "more immature, dependent, coddled, and entitled" (xiii) than previous generations they have studied. They have been protected from failure in school and at home, and they have not learned how to take recoverable risks such as one might experience in competitive sports and science projects where achieving top scores are rewarded over mere participation. As a result of growing up protected from some necessary failures, to them, merely completing a school task equals having accomplished the maximum; according to Levine and Dean: "They confuse effort with excellence and quantity with quality in an age in which the economy elevates outcomes over process" (163). Indeed, the authors express that today's students "truly do not know the rules by which adults are expected to live their lives and by which their colleges work" (52). While these generalizations (fortunately) cannot be applied to all younger students, they do speak to professors' experiences of students who are perplexed or angry at getting low grades when their work is average or completely inadequate.

College is an off-putting project in that it is intended to put us out of our element—to put us in a new environment where our beliefs, thinking, and sense of self can be shaken up and remixed, moving us somehow forward in our lives. When Nathan (2005) registered as a freshman at the university where she was an associate professor, she wanted to learn what student life was like from an ethnographic/anthropological point of view. Regarding her experience as a whole, Nathan expresses: "I was shocked at how vulnerable and out of my element I felt" (11). Given that she was a successful and experienced academic and lifelong learner in her fifties, Nathan's words aptly convey the destabilization of self that young students experience when they begin college. As Nathan's experiences reveal, young students are not the only ones destabilized by college.

The "Old" Nontraditional Student

Continuing a forty-year trend of returning to school after achieving adulthood, more than 40 percent of college students are adult students older than twenty-five and ranging into their sixties or beyond. Research reported in the Lumina Foundation's *Returning to Learning: Adults' Success in College Is Key to America's Future* indicates that the average age of the nontraditional student is between 30.7 and 40.7 years old. Older nontraditional students are people who typically have entered college well after high school. Some may have tried college coursework before and withdrew because of lack of interest, failure, financial difficulties, or any of a number of issues that arise for younger students. Some have returned to school from a desire to improve their promotion potential or to change career fields. Others have been stuck without work in a bad economy and are searching for new skills. Such students bring to their classes their previous experiences, concerns about school, and worries about their careers. They, too, work many hours that makes college an adjunct to their life rather than its focus. They, too, have family and community connections outside college that curtail participation in traditional campus life. Nonetheless, with their college education, these students are positioning themselves for many additional, fruitful employment years given that currently "most individuals intend to work beyond the age of 65" (Pusser et al. 2007, 9).

The Emerging Pathways project funded by the Lumina Foundation reports the following findings about adult learners: (1) they are unique, individual, and not easily characterized; (2) their frequent uses of noncredit learning is poorly understood by educators (and can compromise students' goals of earning bachelor's degree); (3) they choose nontraditional educational paths because traditional ones simply do not meet them at their life circumstances; and (4) they need a guide to help them map their "path to success." In other words, adult college students should not disregard the value of career counseling to meet their specific needs (Pusser et al. 2007, 4, 6).

One thing we can surmise with some confidence is that most adults returning to school are doing so in connection with employment potential. Adult students typically do not have the leisure to try on a variety of academic majors in search of the right fit. Adult students' life experiences impact their studies in terms of time, geographical choices of schools, money, and interests. When they attend an OWC, they do so from necessity as well as from a potential awareness of weaknesses in their writing skills.

Frederic Jacobs and Stephen P. Hundley (2010), authors of *Understanding and Supporting Adult Learners: A Guide for Colleges and Universities*, characterize adult students as seeing the classroom as their defining educational context. When in an onsite course, for example, they do not use the campus in the same way as younger undergraduates. Typically coming to class and leaving directly afterward, their uses of the campus are more purposeful regarding completing their education (9). They tend to draw from their lives and prior educational experiences and link new learning to old learning. Because adult students are involved with their families, communities, and careers, they are thought to be able to bring these connections to college and use them to help make good use of the time they have in their classes (10).

Adult learners appear to have a strong need for safety in the environment in which they will be working (Jacobs and Hundley 2010, 21). Risk taking is a part of all teaching and learning environments, so instructors need to help adult students become more comfortable because many have learned in prior educational settings that negative consequences come from taking a risk, particularly if a project fails to go as expected. Rules for the classroom must be as clear as they would be in a work setting; surprises or changes often are not appreciated, and sometimes adult students do not deal well with them. For example, they may feel cheated when an assignment is adjusted for classmates while they worked hard to complete it as originally described. Adult learners also need opportunities for self-reflection and learning by doing. Similarly, they require respect from the instructor, a sense of immediacy in the learning, appropriate uses of teamwork in small groups, and help with metacognitive and accountability strategies (21–22).

It is well recognized that adult students are motivated differently from their younger peers, leading to a study of adult learning called andragogy (Knowles, Holton, and Swanson 1998) that is distinguished from pedagogy by various traits. The word *pedagogy* comes from Greek, meaning "leading the child"; in other words, pedagogy is considered to place the student in a dependent position and the teacher in a leadership position. It is believed that learners are rewarded externally as with grades and teacher approval. *Andragogy* is a word that comes from German and means a "leveling of power between student and teacher." In other words, the learning environment is more cooperative and the learner is expected to be more self-directed in the learning process (Knowles et al. 1998, 19). Another way of looking at pedagogy is that it has a "subject/topic orientation," uses lecture and other memory-based techniques, employs rewards and punishments in terms of grades to reinforce and encourage learning, and gives the teacher the primary role in the classroom. Andragogy, in comparison, has a "problem/project orientation," uses experiential learning, looks to students to motivate themselves and encourage their own learning, and places the responsibility for learning on the student (Marshak 1983, 92).

Andragogical traits include the individual (1) being self-directed; (2) having experience that serves as a "resource for learning"; (3) having motivation to learn when it applies to one's "social roles"; and (4) wanting to apply the learning immediately (Henning 2012, 45). Jacobs and Hundley (2010) state that adult students exhibit "a high degree of goal orientation, seeking programs with clearly defined steps that help them realize their aspirations. . . . They seek relevancy in their studies . . . and are also practical, assertive, and demand respect" (9). When supported, adult students will learn new concepts by analogy to what they already know, which is a feature of learning transfer (Cleary 2013). Educating adult learners requires understanding "that adults have accumulated knowledge and experience that can enhance or hinder the learning experience" (15). This observation is important to understanding that returning to school is not a smooth sail for many adult students, who may need help in fitting formal education into their life-learned wisdom. Jacobs and Hundley (2010) also note that "andragogy organizes learning experiences around applications to the real-life situations of learners, and learners become ready to learn those things they need to know in order to cope effectively with their real-life situations" (2010, 20).

Having lived independent of formal education and in the work world for whatever period of time, it is natural that adult students would bring different expectations and behaviors with them to college. Life experience informs learning because it provides a connection on which to hook new knowledge and with which to frame that knowledge usefully. For example, adult writers in Michelle Navarre Cleary's (2013) study of learning transfer tended to invest most "in writing that allowed them to make things happen in the world or to explore topics, ideas, and questions important to them, even when that writing did not travel beyond the classroom" (679). Having worked with many adult students, I can attest to the overall truth of these generalizations. However, anecdotally speaking, many adult students remain concerned about grades and what others think of them; they worry about how their teachers and peers may judge their work—often internalizing grades as the proof of their learning—and they express that they have stress when the requirements of work or life conflict with their courses (and vice versa).

Teresa Henning (2012), who studied her own learning in an online environment, notes that adult students do not always behave in what may now be the andragogically expected manner. Traditional education has inculcated a more teacher-focused learning environment that many adults will recall and anticipate when they return to college. They may not see themselves as independent learners in that environment and, therefore, they may give up some of their proactive postures until (and *if*) the instructor helps them to reshape their view (11). Robert Marshak (1983) gives this type of learning the name *adolegogy*, which applies adolescence as a midpoint between child and adult on the pedagogy–andragogy spectrum. This model for learning offers language to address mixed situations where, for example, the adult learner requires great detail in instructions but then acts independently or outside of those instructions once given. Adolescents sometimes are highly dependent, while other times they are extremely independent — a frustrating but natural part of human nature at various life stages. Sometimes adolescents greatly desire external rewards, but other times they refuse those rewards and/or punishments as not applicable to their situation or extraneous to their learning. From another perspective, adult students may not find that they need their adolescent school-based writing experiences until they enter the work world and, conversely, that work-world writing strategies then accompany them back to school (Cleary 2013, 676); in other words, they find exigency for using school and work experiences in the just-in-time writing processes themselves.

Table 1.1 outlines some differences between child, adolescent, and adult learners. It is important to remember, however, that while chronological age applies to learning style, age does not define learning style as much as one's approach to learning does.

With this table in mind, it can be useful to understand the reentering adult student as one with mixed approaches to education that are like those of younger students. For example, look at the third row in Table 1.1 regarding the role of the learner's experience. This characteristic presents a range of responsibility taking for one's learning among students of different ages. The role of one's experiences in learning can take the real-life form of deciding what to write and how to accept its reception with the teacher in OWI or other writing courses.

The child learner's life experiences may not be recognized as especially valuable in the classroom, possibly because she has experienced so little of life when compared with the teacher's experiences or the textbook's breadth and depth. The child, therefore, often takes the teacher's lead when talking or writing about herself or other issues. She tends to accept the topic and the grade given as what she deserves.

The adult learner's experiences, on the other hand, are more valued both by the student and her teacher. College composition courses are known to bring such experiential techniques into play, prizing what the student can bring to her writing. In this situation, the adult student would write about what she wants to study within the parameters of the assignment; sometimes, she might go outside those parameters if there is another topic that interests her more or that seems more immediate to her needs. In true adult-learning style, if the grade is not what she believes she deserves, she might question the teacher's reasoning or profess to want to learn how to do better, but eventually she would tend to posit that what she learned was more important than the grade.

It can help to understand that between the child and adult learning styles, younger and older adult learners may have similar adolescent-like characteristics that can be understood as a learning phase that moves between the familiar (pedagogical) and the unfamiliar (andragogical). Teachers can engage the characteristics of adolegogy deliberately to help their students grow into more andragogical stances in OWI as well as in other subjects.

The Digital-Era Student

Chronological age and the pedagogy-andragogy spectrum are not the most useful measures for understanding contemporary college students. Indeed, neither age nor learning style accounts for the complexities that digital technology brings to the classroom and how such technology affects students. It helps also to consider students in relation to the digital age in which we currently live.

Hence, another way to categorize students by age is through such labels as Matures (1900–1946), Baby Boomers (1943–1960), Gen X (1961–1981), and Millennials or the Net Generation (1982–present) (Stapleton et al. 2007, 100–101). With these categories, the younger students are presented as having qualities in relation to the Internet as well as to the twenty-first century—also inherently connected to a digitally focused global society. As some theorize, younger undergraduates may be different from previous generations because of their typically close relationship with digital technologies from an early age (Thurlow and McKay 2003). Marc Prensky (2001) differentiates the older students who grew up in years prior to the Millennials as "digital immigrants," categorizing the younger students who have grown up with digital technologies as "digital natives." However, the *native* and *immigrant* monikers are not universally accurate because only some of the younger students have grown up using digital devices and some older students reveal greater comfort levels with digital technologies than their younger peers. While the native and immigrant designations attempt a point of departure from chronological age alone, there is a particular veracity to the term *Millennial* given that it speaks less to age or an assumed relationship with technology than to the general cultural influences on a generation.

Generalizations always fail to capture the uniqueness of students, potentially creating caricatures of the thinking and feeling people who inhabit our classes; yet, they are useful in discerning what students need from educators in an OWI setting. For example, it is helpful to realize that younger students

TABLE 1.1 Three Learning Stages*

From the Learner's Perspective	Pedagogy	Adolegogy	Andragogy
Need to know	Must learn what teacher teaches if she/he wants to pass; no need to learn how material applies to life.	Will learn if she/he wants to. May not be persuaded by grades or life-applicable reasons for learning. May be stubborn in decisions even when teacher or authority or even peers try to dissuade.	Must know why she/he needs to know something to learn it, to include benefits of learning it and negative consequences of not learning it. Must go beyond desire for credits or degree.
Learner's self-concept	Teacher and learner see student as a dependent personality with slow independency growth rate.	Sees self as sometimes dependent (and rebels against this) and sometimes independent (and feels uncomfortable with this, too). Is okay with the label of irresponsible if it means not moving out of comfort zone.	Takes responsibility for own decisions and life, and the learner needs to be seen by others as responsible; self-directing.
Role of experience	Learner's experience is little valued as a resource for learning; instead, teacher, books, and learning aids are valued.	Brings own experiences to the learning, but also relies on the teacher or text for the right answer. Expresses desires for experiential techniques of learning, but may not participate fully or with confidence. Is learning how to do so.	Needs to bring in own experiences, which leads to emphasis on experiential techniques.

Readiness to learn	Readiness depends on when and why teacher says it is time to learn with passing and promotion often cited.	Readiness to learn depends on the student's semester choices rather than on life choices. May take courses for expediency rather than for need to know or desire to learn regarding life needs.	Timing of learning experience is critical to the developmental task it supports. Adults ready to learn and find themselves ready to do so in accordance with real-life situations.
Orientation to learning	Subject-oriented learning (knowledge acquisition); learning organized according to subject matter.	Focuses heavily on subject-oriented learning with a desire to put the learning in the context of the life knowledge. Concedes to the teacher's authority over applying learning to life unless the teacher is otherwise focused himself.	Life-oriented and life-centered learning versus knowledge acquisition alone. Gain new knowledge, understanding, skills, values, and attitudes in context of application to real-life situations.
Motivation	Motivated by external factors such as grades, teacher approval, parental pressures, and possibly peer pressures.	Motivated by need for grades as related to student loans/finances, parental pressure, but not necessarily teacher approval unless that is perceived to relate to grades. Moves toward the need to succeed in school as a way to guarantee success in life—almost to a fairy tale degree or fantasy of connection of college grades to life achievement.	Responsive to external motivators like job retention and promotion. Most responsive to internal pressures for greater job and life satisfaction and quality of life.

*Descriptions for pedagogy and andragogy were adapted primarily from Knowles (1990, 54–65).

have a more recent connection to reading and writing—or should have one—from their high school English classes. They likely will have more current scaffolding on which to link certain kinds of reading or writing presented online. Adult students, on the other hand, might need a different kind of guidance to help them feel familiar with academic writing or certain types of reading assignments in an online setting.

Although categories of student demographics have worked to help educators discern strategies for reaching them and for shifting pedagogies, updating the distinctions can help to understand how students may approach OWI. To this end, we must recognize not so much the chronological age of our students—although age certainly matters—but other contexts that they bring to their education such as their connections to digital technology—especially regarding reading and writing—and how such technology may be used in the OWI setting.

THE "NEW" NONTRADITIONAL STUDENT

For the many young students who historically have not fit the common definition of a traditional student even though they were between the ages of seventeen and twenty-four, it is easy to categorize them as anomalies. In reality, such a definition is deficient because it does not include the students who commute (my college had a "day-hop" room in the basement of one of the dorms devoted to commuters in the 1970s) or those who have to work twenty to forty hours per week to buy gas and make the rent. It does not include students who are thrilled to enter community college and proudly wear their college's mascot clothing because they are the first in their families even to attempt college. It does not include students who drop out of school or who are single parents with children to feed and care for. Nor does it include the disabled, who may receive government help sufficient to pay for rent and classes but not enough funding to cover food, gas, and school supplies. Finally, it does not include the Millennial generation's connections—or lack of connections—with digital technology. The common view of younger traditional students is oddly anachronistic and incredibly narrow.

As an alternative, I categorize all OWI students as generally nontraditional given their various backgrounds and learning needs. Their characteristics differ from educators' conventional understanding of college students. By instead considering all of these students nontraditional because of their experiences with digital technology, we gain a different lens through which to understand the literacy needs they have in OWI. Examining them specifically regarding differences relative to the increasingly digital world, in this section, I look first at younger students—the "new" nontraditional students—and their relationship with digital technology given that many are born to it; then I demonstrates how the "old" nontraditional students are similar to, yet differ from, their younger counterparts given that adult students typically are developing a relationship with digital technology. Finally, I consider how all these nontraditional students of our digital era have literacy needs influenced by technology.

The Younger Generation

The "new" nontraditional students are young people who have entered college directly from high school or within a few years of graduation. These students have limited life experiences when compared with adults, yet many have lived through life-changing challenges like parental divorce, deaths of family members or friends, and other upheavals that inform their lives — and their writing. Their experiences are unique; some have been communicated and filtered through technology because they have grown up in a world that always has had cordless phones, computers, and mobile devices.

Certainly, these students' experiences should not be oversimplified. Some students have been exposed to the latest in computers and cell phone technology all of their lives. As toddlers, they played and learned with computing toys. Many have watched their parents upgrade their technology every few years; the students may have received the older devices or they may have received new devices. Some younger students have owned the latest games and gaming devices, using such play as their primary interaction with digital technology. These students most likely grew up with increasing computer access and emphasis on using computers in school. Other students from different socioeconomic backgrounds may never have owned a computer — using the school or public library when they wanted to access the Internet or to type homework. Indeed, some of these less affluent students may never have used the Internet beyond a simple Internet search and they may be less familiar with the complex features of common word processing programs; as such, they may not know how to insert footnotes or track changes, for example. And, while they may own a cell phone, it might merely make phone calls (and possibly enable rudimentary texting) without camera, voice activation, or Internet capabilities. There remains a vast digital divide, and our youngest students' experiences most certainly will reflect that.

Beyond a technological divide, these students will demonstrate a difference in preferences. Some students who have been exposed to computers and other digital technology all of their lives choose not to interact through IM chat, e-mail, texting, and the like. They may profess to hate dealing with computers or they may feel incapable of understanding how to use them. Others who have had limited access may be quite dexterous with the technologies, professing to learn them naturally. Some will not be able to stay away from Facebook — having different pages for different types of friends—and they will do most of their interactions via texting or other social networking chat, assiduously avoiding voice or face-to-face interactions. On the other hand, some peers will reject a life lived in social networking technology for simpler interactions. We must respect that being born to digital technology does not equal enjoyment of, comfort with, or preference for it.

One trait that we can count on is that our younger students likely have had little to no experience with educational computing that transfers naturally to OWI. Particularly when OWI is taught asynchronously, younger students may find themselves struggling both with the relative slowness of the interactions asked of them (e.g., discussion posts and peer group work) while they grapple with learning to write academic prose through a system that requires them to read academic prose and instructions, interpret them, and apply them to their own writing. It is at this juncture that—despite varied comfort levels with digital technology—our youngest students will be most alike.

What Shapes the Young Undergraduate?

Based on their 2006–2011 study, Levine and Dean (2012) paint a picture of young college students with broad strokes: "Today's college students are the most diverse generation in higher education history" (xii). They express a high comfort level with multiculturalism and diversity, and they "are global in orientation"; however, they have a more limited, local focus and "little knowledge about the world" (xii, 163). These attitudes can be connected, I think, to generally more diverse and welcoming elementary and secondary school settings than those their parents experienced. Today's young college students are connected globally to others—often digitally—yet isolated because they are "weak in interpersonal skills, face-to-face communication skills, and problem-solving skills" (xii, xiii; see also Jukes et al. 2010, 13). Digital connections can become such a habitual way of communicating that they can supersede in-person and voice communications, leaving these interactive modes rusty and, in some cases, unlearned.

The world these young undergraduates live in is one of rapid, "unrelenting and profound change at a speed and magnitude never before experienced" (Levine and Dean 2012, xiv). As many educators can attest, this world is "dramatically different" from the one they and their students' parents experienced (xv). Indeed, according to Levine and Dean, "the pace and scale of change will accelerate for the nation and its college students" (xv), and the changes will be "relentless" in their lifetimes (158). Using the digital information economy as a benchmark, Levine and Dean distinguish between what they call the digital 1.0 world in which contemporary educators have learned to work with digital technology since the late 1980s and the digital 1.5 world of today that is moving toward a completely digital 2.0 information economy. Such a distinction places these young students on the cusp of yet another change in the degree to which people rely on and use digital technologies. Our current youngest undergraduates "will not only need to learn to live successfully in a world hurtling between its 1.0 and 2.0 versions but they also will have to create it" (xvi). To create that world, they will need to be able to think critically about what is happening in it. Ideally, learning to think more critically will occur (or begin to occur) in their undergraduate years because, in later years, many students will need to return to school to advance their skills and update knowledge (165).

Digital Influences on the Young Undergraduate

"Today's undergraduates are the first generation of digital-age natives," claim Levine and Dean (2012, xii). As digital natives, today's students — at least those with adequate access to the marvels of the digital age — speak "digital as a first language" (Jukes et al. 2010, 15). In addition to watching television programs like previous generations, many learned to read and follow directions by playing computer games. They can type or swipe a text message faster than they can recite the ABCs, and do it surreptitiously while talking, walking, or attending class.

How can traditional, formal education compete with a digital world? Indeed, some would say that it cannot. Levine and Dean (2012) state that "higher education lags far behind its students technologically and pedagogically and must transform itself if it is to educate current undergraduates for the world in which they live" (xii). Jukes et al. (2010) studied high school students to learn more about why and how "the traditional teaching methods are not producing the results we expect" (Prensky, in Jukes et al. 2010, Foreword). Their research leads them to believe that traditional teaching methods are not working because the current students are not the ones for whom traditional schools were designed (Introduction). Although their research is written about secondary-level students, it has much to teach college educators who are seeing these recently graduated students in their classes.

James Stapleton et al. (2007) studied how students of different generations perceive online learning. Using their preferred term, they find that Millennials were more likely than people of other generations to believe that online technology actually reduces learning although they "tended to have higher levels of interaction with students" (and fewer interactions with teachers) and "were more comfortable participating in discussions" (105–6). Perhaps these students did not view online learning as being aided by technology because they also "tended not to develop an online study plan and stick to it" (106), an issue of self-motivation and determination.

From what Levine and Dean (2012) and Jukes et al. (2010) suggest, however, it also is possible that the students in Stapleton et al.'s (2007) study simply found the technology used in their classes to be slow, clunky, or outdated. For example, when it comes to technology used for OWI — whether fully online or hybrid — there is a great disparity of available tools. While some institutions are set up to provide synchronous courses through voice and video, most OWCs are offered asynchronously. Also, while a few more economically privileged institutions are prepared with the technology and teacher training to teach writing with multimodal and multimedia technologies, the vast majority of institutions do not have access to such technological wealth for their OWCs.

A SHALLOW RELATIONSHIP WITH TEXTUAL LITERACY According to Jukes et al. (2010), young students "expect to be able to communicate with anyone or anything at anytime and anywhere" (13). Of course, people are not always appropriate about the anyone, anything, anytime, or anywhere, which means that conscious reflection regarding such communication can help them to become better communicators overall. Jukes et al. indicate that these students are comfortable with "visual bombardment of simultaneous images, text, and sounds" as both "relevant and compelling experiences that can convey more information in a few seconds than can be communicated by reading an entire book" (2010, 14). This statement smacks of hyperbole, but one can imagine that some younger students would believe it to be true — many young students profess not to have read more than a few books in their entire lives.

Today's young undergraduates know how to find answers to questions; it does not seem to be a stretch to say that many learned to research by using Google or another search engine to find a topic and Wikipedia to provide background information. They can search broadly, but they may not see any reason to search deeply. Levine and Dean (2012) note that "digital media produce a shallow ocean of information and encourage students to gather and sift. Of course, they can go deeper if they wish. But they matriculate into analog universities, populated by academics who are hunters, whose interests and work generally emphasized depth over breadth" (22). Indeed, once a question has been answered, however shallowly, their fast world and research inexperience seem to push young college students to the next concern. Many writing instructors have seen this behavior in superficial essay drafts. Much instructional time is spent teaching such research skills as how to use an onsite and online library; how to summarize, paraphrase, and quote from sources; and how to analyze and synthesize sources into the student's earned opinion and perspective. These needs likely stem from the generally insubstantial understanding of research that undergraduates of any age may have, disappointing and frustrating their hunter professors. Educators, too, use Google and Wikipedia to get quick answers to questions. The difference is that experience has taught them when depth over breadth is appropriate and necessary. That said, when students believe that a few seconds on a web page yields more information than reading a book, educators can see an area in which such young students are missing the proverbial boat. Books—even many web pages—are written to delve into a subject more deeply precisely because depth of knowledge in one area can lead to crossover knowledge and greater understanding in other areas.

Jukes et al. (2010) claim that "at least 60 percent of students in any given classroom are not auditory or text-based learners." They "think graphically" and "they're either visual or visual kinesthetic learners or a combination of the two" (28). That students have different learning styles is not a new concept, of course. However, the authors stretch the concept further, claiming that digital-era youths are "wired for multimedia" (28), which would be good for them if the authors were correct in their assertion that "the role of text is to provide more detail to something that was first experienced as an image or a video" (37). But text is more than an adjunct explanation for a visual image and more than a narrow part of overall literacy. Although the orality versus text discussion started in Western culture with Plato's depiction of Socrates in the *Phaedrus*, it has not yet been resolved in favor of pictorial representations. To that end, it seems certain that not being able to read a book or even a well-considered shorter article without visual aids can put young students at a distinct disadvantage both educationally and in the world more generally. As Chapter 2 discusses regarding reading skills, visual images—moving and still—and voice are potentially powerful forms for information dissemination; yet they cannot and do not replace alphabetic text in our world.

Some believe that using digital tools like the Internet as a primary knowledge source has affected students' learning. Jukes et al. state: "The rapid access, skim, and leave reading behavior fostered by surfing the Internet, coupled with multitasking that is done in the digital world, has made the digital generation less likely to work their way through documents that require a more patient approach to follow the thought of longer and more challenging opinions and arguments" (2010, 4). Such "twitch speed" (Prensky 2001) interaction and lack of patience suggest reasons for the flaws educators see in younger students' schoolwork, such as patchwriting (Berrett 2012; Howard et al. 2010), plagiarism (Levine and Dean 2012, 50; Wolfe 2010), and other insufficiently deep analytical writing. As indicated earlier, it also may be the cause of the dissatisfaction with contemporary online learning that Millennials express in Stapleton et al.'s (2007) study.

DIGITAL MULTITASKING AS A SKILL THAT INFLUENCES LITERACY Multitasking is another trait of this new nontraditional generation. Jukes et al. (2010) define multitasking as "continuous partial attention [that] involves randomly toggling between tasks, deciding on which one to do next" (36). Even though both younger and older students frequently may perform "multiple digital tasks simultaneously," the authors acknowledge that "trying to multitask while attempting to complete a challenging new task goes against our biology" (3; see also Medina 2008, 85).

Despite research claims "that effective multitasking is really about having a good memory capable of paying attention to several inputs at one time and being highly adept at task switching" (Jukes et al. 2010, 36), in fact, we are not doing multiple tasks at one time but jumping from one task to another and back again without full concentration on any one task. That understanding is important to realizing that multitasking is a skill that can add to or detract from overall literacy at any one time. We gain something when we multitask—getting some job done sooner or before forgetting about it, for example—but also lose something in concentration and depth of thinking. We may forget what we have read or interrupt a chain of thought and cheat ourselves of what it would have led to, for example.

In *Now You See It: How the Brain Science of Attention Will Transform the Way We Live, Work, and Learn*, Cathy N. Davidson (2012) describes this kind of work as "really multidistraction, with attention not supplemented but displaced from one point of focus to another" (31). She explains that distractions exist everywhere in life and can be helpful to seeing the world differently and as a key to learning: "Many distractions happen and are simply forgotten. Others we take with us. We apply information from one experience when we need it in another. What makes the difference between the forgettable and the important is what I call learning" (31–32). For some people, however, distractions detract from learning. Indeed, for students with attention deficit disorder (ADD) and other learning challenges, distractions in the form of multitasking can help them to procrastinate (Lewis and Alden 2007, 124–25). Although some might consider multitasking more efficient than addressing one task at a time (e.g., having a preference for getting three school tasks partially done rather than one or two finished completely), researchers have indicated that multitaskers make up to 50 percent more errors and take up to 50 percent longer to complete a task than nonmultitaskers (Medina 2008, 87).

The habit of multitasking with digital technology cannot be underestimated as a factor in young students' learning processes. In some ways, the ability to move (apparently) seamlessly among tasks might be considered a higher-level thinking skill, but the wide range of computer-based distractions—such as the unlimited number of tabs one can open in an Internet browser—truly are disruptive both in and out of class. Learning to multitask digitally from an early age can detract from the necessary job of learning to apply sustained focus and diligence to a task. Reading and writing, the literacy concerns of OWCs, demand a level of continued attention and focus that can be learned by many students, but these skills are easy to dismiss as hard or boring. The propensity to jump among tasks eats into that focused time and effort necessary for reading, writing, and thinking deeply. When students measure their time for school tasks at little more than ten hours a week per Nathan's (2005) research, every minute not focused on that work is learning energy lost.

While digital immigrants have had to learn to multitask, younger students with access to digital technologies have grown up multitasking and receive a reinforcing message that it is the best way to complete their work. For instance, an AT&T (2013) cell phone commercial, aired on television and viewed over 136,000 times on YouTube, illustrates this point. In the commercial, an interviewer talks with a small group of elementary school children. He asks them which is better: doing one thing at a time or two things at once. The obvious answer for the cell phone being advertised is that doing two things is better, and the children eagerly provide that answer. The advertising message is that people should be able to surf the Internet and talk on phones simultaneously. As part of a more-is-better culture where interpersonal interaction is not prized, the lesson is heard clearly from the youngest of children: no communication or task — not even talking with someone on the phone — is worth taking time away from the multitude of other things we could be getting done by surfing the Web.

When digital-era students grow up with such messages, getting them to pay attention in their writing courses and to read deeply can be challenging. Levine and Dean (2012) rightly question what students are doing in the classroom, such as ordering things online, text messaging, and checking e-mail (51); many times in a traditional or hybrid classroom, instructors do not know this multitasking is happening or do not know how to stop it. Recent professional listserv discussions have supplied various antidotes for the problem, including banning laptop use and cell phones from the classroom. In a fully online or hybrid OWI setting, such multitasking happens, yet it is out of the teacher's control because the computer and the Internet are central to such classes; they cannot be banned!

Young students are not the only ones guilty of such jumps in focus, of course; the adult students discussed in the next section have these issues as well. The difference may be the degree to which one has grown up multitasking versus having learned it as an adult. We teachers are equally guilty. Last year, I delivered an onsite, professional workshop at a university where we met in a computer classroom because much of our work involved OWI teaching skills. Every single participant used the computer to multitask both while I talked and during the work time dedicated to completing workshop tasks. Some did not complete the workshop tasks — possibly because of their attention to e-mail and the like. In a similar situation at another university, writing tutors being trained for online tutorials mixed checking e-mail and texting with incomplete attention to training scenarios. Although learning certainly can occur when students (and teachers and tutors) multitask, it is important to understand the potential for distractions from educational goals.

There is yet another challenge to the bouncing attention span of multitasking that bears mention in light of students' literacy needs. Jukes et al. (2010) claim that it is the younger students' "second nature to multitask" and "still be bored" (14). I am not moved by this argument. Perhaps these students are bored because they never are deeply engaged, and instead they have mere surface-level interactions both with learning material and people. Boredom should not be an acceptable response in college. Even though the baccalaureate often is considered the new high school diploma, students presumably matriculate voluntarily with some desire to learn. People who want to engage with learning can learn to do so. Jukes et al. accept student apathy toward their learning: "As a result, the digital generation, who are accustomed to the twitch-speed, multitasking, random-access, graphics-first, active, connected, fun, fantasy, quick-payoff world of their video games, MTV, and the Internet, are incredibly bored by most of today's education" (22). The authors urge educators to change their approaches to include more digitally stimulating methods. While Stapleton et al.'s (2007) research supports the need to use more robust technologies that can stimulate student's peer interactions, for example, students must learn how to self-regulate their boredom and find their own interest in learning.

OWI certainly is poised to stimulate writing students more than traditional onsite courses if, indeed, digital writing experiences do stimulate students. My problem with Jukes et al.'s (2010) thinking is that it places on educators the students' own problem of needing to learn challenging thinking, reading, and writing skills—just because they are not easy to do. Reading and writing are, indeed, painstaking experiences we may not be able to make less painful because they require time, effort, and personal investment. Although today's younger, digital-era undergraduates may be different thinkers, as Chapter 2 suggests, they still have responsibility for their own learning. Because they are responsible for their own success, students need to self-engage with the world and with learning in general. I am at odds with the expectation of keeping kids interested at twitch speed when college is about helping students to find their own paths of self-engagement. Indeed, sometimes boredom is a sensation that occurs because students need to learn how to self-stimulate the learning. At times, the sensation of boredom may arise from fear, laziness, or simply not being able to read well or comprehend what they read, which is why the literacy strategies in this book are crucial. As Levine and Dean (2012) point out, in essence, students need to negotiate their primary digital world, but they also must navigate the changing rules of the analog world in which they concurrently live (x). Regarding the literacies of reading and writing, students will find that they need to read and write more in the new digital information world than they may have thought possible.

The Older Generation

Adult students also are influenced by their relationships with digital technology. As with younger students, they must develop a working relationship with digital technology in their home and work lives. By attending college, they also must employ such technology in an educational setting, where its use may differ from other areas of their lives. Like younger students, some adults are quite comfortable with using digital tools in their work. While they may not have been born to it, some adults born in the early 1980s have been interacting with computers since they were in their early teen years. They were adolescents when mobile phones stopped being tethered to automobiles and morphed into portable, if somewhat unwieldy, cellular devices. They joined their parents' generation in giving up desktop machines for laptops, notebook computers, and now tablets. They cannot remember doing schoolwork with a typewriter because they never used one.

Older adult students did give up a typewriter for the family's first computer. They marveled as phones became cordless and wondered whether they really needed a cell phone. Now, they cannot imagine life without one and may feel lost if they leave it at home while on a jaunt to the store. Many adult students have Facebook accounts to keep up with their own friends as well as with their families. The adult student's relationship to digital technology is similar in many ways to that of the younger student except that most adults can remember a time without the technology and they likely have a sense of what they have gained and lost through it.

As with younger students, however, educators should not overgeneralize and they cannot assume a single comfort level that their adult students have with digital technology. Many people use the Internet to connect with colleagues for work purposes, for example. They can be assumed to have some skills that they realize are transferrable to school settings. However, adult students are even less likely than younger ones to have used their digital tools and technology skills for educational purposes. In an OWC—whether fully online or hybrid—they might be fluent with word processing but unfamiliar with the notion of posting a discussion comment or being graded on the number or quality of words in that comment. On the other hand, some adult students who have never been to college before also will not have used a computer much, if at all. These students would join their younger peers in worrying over how to format a paper and fearing they have broken something when the printer will not print. OWI teachers will encounter all of these students in their OWCs and will need to keep their varying digital literacy abilities in mind as much as their reading and writing skills.

What Shapes the Adult Undergraduate?

In a report from the Lumina Foundation regarding adult students who are returning to school, Pusser et al. (2007) explains that as many as 54 million American adults in 2007 did not have a college degree; of those people, as many as "34 million have no college experience at all." Claiming that these numbers are unsustainable in this century of digital (hence, global) growth, the authors made the dire prediction that continuing this trend would cause the United States "to trail global competitors on a number of key measures of educational achievement" and "limit our adult citizens and erode the vitality of our essential institutions" (1). Assisting adult students in their ongoing education is not as simple as getting them to matriculate, however.

According to Jovita M. Ross-Gordon (2011), adult students return to school with a wider variety of life experiences compared to younger students. They are married, unmarried, divorced, or widowed. They have children; are childless; or are caring for children, grandchildren, or parents. In fact, one characteristic that distinguished "reentry adults" from their younger peers is this juggling of roles while in school; she considers such roles "assets" because they bring with them certain levels of support, but they also bring "multiple challenges" to the study table.

Indeed, most adult students work while they are in school, making opportunities and expediency clear values and part-time education a necessity. If there is a choice that must be made between completing a work or a school assignment, work likely will win. For soldier- or other military students, for example, there will be times when being in the field or going on temporary duty—much like a business trip—makes completing a school project difficult to impossible without an extension or some other consideration.

As part of their quest for education that will serve adult needs, Ross-Gordon suggests that these students "look for degree and certificate programs that provide them flexibility in time and locations for both course completion and for access to key student services." To help meet those needs, a variety of postsecondary institutions "have been designed around the needs of adult students, such as Empire State University [*sic*], Fielding Institute, Regis University, and, more recently, the University of Phoenix and many other institutions in the for-profit sector" (Ross-Gordon 2011; see also Pusser et al. 2007, 2). Just as they look for institutions that cater to adult reentry student needs, they also tend to look for accelerated courses, compressed certificate programs, and other nontraditional offerings that meet their life challenges and preferred learning styles (Ross-Gordon 2011). They seek out noncredit-bearing, continuing education courses if other programs are not available, which can be to their overall detriment because earning a baccalaureate is a key goal for many in this student population (Pusser et al. 2007). Adult learners particularly value "convenience, service, quality, and low prices" (Levine and Dean 2012, 9) when choosing an educational institution, which is one reason that they are attracted by institutions that advertise themselves as helping the returning student to move more quickly through their programs.

One of the results of adult students' reentry into education is that online writing instructors will see many of them in their classes. Reading and writing are critical literacy skills in many workplace settings. Although hourly employees (e.g., those working in the transportation, utilities, and fast food industries) write infrequently on the job, these skills still can be important. Some people will never be interviewed for a desired job because of the poor quality of their written application materials (College Board 2004, 9, 10). According to "Writing: A Ticket to Work . . . or a Ticket Out" (2004), a College Board report on writing and work, 80 percent of employees need to write in their jobs in the finance, insurance, and real estate sectors and the services, construction, mining, and similar industries (9). Even if they are not expected to write regularly, many employers assume their employees can write; indeed, writing ability more often is connected to dismissal than to promotion decisions (15).

This same report indicates that workplace writing responsibilities "frequently" to "almost always" include e-mail, oral presentations with visual aids, and written (technical and formal) reports, as well as memos and other correspondence; increasingly, IM chat, video chat, and other aspects of unified communication technology also are required on the job. Accuracy and clarity are highly valued with concision often valued (11). Employers require documentation of meeting minutes and other "core points" (12). They expect cogent and appropriate e-mail for documentation and communication. Other frequently written materials include executive summaries, after-action reports, and summarized points from broader and multiple documents and meetings.

Writing effective work-related documents relies both on reading well and writing summaries. Charles Taylor, chief operating officer of Meridian Institute, a nonprofit dedicated to helping the people within organizations connect by mediating problems, explains that the company's interns, who are advanced undergraduates—"some of the best and the brightest in the country"—"often have great difficulty with summarizing" both situations and written material (January 28, 2013). This master skill requires that people analyze a situation or text, understand the audience for which they are writing, and write about the most important concerns. If the "best and the brightest" undergraduates struggle with these skills, it is not hard to imagine that other undergraduates—especially the currently employed students reentering the educational arena—will need ongoing and focused practice with them.

Retraining deficient writers in workplace settings is like training them in the first place, and it is something for which employers pay dearly. The high cost of retraining ranges from under $1,000 for online writing tutoring to many thousands of dollars for in-house programs and professionally produced writing workshops (College Board 2004, 16). According to Pusser et al. (2007), employers paid as much as 50 billion dollars in 2004 to educate their employees (13). There is no question that writing functions both as a "marker" of ability and as a "gatekeeper" to cull less-skilled people in workplaces where writing skills are needed and valued (19). Thus, the literacy skills addressed in this book are ones that adult undergraduates would recognize as important to their later employment-focused writing.

Digital Influences on the Adult Undergraduate

Technology use is one area in which adult students may give up their autonomy or find themselves unexpectedly challenged and reverting to an adolescent-like stance. Here, it may be useful to understand them as Prensky's (2001) digital-era immigrants in that they were not born to this digital information society. Those who grew up without computers, cell phones, game devices, and other digital technology are somewhat disadvantaged (and this includes socioeconomically deprived younger students who have missed out on earlier digital experiences). Our world is changing rapidly in ways that contrast sharply with our upbringings. Many adults longingly recall their outdoor after-school play when computer games were unknown or when a missed phone call could not be returned because there was no way to know who had called. They may have been excited when computer/ television games debuted, but honesty compels many to admit that they had at first feared breaking the machine or ruining the game. Programming a digital video recorder (DVR) or learning how to download an app creates anxiety for some adults, but now that such programming is ubiquitous on ever more sophisticated technology, adults have had to learn what to do. In contrast, those born to active involvement in the digital age are said to be fearless when getting a new electronic device, knowing that if something goes wrong, they can always reboot (Jukes et al. 2010); alas, this is a lesson that I have had to relearn repeatedly.

Adults live in the moment in their educational lives. They seek direct connections between what they are learning and what they are living. Often called *just-in-time learning*, it "is about having the skills, knowledge, and habits of mind that will allow them to continuously learn and adapt just in time, when that next window of opportunity or area of interest briefly opens to them" (Jukes et al. 2010, 39). Just-in-time learning contrasts with the *just-in-case learning* of most formal (and pedagogically focused) education. Such learning includes memorizing presidents' names or state capitals, as well as being able to name the genus and species of hunting birds in one's county (one of my sharpest memories of college biology).

While these activities exercise the memory, they do not promote learning that helps to address real problems as they arise. From this point of view, a great deal of what students learn in lower and higher education is not necessary to what they need to do in the moment, making it quite unnecessary to adult learners who are purpose driven in their educational goals.

When adult learners reenter school, they want to advance their literacy skills quickly. Therefore, it may surprise some of them that even the notion of what constitutes literacy is changing because of digital advancements. According to Cynthia Selfe and Gail Hawisher (2007), the computer game is a new literacy that can be used in the classroom or for training purposes. In the foreword to their book *Gaming Lives in the Twenty-First Century: Literate Connections*, James Paul Gee argues for a broader view of literacy to encompass computer games because "literacy is something that happens out in the world of social, cultural, and institutional activities" (ix). He suggests that a "verbal understanding of the text" is all that comes from written text as opposed to the addition of "images, actions, and dialogue" that create "situated understanding" (ix). Gee indicates that life experience, which he calls the "game," is what contextualizes learning (x). From studies of adult learning, we know this notion has some truth, and we know that adult learners have life experience in abundance. Younger students, who do not have that experience, may gain some of it from their games, which puts gaming in a different light. Gee asserts that the social consequence of viewing computer games as a learning venue is that such games provide experiential learning to people who otherwise might not have access to it. Those with experiences will have a different level of knowledge and understanding from those who are merely able to read a book (xi). Nonetheless, if they are introduced to gaming in an OWC, adult students might have difficulty seeing the game as a literacy-based strategy, thinking instead that their precious time is wasted. Instructors who use game-based lessons need to be explicit in expressing their reasoning to appeal to adult students.

What their younger counterparts in the classroom may see as literate behavior will appear much different from the reading and writing that adult learners expect from school—particularly since FYW and other writing-intensive courses should meet their understanding of usefulness in addition to credit requirements. According to Jonathan Alexander (2006), digital-era youth-produced texts (often web-based texts with images and audio/video) are more than text-based and there—in spare language—the younger students he studied seemed to shine (384). Today's digitally literate youth can be described as interested and adept in "manipulating media images, texts, and even whole genres through hyperbole, irony, and parody." These are "different literacy emphases" (26) from what the adult student may understand as valid learning about writing.

Change is happening to be sure. While the OWC typically is one where learning to produce text-rich genres and forms is the focus, in select—often privileged—settings that value digital rhetorical awareness, composition is becoming more than a text-based endeavor. It also is one where text meets visual imagery, voice, and other media. Nonetheless, I think that learning to produce text-based genres will continue to be the goal of most writing courses, which keeps reading and writing alphabetic text a familiar goal of OWI.

Indeed, returning adult students for whom a more traditional piece of writing is a significant key to success at work may struggle with the new literacy possibilities of the digital world. Jukes et al. (2010) indicate that the "use of digital tools for work is often overlooked" in favor of their recreational uses. They continue: "The cognitive skills required to solve complex problems using the digital tools they know so well are often underdeveloped" (48). If true, then the digital-era adult learner is at a distinct disadvantage both in the classroom and at work.

Henning (2012) explains that technology use in teaching and learning situations can frustrate both faculty (as adult learner-teachers) and their adult students and make them reluctant to try educational technologies (p. 11). This posture can contrast sharply with the students' facile uses of digital technology in the work world or in private life. Indeed, the ability to link an iPhone, iPad, and iPod for work and pleasure may not translate well to using a learning management system (LMS) in the classroom, where there are different stakes informed by a childhood of grades perceived as judgment. In online learning settings, adult students are not always comfortable with new uses and applications of technology. This lack of comfort sometimes translates to a need for teachers to take the lead and actively pull students along to where teachers would like them to go; this is a strategy of adolegogy. For example, such students may benefit from a phone call where the instructor walks the student through how to post a paper assignment in the LMS or discusses the point of an assigned journal entry; the goal is to validate the students' challenges and empower them for the next independent stage.

Stapleton et al. (2007) find that the Millennials they studied shared with older adults a perception of satisfaction and a sense of learning with online courses. However, the adult students of varied ages expressed lower comfort levels with online course discussions while indicating they were more comfortable initiating interactions with teachers than the Millennials (105–6). Both being uncomfortable with online peer discussions and wanting or needing to be in greater communication with teachers suggests that such older adult students may be leaning on adolegogical learning strategies in online settings. In an interesting contrast, Xu and Jaggars (2013) learn from their study of the Washington (state) community college students "that older students adapted more readily to online courses than did younger students." However, they label that finding "intriguing, given that older college students tend to have poorer academic outcomes overall" and that they "did more poorly in online than in face-to-face courses" (23). It seems important to understand the returning adult's needs more completely since the adaptability that Xu and Jaggars found did not transfer into their unqualified success in the online courses. Given that online courses are a more flexible educational choice when juggling other life responsibilities, one would hope that adult students would experience more success overall in this environment.

I do not consider such currently mixed results to be reason to reject OWI for this population. There are many considerations that researchers still need to study and equally as many ways that teachers can change their approaches with older nontraditional students. As Jacobs and Hundley (2010) suggest, there are some circumstances for which pedagogy is more appropriate and ones for which andragogy is more appropriate, to which I would add that there are yet others for which a thoughtful adolegogical blending of the two approaches is most appropriate. Teaching reading and writing in an online setting, as this book explains, is one of those circumstances. To this end, it is useful to see online adult learners as a blend of the two types of learners and adolegogy as providing a strategy with potential for meeting their literacy needs.

REMIXING THE NONTRADITIONAL, DIGITAL-ERA STUDENT

From these descriptions of students—youth and adult—we can begin to see why educators are struggling with understanding and teaching them in this digital age. In addition, within these two groups are students with a variety of reading and writing skills and physical, learning, linguistic, and socioeconomic challenges. Students with physical challenges like blindness, deafness, or paralyzed limbs often require different hardware, software, and formats for their written instruction. Those with learning challenges like ADD, dyslexia, and audio processing disorders have other needs. Linguistically, some of these students are speakers of multiple languages with different degrees of fluency in each. Socioeconomically, some young students are immigrants to technology as much as their adult counterparts. Providing access to all students complicates the picture.

In our *A Position Statement of Principles and Example Effective Practices for Online Writing Instruction* (2013), the CCCC OWI Committee delineates fifteen core principles. We recommend that providing inclusion and access for all students (and teachers)—particularly those with physical challenges, learning disabilities, multilingual histories, and socioeconomic disadvantages—should be considered the overarching principle for effective teaching and learning in OWI. In other words, rather than retrofitting an OWC for accessibility, they should be developed with accessibility as a foremost consideration. Because the presence of such diverse students often is masked in the online setting where students may not disclose their special needs, the question becomes not whether such a student is in a course but how to provide improved access for all students from the outset — such that accommodation generally is unnecessary and yet easily accomplished if additional inclusive actions are required. Indeed, whether or not students' learning needs are masked, it is a big job to teach all of them appropriately and effectively in an online setting. Thus, the complexity of teaching contemporary college students both online and in the onsite classroom is clear. The important concerns of inclusivity and access are more completely addressed in Chapter 2 and then acknowledged throughout the rest of the book.

This chapter has developed a snapshot of OWI students in terms of their relationship to learning and to digital technology. Unquestionably, writing instructors need to focus on a variety of literacy skills when teaching online because students of all types have diverse needs, approaches to education, and connections to digital tools. In particular, writing students have the following literacy needs:

- Conscious reflection of anytime, anywhere communication
- Deep reading with and without visual/audio guides
- Reading for research
- Addressing challenging texts
- Learning strategies for fast, slow, and skim reading
- Reading situations in social and transactional settings
- Choosing when and why to multitask
- Analyzing the relative values of digital tools for education, social life, and workplace settings
- Taking educational risks
- Developing the habit of mind necessary to distinguish just-in-time from just-in-case learning
- Writing of various genres outside academic writing
- Collaborating confidently and at different levels in writing projects

These literacy needs may have somewhat different qualities in OWI settings, which are addressed in this book. The emerging picture conveys some of the literacy challenges facing writing students in online settings, setting the stage for Chapter 2 and the reading and writing strategies in Parts Two and Three of this book.

2

Reading and Writing in Sync

At the college level where the traditional classroom approach to learning is disrupted by digital tools, we need to pay more—not less—attention to basics like reading. The Introduction uses the analogy of needing different, amped-up muscles to learn and teach well in OWI. As Chapter 1 indicates, there is a touch of the adolescent in many OWI students in terms of their approaches to learning. Cathy Fleischer (2010) writes in *Reading & Writing & Teens: A Parent's Guide to Adolescent Literacy* that adolescent learners face a number of challenges. The literacy demands on them constantly shift because the digital literacies in which many students are immersed change rapidly and frequently (which is not to say that they cannot learn even as toddlers using digital venues as much as they can learn using print ones; see, for example, Hanna Rosin 2013). Nonetheless, audio/video or image-based, touch-and-swipe literacies differ from alphabetic, textual ones. And, as a result of the plethora of digital tools and their educational and game apps, traditional paper-based or lengthier texts may seem less important than they really are. Indeed, both younger and adult college students live with multiple literacies, some of which are taught to them deliberately (i.e., hand-lettered and typed alphabetic text and numbers) and others of which are not (i.e., digital communication in venues like e-mail, IM chat, and Facebook). Hence, college learners—those in their teens and those who are adults with a mixed adolegogical learning style—come to the writing classroom with their own literacy issues that must be addressed by thoughtful teachers.

READING FOR THE COLLEGE STUDENT

In *Framework for Success in Postsecondary Writing* (2011), the Council of Writing Program Administrators, the National Council of Teachers of English, and the National Writing Project emphasize the importance of "critical reading and writing" (7). They also suggest strategies for helping student writers develop critical thinking capabilities through "opportunities and guidance to:

- read texts from multiple points of view (e.g., sympathetic to a writer's position and critical of it) and in ways that are appropriate to the academic discipline or other contexts where the texts are being used;
- write about texts for multiple purposes including (but not limited to) interpretation, synthesis, response, summary, critique, and analysis;
- craft written responses to texts that put the writer's ideas in conversation with those in a text in ways that are appropriate to the academic discipline or context;
- create multiple kinds of texts to extend and synthesize their thinking (e.g., analytic essays, scripts, brochures, short stories, graphic narratives);
- evaluate sources for credibility, bias, quality of evidence, and quality of reasoning;
- conduct primary and secondary research using a variety of print and non-print sources;
- write texts for various audiences and purposes that are informed by research (e.g., to support ideas or positions, to illustrate alternative perspectives, to provide additional contexts); and
- generate questions to guide research." (7)

The key to all of these strategies is the integrated nature of reading and writing. Particularly important is how the act of reading in different ways and with different purposes can enhance the thinking and writing that often follows in a college writing course assignment.

Jukes et al. (2010) assert that although reading and writing remain important skills, "people are reading less and they are reading differently" (113). This statement makes sense; we know from the Web that reading is different when it is chunked, hypertextual, highly visual, and symbolic rather than purely alphabetic. Indeed, even reader-based print media — newspapers, web pages, magazine articles, and advertisements — are becoming observably more image-focused. There are fewer words per article, as lovers of earlier versions of periodicals (e.g., *Smithsonian* magazine, *National Geographic*, and the *Reader's Digest*) can see. According to Jukes et al., "this shift is having a significant impact on traditional reading" because "university training has inculcated a love for words and books that is deeply rooted in the paradigm teachers have for what reading is. However, communication in the world of today is not done exclusively with text" (118). Perhaps not, but text remains crucial to college learners in writing and most other courses.

What kinds of reading do college students typically do? If they are like their high school counterparts, they read functional texts needed to operate daily in the world; such texts are highly influenced by the Web and use icons and symbols to guide and interest readers (118). For communication, functional texts include e-mail and the truncated, IM-ular writing common to texting, IM chat, and tweeting (Hewett and Hewett, 2008). Jukes et al. (2010) note that students also read for enlightenment and enrichment; these kinds of reading would include texts employed for formal learning, sports development, self-help, and religious understanding. A final kind of reading that the authors list involves texts for entertainment and leisure, which encompass online news, blogs, and fiction; the authors claim reading of newspapers and books is a casualty of the digital age, and the increase in alternative types of recreation may support their assumption (118).

Lack of overt reading instruction is especially detrimental in the text-rich OWI environment. Fortunately, reading as a college English skill has enjoyed a sort of revival, becoming "relevant again" (Salvatori and Donahue 2012, 199) because reader-response theories have "situated readers at the center of the interpretive enterprise" (202). Even where a focus on reader-response is now passé, our understanding of students as readers and writers has been enhanced. Nonetheless, according to Mariolina Rizzi Salvatori and Patricia Donahue (2012), in professional conferences at least, the use of the word *reading* in relation to writing is scarce. This rarity suggests a low conscious focus on reading, making reading appear invisible and commonplace (212). In other words, professionally speaking, writing teachers can and should pay more attention to reading. One might surmise that the distancing of literary studies from composition instruction leaves a gap in writing instruction where there once was at least minimal focus on close reading. If we examine our current practices for evidence of deliberate reading instruction outside of developmental reading courses, it appears that there is little overt reading instruction in composition studies, which is to the detriment of students overall (Bunn 2013).

Reading is not a skill that everyone has learned and integrated comfortably into life — as the very presence of college developmental reading courses demonstrates. Mike Rose (2012), whose work in adult literacy is well known, states:

> Some students arrive at college with pretty limited skills, reading at an elementary school level, unable to do more than basic arithmetic, writing undeveloped and error-ridden prose. But students with better literacy and mathematical skills can still have problems with literacy-related academic routines. These can include strategies for reading a textbook, how to use its apparatus

(index, glossary), its layout and format, and its illustrations and changes in font to help the reader determine what's more or less important. How to annotate the book and take notes from it also presents challenges for many students. (n.p.)

This chapter explores some reasons why students enter college with suboptimal reading skills. It considers how we define reading, digital stressors on reading, the brain's relationship to reading, the convergence of reading and writing in OWI, and educators' responsibilities in OWI settings.

WHAT IS READING?

To best understand the deep connections of reading to writing in an OWC, it is helpful to consider the nature of reading. Reading is the alphabet-based literacy skill that changes thinking and opens imaginations through books, magazines, letters, reports, web pages, zines, and blogs. It enables interpersonal communication via e-mail, IM chat, and text messaging. For some of our students, reading began with a favorite lap, adult hands holding a print-bound book, an animated voice, and hearing the same words recited whenever the book was opened. According to neuroscientist Maryanne Wolf (2007), author of *Proust and the Squid: The Story and Science of the Reading Brain*, not everyone has received the same benefits when learning to read:

> The richness of this semantic dimension of reading depends on the riches we have already stored, a fact with important and sometimes devastating developmental implications for our children. Children with a rich repertoire of words and their associations will experience any text or any conversation in ways that are substantively different from children who do not have the same stored words and concepts. (9)

The difference in vocabulary and words spoken to or in front of a child can be as many as 32 million words by the age of five (20). An average five-year-old has a repertoire of 10,000 words (87). Regarding the "devastating developmental implications" of growing up on the lower range of vocabulary exposure and acquisition, Wolf argues that children absorb more words when they learn to read with a caring person — with human interaction — listening to words while looking at the book and connecting reading to something loving and positive; these experiences presumably lead to a richer vocabulary in a deeper contextual and intellectual connection with reading. (Certainly, studies need to be devised to understand better whether and how digital, human-adaptive interaction with words can do what Wolf believes "a caring person" can accomplish regarding vocabulary exposure and acquisition.) Interestingly, socioeconomic stability may not be a strong marker of reading literacy given that children who grow up in financially secure homes may be impoverished in their literacy if they do not receive this kind of early attention that helps to shape and form their brains for reading.

For many children, reading on their own becomes an owned, personal skill sometime between late preschool years and kindergarten classes. Then, somewhere in the late second to third grades — certainly by the fourth grade — teachers shift student attention from *learning to read* to *reading to learn* (135). At that time, some students become lost because their reading skills are weaker than their peers, they have undiscovered learning/reading challenges, they unknowingly need eyeglasses, or they miss the import of this significant shift in reading emphasis. Some of those students lose ground year by school year while their peers gain fluency and skill. Those who have lost ground struggle with meaning making and steadily decreasing confidence. We meet a sampling of these students in refresher reading and writing courses; we also meet many of them in OWI.

Defining Reading

Despite my attempt at the beginning of this section, reading is not easily defined. According to Salvatori and Donahue (2012), "Reading ... is a complex term that signifies a range of ideas, practices, assumptions, and identities" (203). As important as ideas, assumptions, and identities are, when we think of reading in educational settings, we typically think first of the practices involved in acquiring and improving the basic skill. Wolf (2007) outlines five crucial parts of learning to read:

1. phonological development (hearing, segmenting, and understanding the small units of sound that make up words),
2. orthographic development (learning that the writing system represents oral language regarding what letters look like, common letter patterns, and "sight" words),
3. semantic and pragmatic development (learning the meaning of words and how they work culturally and idiomatically),
4. syntactic development (learning the grammatical forms and sentence structures), and
5. morphological development (recognizing small, meaningful units of words like prefixes, suffixes, and tense/number markers, and using them rapidly for meaning making) (113).

Of these five skills, phonological, orthographic, and semantic skills are considered the three primary "code-cracking strategies" for eventual reading fluency (117). A circular learning process develops with children who are offered access to words through vocabulary exposure and who comprehend the meaning of those words. Knowledge improves reading, and reading improves vocabulary (123).

According to Linda Adler-Kassner and Heidi Estrem (2007), reading is "a complex interaction between reader, text, and context" (45). "Good reading," on the other hand, is "evidenced by a dialogue between the writer's ideas and those in the text she is using, as well as an understanding, demonstrated through writing, of the conventions of source use—from interpretation to citation practices" (37). They continue: "good reading involves at least an awareness that interacting with and interpreting text is not neutral, that it is always 'sponsored.' But this definition also suggests that readers must play an active role in 'good reading'" (38; see also Maclellan 1997; Wolf 2007). The conscious understanding that one must be active in reading is appropriate to college-level instruction. Students need to understand reading as part of their purposeful learning enterprise; they should be developmentally ready for self-reflection and awareness so that they can choose either a surface or deep approach to their reading. Effie Maclellan (1997) states the following in her seminal article "Reading to Learn":

> Students who conceive of learning only as "more things to know or remember" are going to treat the text as though it were a repository of facts to be raided. On the other hand, students who recognize that a text might radically affect the way they think about aspects of reality are going to engage with the line of reasoning expounded and evaluated in terms of a range of criteria. (285)

When composition students look to their reading assignments as merely a fact base, they may gain some knowledge but not necessarily a sense of how to use it in their writing or for their writing development. Such shallow reading—sadly linked to some shallow writing assignments—naturally leads to the kind of patchwriting and plagiarism that Rebecca Moore Howard, Tricia Serviss, and Tanya K. Rodrigue (2010) report in "Writing from Sources, Writing from Sentences."

The Textbase and the Situation Model

While content knowledge can lead to a shallow understanding of "one's physical, social, or psychological world," it provides only a "textbase" of information (Maclellan 1997, 278). On the other hand, critical conceptual information, gained from a deeper reading, is necessary to understand the meaning in a text regardless of one's ability to read and understand the words. Using the language of Walter Kintsch and T. A. van Dijk (1978), Maclellan (1997) contrasts a "textbase" whereby students can "construct a representation of what the text says" with a "situation model" whereby they can "construct a representation of what the text is about" (278). Extant

or even add-on knowledge has a place in reading, but the ability to build a situation model is more important because it enhances deeper learning.
In constructing the textbase:

> the reader will activate a whole range of seemingly pertinent information. This knowledge will include both information retrieved from long-term memory and inferences which are generated by the reader to make the text more coherent. However, much of the information which is activated will turn out to be irrelevant to, or inconsistent with, the particular context of the text. The reader must then decide which information to "dump" and what to retain. It is in the excising of irrelevant information and the integration of pertinent information that the reader constructs the situation model. The significance of the situation model is what it allows the reader to do as a result of reading. Having constructed a situation model, the reader can use the instruction manual to operate the computer, can use the set of directions to travel from one place to another, can successfully modify the cookery recipe to take account of available ingredients. In other words the availability of the situation model allows the reader to use the text to solve problems or effect appropriate action. (278)

Although constructing a textbase of information can lead to learning for writing purposes, constructing the situation model enables deeper writing. For example, in research reading for an article or book, educators-as-writers dig into the information to see how it connects meaningfully with a theory or argument being developed. Sometimes, the connection is not an obvious one, but once something has been read, it changes the writer's thinking on some level, causing a new line of thought to arise. Student writers, however, often read at the level of building a textbase merely to complete an assignment in a just-in-case learning scenario, as discussed in Chapter 1. When they do so, they often are left with an uncritical view of how to use a source and may employ it to patchwrite and copy from a text where they think it might be useful.

Patchwriting occurs when students "don't understand [what they have read] and don't know how to do anything but grab a few sentences and go" (Berrett 2012, n.p.). In their study, Rebecca Moore Howard and Sandra Jamieson (quoted in Berrett 2012) learn that students use sources often to patchwrite, but never to summarize an article's meaning. Students often inadequately reference, quote, or cite direct uses of text and paraphrase (179). Howard and Jamieson also investigate students' uses of sources for researched writing. Howard was quoted as saying: "'Habitually grazing texts online may also play a role. . . . It is true that the new literacies are changing the way we read, and many of us, including me, do a lot more skimming than we used to do. The trouble is, [students] are not also learning how to read deeply'" (n.p.), which suggests that they may not be able to contextualize their reading as mind-broadening information. Patchwriting is a poor sub-stitute for students' need to understand and summarize text they read for research, and its use indicates lack of deep reading and/or analytical ability.

Most writing teachers and tutors are familiar with the result of this kind of reading in student essays. For instance, while students may recognize the thinness of peers' evidence or authoritative support for their claims, they lack the language for helping each other to go deeper into the reading, which would help them to write more critically. I frequently have heard peer group members say to each other, for example, "Add more quotes," by which I think students mean "You're missing something here. Deepen the argu-ment with more support and pertinent sources." A typical student response to that guidance is to supply a single-sentence quote here or there instead of substantive and meaningful support from an outside source. The genuinely critical readers and writers that we hope to train in writing courses need to learn how to build a situation model from the reading, excise the irrelevant information, and integrate only the pertinent information into the writing.

Context Clues

Savvy student readers will have learned (or will relearn easily from exercises such as those found in Part Two) to find context clues in a text's organiza-tion. Such clues help readers to understand the information in the genre in which it is being provided. For example, Maclellan (1997) points out that there are logical patterns that we consciously and unconsciously know to be a part of exposition, which is writing that explains something to us. In exposition, we may see thought patterns of comparison, contrast, definition, and classification. We likely will see a formal type of discourse, and we may be able to find the main point, or thesis, fairly quickly. Such text differs radically from narrative, which tends to be organized more chronologically, reflects a narrator's point of view, and has a decidedly more informal feel.

Students typically begin their reading life with narratives — from a toddler's storybooks to early school experiences with fiction — moving to exposition later in their reading years and into such sophisticated genres as argument in still later years. This reading development nicely mirrors the writing developmental process that James Moffett (1983) claims most helps writers — moving from recording and reporting (narrative) to generalizing (exposition) to theorizing (argumentation). Maclellan (1997) states that the well-known structure of the genres with which students are familiar enables them to read at a higher level of meaning because they do not have to work out the type of writing they are encountering. Organizational signals such as headings, subheadings, paragraphs, summaries, abstracts, and font changes announce focal points and help readers process the text. Nonetheless, text will not always be structured or presented as well-organized. Some texts will be difficult to read for that reason, and some of those texts can be found in any discipline and from any set of readings provided to students. Such structural disruption requires a strategic response to text (283), which stronger readers can provide because they recognize a genre's features, allowing them to read even poorly organized texts or those without structural signals for meaning. Those who can do such reading tend to gain more conceptual knowledge. Stating that "the role of extant conceptual knowledge is very important," Maclellan frankly remarks that "those who know more, learn more" (279).

Reading Critically

What we ask students to do with the texts they are reading has major importance for whether they will absorb it into their learning lives. Because good reading requires both content knowledge and an ability to take information and use it conceptually, if students cannot:

> construct a situation model but [their extant knowledge] is nevertheless sufficient to construct the textbase . . . , we must be clear about what products we expect from their reading and what value we can place on such products. If the only demands which are made of students are that they recall or report the gist of their reading, or make some low-level inferences from information in the text, or otherwise engage in tasks that would fall into the category of "knowledge-telling" (Bereiter & Scardamalia, 1987), the extent of their learning must be recognized for what it is: as limited and possibly not fulfilling the aims of higher education. While students may indeed require [sic] to learn facts from their reading material, most higher education would have as an aim that learners go beyond the specifics and confines of a particular course and use content in successively more sophisticated ways of understanding the world (Biggs & Collis, 1982; Ramsden, 1992). (Maclellan 1997, 279–80)

Maclellan's argument that college-level students should be able to read and apply their learning in ever more critical ways seems apt. Developing such sophisticated reading, however, relies on students to self-engage with and work their way through sometimes challenging material. As Chapter 1 points out, students who give in to a sense of boredom when their desires for twitch-speed learning are not met likely will miss this mark.

For OWI or any college-level writing or writing-intensive course, critical thinking and writing are the primary aims of reading whether that reading is research for an essay, content about how to write, or other instruction pertinent to the course. To that end, instructors ask conceptual understanding of students and, therefore, require of them a higher-level reading skill. Such skill is more sophisticated than what Nathan (2005) indicates undergraduates, first-year students in particular, are willing to engage unless instructors do something specific to provide them with direction, skill, and an impetus to do so.

THE DIGITAL READING ERA

How does the digital era in which we live and teach affect reading? Wolf (2007) suggests that "ironically, today's hypertext and online text provide a dimension of virtual dialogue to reading computer-based presentations" that "requires new cognitive skills" (220). Indeed, there are new types of reading involved in the digital age that include analyzing and understanding URLs, their syntax, and cookies. Shopping tags have changed the way we read advertisements online and computers market to us, providing intelligent guesses about what we might want or need to read next as well as what we might want to buy next. These types of readings demand their own kinds of analyses about which we are only now learning. Wolf expresses concern that digital-era readers may not question or fully comprehend the information that they find so quickly online, much of which is found without critical effort and often is read on a shallow level:

> And within children's particularly vulnerable transition to the level of fluent, comprehending reader we must exert our greatest efforts to ensure that immersion in digital resources does not stunt our children's capacity to evaluate, analyze, prioritize, and probe what lies beneath any form of information. We must teach our children to be "bi-textual," or "multi-textual," able to read and analyze texts flexibly in different ways, with more deliberate instruction at every stage of development on the inferential, demanding aspects of any text. Teaching children to uncover the invisible world that resides in written words needs to be both explicit and part of a dialogue between learner and teacher, if we are to promote the processes that lead to fully formed expert reading in our citizenry. (226)

Such overt teaching should happen at all levels — the college level in particular — because everyone's reading strategies will need continuing adjustment as digital materials become ubiquitous.

Reading from Digital Technology

Like many scholars, Wolf expresses concern about how today's digital-era children will differ from those of her generation as they read text presented on the computer more than hard copy text: "In other words, when seemingly complete visual information is given almost simultaneously, as it is in many digital presentations, is there either sufficient time or sufficient motivation to process the information more inferentially, analytically, and critically?" Or, she wonders, "Does the potential added information from hyperlinked text contribute to the development of children's thinking?" And, finally, she poses a key question for OWI: "Should we begin to provide explicit instruction for reading multiple modalities of text presentation to ensure that our children learn multiple ways of processing information?" (16).

The vagaries of reading text from digital devices are directly connected to the different literacy skills necessary for reading from a computer or mobile device. In *Writing Technology: Studies on the Materiality of Literacy*, Christina Haas (1996) published seminal research into reading and rereading just as the computer boom was influencing today's adult students. Her research occurred from 1983 through 1991 with writers from eighteen to fifty-two years old. Among other issues, she investigates whether and how writers read from hard copy versus the computer screen with a focus on spatial recall, retrieving information, and reading to revise.

While all the writers that Haas studied indicated satisfaction and comfort with their computers for writing, they expressed reading difficulties from the computer screens alone. Given that "writers move back and forth between writing and reading as they produce text" (and in writing classes, they also move between instructor and peer feedback and their revisions), the participants complained about several scenarios (55). First, they had difficulty finding certain parts of their writing and moving to it quickly. This problem has to do with spatial recognition, which is what we use when we remember and can retrieve information from the relative vertical position it has on a page and whether, in a book, that page is to the right or the left. Although most word processing programs now have a number of ways to search text, doing so requires remembering some of the exact wording. Those who read books from a tablet, Kindle, or other mobile device might have a similar problem with finding a memorable line or something they want to cite. It is challenging to recall first a chapter and then how many times one clicked or touched the screen to find the right "page." Some of these devices now provide digital bookmarks to help with spatial recall, but it still may present a problem. Indeed, reading from a cell phone, which some students do regularly, offers no spatial cues if the reading involves continuous scrolling.

Another problem that participants indicated was that the text they wrote on the computer led to a decreased sense of "intimacy" that they believed was made possible "with pen and paper" (55). They had increased difficulties, as well, in reorganizing texts online and finding errors. Screen reading interfered with these tasks, leading many of the participants to print and use hard copy as a natural part of their writing process: "Even writers who called themselves 'adamant' computer writers took it for granted that computer writing does not mean that one forgoes a hard copy" (55). This lesson, natural to computer writers in the 1980s and early 1990s, might be one that contemporary OWI students need to learn from explicit teaching.

One of Haas's most important findings is that "a computer is not a computer is not a computer" in that different hardware (screen sizes and types) as well as software configurations led her research participants to different reading experiences (51). Even the interface software—using a keyboard or a scroll bar to move the text vertically and whether one used a mouse, for example—led to different reading experiences. Add today's eraser mouse, scratch pad, and swipe technology, and the reading experience changes again. Haas learned that while readers had similar experiences of reading text on a hard copy page and a large screen computer, reading from a smaller screen was "significantly slower" (67). Studying these kinds of conditions for reading is important given the various types of devices from which students are reading today: full-sized desktop screens, mini-notebook screens, tablet and other mobile reading screens (e.g., Kindle or Nook), and mobile cell phone screens.

From these findings alone, it becomes obvious that it is vital to understand how reading and rereading changes from one digital device to another. Per Wolf's (2007) earlier question, such an understanding absolutely needs to be conveyed to students in explicit ways to help them become more critical readers and thinkers about what and how they are reading with digital technology.

Scholars and educators worry about the rapid changes that are occurring in communication strategies and digital tools—how and what students learn. They express concern that students are not learning what they need to learn while they engage with technology. Wolf explains that written language enables us to think beyond what we know before reading what we do not know. This generative capacity of reading is essential, and Wolf stresses that "we must not lose this essential quality in our present moment of historical transition to the new ways of acquiring, processing, and comprehending information" (17). In other words, reading is central to thinking critically and learning beyond our direct experience. Even though digital technology infuses our lives with different reading forms for which different reading strategies are necessary—such as the need to read images for meaning—the act of learning to read alphabetic text remains important. It is equally critical to understand how text written on and read from digital devices changes that act.

THE BRAIN ON TEXT

Wolf (2007) notes that reading is the most important step in a human's intellectual development—particularly now as the digital world continues to encompass more of our lives (ix). By recasting all students as nontraditional given their relationships to digital technology, we validate the assumption that students today are different. However, that is not to say that one kind of reading skill—paper, hard copy versus digital text—is more valuable than the other. Both skill sets "are equally essential today" (Jukes et al. 2010, 38), which means that some aspects of twentieth-century learning should not be abandoned to accommodate a completely digital, twenty-first-century world. Reading instruction from traditional text is one of those aspects.

The Plastic Brain

What does neuroscience teach us about the brain and its relationship to text—whether traditional or digital? It is becoming common to hear that the brain is "plastic" in its adaptive nature. Many researchers are talking about how the brain's neural pathways are changed by our experiences, particularly those experiences with digital media (Davidson 2012; Jukes et al. 2010, 2; Small and Vorgan 2008; Wolf 2007). Davidson (2012) defines learning as "the constant disruption of an old pattern, a breakthrough that substitutes something new for something old" (5). It follows that humans are genetically programmed for breakthroughs, and technology for learning is one of those breakthroughs: "Reading can be learned only because of the brain's plastic design, and when reading takes place, that individual brain is forever changed, both physiologically and intellectually" (Wolf 2007, 5). That change is so profound that people who learn a language other than or in addition to English have different neurological connections, which a brain map would illustrate.

Wolf (2007) believes that the foundation for reading stems from the following three brain-design principles: "the capacity to make new connections among older structures; the capacity to form areas of exquisitely precise specialization for recognizing patterns and information; and the ability to learn to recruit and connect information from these areas automatically" (12). As the brain begins to connect "the visual, auditory, semantic, syntactic, and inferential information" from any text, the reader makes connections between her "own thinking and personal insights"; hence, the brain does its work and the reader does hers (15).

Wolf explains that because of the brain's plasticity, it naturally is reshaped and rewired by our experiences. Indeed, younger students born to the digital age are said to be neurologically wired differently from adult students newer to digital technology. According to neuroscientist Gary Small and coauthor GiGi Vorgan (2008), younger students "process information in a parallel or simultaneous manner, not sequential[ly] like ours" (19). Because the brain changes and learns with experiences, when our experiences and learning are as vastly different as those for people born prior to 1990 and those born after, the ways that we read, think, and write critically will differ proportionately (Wolf 2007). To that end, Jukes et al. (2010) suggest that traditional literacy creates a left-brained, linear, logical, twentieth-century learning style and that the new digital literacy creates a right-brained, "non-linear, light-, and sound-based" style (22–23).

According to Wolf (2007), "Knowing what reading demands of our brain and knowing how it contributes to our capacity to think, to feel, to infer, and to understand other human beings is especially important today as we make the transition from a reading brain to an increasingly digital one" (4). The capacity to learn to read—in theory—exists in each of our brains (albeit differently for those with certain learning challenges); in other words, most human beings possess the innate capacity to learn to read. However, while the brain is hardwired for many things, reading is not one of them. Reading is a skill that each person has to develop individually because reading is purely a cultural invention. It cannot be passed genetically through the generations and it must be learned by each individual brain through similar painstaking and multidimensional processes. Each person and each generation must learn to read on its own (11). As the current generation born to the digital age grows older and produces new generations, the reading brain—per Wolf's terminology—that many readers of this book developed will give way to an increasingly digital brain in that reading will look different and, hence, so will the brain's wiring.

The Fluent Reading Brain

Fluency in reading is a highly desirable skill, one that all too many students have missed. One of Wolf's concerns is whether digital learning, which she believes involves often shallow reading and significantly more image processing, may negatively affect alphabetic-text reading fluency: "Fluent word recognition is significantly propelled by both vocabulary and grammatical knowledge. . . . For the word-poor child, reality actually worsens because of the usually undiscussed fact that precious little explicit vocabulary instruction goes on in most classrooms" (2007, 129). The combination of too little vocabulary instruction and digital learning from an early age certainly may affect reading fluency.

Fluency is a tricky subject to discuss with readers because feelings of embarrassment or shame may be attached to the word. One older student, for example, explained to me that she sees herself as a poor reader because she reads very slowly and may need to reread passages for clarity. Nonetheless, she usually can explain what she reads and connect it in a situation model, as Maclellan (1997) suggests is necessary for higher-level reading. (Rereading, by the way, is a strength and key literacy strategy, as this chapter later suggests.) However, as Wolf (2007) explains, fluency is not speed-related; rather:

> it is a matter of being able to utilize all the special knowledge a child has about a word—its letters, letter patterns, meanings, grammatical functions, roots, and endings—fast enough to have time to think and comprehend. Everything about a word contributes to how fast it can be read. The point of becoming fluent, therefore, is to read—really read—and understand. (130–31)

Enlisted in this goal are "key executive functions such as working memory and comprehension skills such as inference and analogy" (131). It is hard to overstress the importance of fluency over accuracy, the need to be a *fluent* reader rather than merely a *good* decoder. As noted earlier, American fourth graders who have not yet acquired fluency may be set up for years of frustration because "through no fault of their own, most fourth-grade teachers never take a course in teaching reading to children who have not acquired fluency" (135). Sadly, at this time in their education, many nonfluent readers begin to fail both grade-wise and in self-image.

To improve fluency, students must learn reading comprehension strategies. Comprehension is more than learning facts or simple content; it reflects "an increased capacity to apply an understanding of the varied uses of words — irony, voice, metaphor, and point of view — to go below the surface of the text" (Wolf 2007, 137). The knowledge of figurative language and style provides tools for finding new and deeper meaning in texts. Thus, we "unpeel the layers of meaning in a word, phrase, or thought" (138). It is this kind of comprehension — developing a situation model over a mere textbase — that writing instructors seek when they ask students to read material as research or source material for their writing as well as for genre and writing technique models.

According to Wolf, the main benefit of reading fluency is that it leads to more time in their lives. The "fluent comprehender's brain doesn't need to expend as much effort, because its regions of specialization have learned to represent the important visual, phonological, and semantic information and to retrieve this information at lightning speed" (142). With this level of fluency, "the brain becomes fast enough to think and feel differently," providing a "gift of time" — a precious commodity in our day, indeed (143).

Given enough reading history and practice, the fluent reader may become an expert reader. Being an expert entails "the almost instantaneous fusion of cognitive, linguistic, and effective processes; multiple brain regions; and billions of neurons that are the sum of all that goes into reading" (Wolf 2007, 145). The expert reader is "equipped with circuits in the visual cortex that did not exist prior to reading," demonstrating one of the ways that literacy changes the human brain on a person-by-person basis (149). In reading, we use our brains — particularly our executive processing — to predict, anticipate, plan, infer, hypothesize, and check our intellectual responses against what we are reading to see whether we are correct. The actual text confirms or denies our hypothetical thinking about what might or should occur in it; any mismatch requires a rereading and revision of the thinking-to-text connection (160). Reading expertise is demonstrated when a reader's lexical and syntactical skills combine with previous linguistic knowledge and reader experience to fill in conceptual gaps (Birch 2008, 77). Wolf (2007) explains that "the expert reader is living testimony to our consciously expanding intellectual evolution" (160).

Saccades, Fixations, and Regressions

Brain science also has provided ways to understand more about the processes of reading, which may help to answer how reading changes when alphabetic text is written using and read from digital devices. There is a great deal that technology can teach about the brain on text:

> The dramatically growing use of computer technology in every part of the educational system starting in the elementary grades has created a need to know much more about what students do when they look at and interact with screens; this activity includes reading, scanning, selecting, and focusing on a range of textual information, still and moving images, and elements of the screen used to control what is seen next. (Anson and Schwegler 2012, 163)

When we read, our eyes move across the page or the screen. The advent of computer or mobile device screen reading enables technology that reads the eyes' movements, called saccades. Saccades are eye glances between point A and point B on a page or screen. A fixation is the moment when the eyes rest on a point on a page or screen. A regression is a backward movement to text previously viewed, potentially done to check or improve comprehension (Birch 2008, 7; see also Horning 1978). As Chris M. Anson and Robert A. Schwegler (2012) state: "In real time, the eyes are still for much more time than they are moving. Readers may feel as if their eyes have seen every word, but their brains are providing more information for their comprehension than what's literally on the page" (156–57). In other words, the eyes convey what they see to the reading brain, which works to decode phonics, orthography, semantics, syntax, and morphology, as well as to engage the processes of prediction, anticipation, planning, inference, hypothesis, and checking out thinking against the reading for correctness—all at lightning-fast speed and irrespective of seeing every single word.

It is useful to teach students that we spend more time with fixations than with saccades, using the fixation to determine important information versus information that can be skipped with the intended meaning relatively intact. Students may not realize that readers regularly skip phrases that are repeated where, for example, an appositive phrase stands in for a noun, as well as patterned phrases (157). We also fixate more on content words than on functional ones, use partial information from consonants better than from vowels, and take "snapshots" of word information a few words beyond where the eyes will move next (Birch 2008, 76–77). Slow readers like my older student may be slow precisely because they use regressions to return to earlier saccades, checking their understanding of previous text. Because we infer a great deal from the text as opposed to reading every word, we may not get the exact same conceptual sense from separate readings of the same text.

Eye tracking devices mediated by computer technology may be able to provide information about the relationship between reading and writing.[1] In their study of eye tracking, Anson and Schwegler (2012) indicate that by looking at eye movements as the eyes track across the page, we learn "not that the text is smoothly offering up its meaning but that you're doing most of the work, actively constructing meaning from the words to create a coherent mental representation" (152). This idea of reading as work is valuable for understanding what students are asked to do in a writing course, whether traditional or online. Students can benefit from learning that what *feels* like work to them actually *is* work in which they can choose to engage. Not only is this an issue of motivation, but it also is a realization that may help students who secretly fear they are suboptimal readers to see themselves more realistically and to renew their energy and efforts for college-level reading.

Anson and Schwegler (2012) also considered how eye-tracking data could help educators understand how students read and fixate or fail to do so with either their own or others' writing: "Currently, we also know little about what students do when they read texts in progress and published texts—whether, for example, they behave differently knowing that one kind of text is in need of further revision and editing while the other, presumably, is not" (165). Their point is well taken because students likely consider instructors' texts—whether content or instructional guidance—to be polished. The kind of attention this apparently finished writing garners can help us to understand how deeply students read instructional text and where they stumble. I speculate that instructional reading is less interesting than other kinds of reading students might encounter, and, at a minimum, I think students pay attention differently when they read instructional text. To pay good attention to such writing, students need to engage their motivation for success. While only a hypothesis, instructors would do well to think carefully about what and how they write instruction for students, as Part Three of this book addresses.

---

[1]Sung-Eui Yoon, Enrico Gobbetti, David Kasik, and Dinesh Manocha (2008) indicate that digital-age immigrants have a Z-curve pattern in reading a page. The Z reflects the eyes finding "an intersection about one-third of the way down the page and one-third of the way in from the left side" (Jukes et al. 2010, 27). Greg Byerly, Jason Holmes, David Robins, Yin Zang, and Athena Salaba (2006) used eye-tracking software and a heat map to study how digital-age natives read, "whether students were concentrating or confused, were reading or quickly browsing, or were engaged in or ignoring parts of the Web pages" (n.p.). From these studies, Jukes et al. (2010) surmised an F-pattern in that "the digital generation typically tends to unconsciously ignore the right side and bottom half of the page and will only read content in those areas if they are highly motivated to do so" (27). Although as reported these results are too sketchy to guide instructional practices at this time, they suggest a future understanding that, for example, may enable teachers who write content for students to format it strategically for improved digital reading.

Attention in Reading

Brain science also can help educators understand issues of attention, which can be applied to reading. Davidson (2012) notes that people simply do not see or miss the same things in any particular situation. She bases this observation on an experiment where viewers were shown two teams playing a ball game with each team wearing a different colored shirt; viewers were asked to count the number of people on each team. After they had time to make their count, they were asked whether they had seen a gorilla (a person in a gorilla suit actually had wandered onto the playing area). Few people saw the gorilla because their focus was on counting the team members.

Davidson's point is that if we change where we typically focus our attention, we will learn more and gain a different perspective on the world. Our world is busier and more information crazed than ever before, and when our attention is divided—such as through multitasking—or hyperfocused, we miss important things like a gorilla in the room. She calls the problem "attention blindness." As a remedy, Davidson recommends using collaborative partners both to share and divide our attention usefully. Cooperating with people to look for other things or to take advantage of their particular attention style, she surmises, helps to create a bigger picture and provide more options for working in an increasingly digital world.

Davidson states that "our ability to pinpoint a problem and solve it, an achievement honed in all those years in school and beyond—may be exactly what limits us" (3). Because we have been taught to see in particular ways, she contends we miss many things that could be considered within our view: "The more you concentrate, the more other things you miss" (4). Davidson's point that we need to teach cooperation fits within the requirements our students have or will have in the globally networked work world. It fits, too, with the need for teaching layered collaboration in writing courses (discussed more completely in Chapter 3), while it highlights that such interactive collaboration must be considered acceptable and desirable instead of as a form of cheating or stealing another's ideas.

THE HARD WORK OF READING

For good reasons, writing often is coupled with reading essays and articles in composition courses. Patricia Dunn (1995) claims that "reading and writing form a whole process of discovery and cannot be separated into parts" (4). Similarly, David Bartholomae and Anthony Petrosky (2002) contend that the writing course is the best place to read and to learn to read better. For students, "the reading/writing connection needs to be made explicit," says Lori Mayo (2000, 74). While reading can happen without writing, Alice Horning (1978) indicates that writing is critically connected to reading:

"In order to write, however, one must know how to read. . . . One must be able to develop the highly specialized reading skills needed to write successfully: the skills of proofreading, of knowing where to look for information on the printed page, sorting, storing, and analyzing the print for the total message" (265).

In other words, reading and writing are inextricably connected as literacy skills especially where a writing course is concerned.

Making that connection work for students is a challenge, however. For Mayo (2000), writing more complex texts can help students to better read more complex texts (75; see also Bartholomae and Petrosky 2002). Such complexity can help students find the music of language, something that they may in fact apply to their own writing, finding rhythm in their writing (76). To reach that goal, however, Mayo recommends that success may reside in "reading *shorter* texts" in the writing course (76; italics mine), whereas Bartholomae and Petrosky (2002) recommend assigning more complex texts that "leave some work for readers to do" (vi).

The Read/Write Cycle for an OWI Assignment

As outlined in the Introduction, in order for students to learn to write well in OWI settings, teachers depend on students' ability to read well even more than in onsite settings where they are afforded oral communication.

Educators may think that if the student is a good reader, he will be able to understand what the teacher, tutor, or peer is saying in the response and then enact that advice, guidance, or required change without any problem. This is not an accurate scenario for a lot of students from various backgrounds. Any student can exhibit problems with reading and using instructional text about writing and about their own writing in particular. To use the instructional text well, the student needs to be able to make an explicit cognitive connection between that written guidance and his own writing.

Certainly a student can be a good reader of various genres — fiction, biographies, lab reports, textbooks (although many students are not, as this chapter makes clear) — but not necessarily a good reader of instructional text about his or her writing. Particularly in an online setting, instructional text includes language about essays, arguments, expositions, thesis sentences, assertions, topic sentences, content development, organization, and various concerns at the sentence level. Students often must decipher the thick jargon of the English and rhetoric and composition disciplines. Furthermore, they must figure out hidden meaning behind timeworn and clichéd abbreviations (e.g., awk, sp, verb conf, frag, shift, tense, and ¶) that teachers still use; edits; and corrections to sentence-level concerns that their teachers might say are far less important than the higher-order content-based concerns, but are belied by the evidence in the markup, commentary, and grade (for seminal work in this area, see Sommers 1982). In short, students have to understand the meaning of these words in application to their own writing without the benefit of the teacher's body/face/voice intervention about their writing. In other words, it often requires a cognitive leap from what the written instruction is supposed to convey to what the student is supposed to do in the writing.

As explained in *The Online Writing Conference: A Guide for Teachers and Tutors* (Hewett 2015), the problem of written instructional intention versus student interpretation can lead to a lack of student success in any given writing assignment. Furthermore, students do not always know what questions to ask when they are unclear about the feedback they receive whether it occurs in the onsite or online setting. In the online setting, particularly, students who are unclear about feedback often have difficulty expressing their lack of understanding because they now have to use writing to express their problems with the written instruction and their own writing (Hewett 2004–2005, 2006, 2010, 2015). The body/face/voice and corresponding visual/oral/aural components are gone. The problem emerges in reading the instructional text and translating what they have read into something they can enact in their writing about that text (to ask a question) or to write from it (to make changes through revision). Students must make a challenging and correct cognitive leap from reading to action, and that requires comprehension both of the feedback and of how to apply it to the draft. Thus, reading instructional text in OWI can strongly affect what students do with the feedback and guidance that teachers, tutors, and even peers give them. It certainly can affect their overall writing development.

To understand the hard work of reading in an OWC, let us look at just one type of reading that students must do in an asynchronous paper cycle: instructional text relative to essay drafts. In an essay cycle, teachers provide written content for students to read and from which to learn. They also write assignments to encourage different genres and levels of writing. Students read the content and assignments, and then submit or publish a piece of writing to their teachers, tutors, or peers, who respond to it in writing and return it to the students for their responses. The students' responses, while dialogic in that they constitute a response to a written message, typically is limited to the choice to revise or not and whether to actually use the feedback provided in a revision. In asynchronous settings, however, unless they deliberately request that students explain their revision choices, readers may be left to guess why the writers have revised as they did.

The following diagrams provide a way to understand the challenges facing students in an online setting because of its reading- and writing-intensive nature. The traditional understanding of writer to reader to text looks something like Figure 2.1's adaptation of Kinneavy's (1971) original communication triangle, in which the relationship was drawn among the encoder (speaker/writer), the signal (message/text), and the decoder (hearer/reader). Kinneavy's theory of discourse did not address instructional

FIGURE 2.1 Kinneavy's Communication Triangle for Instructors and Students

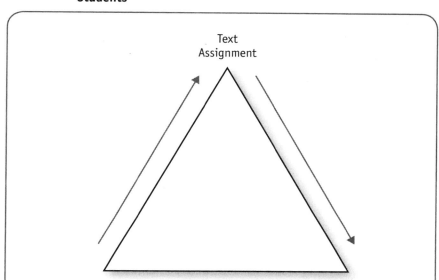

discourse, so Figure 2.1 is an adaptation that attempts to show an instructional relationship, where the writer is the student, the text is the assignment, and the reader is the instructor. This triangle, however, fails to address the complexity of the writer–text–reader relationship in an instructional setting, let alone an online, text-based setting.

A second diagram, Figure 2.2, addresses some of this complexity by using arrows to represent the back-and-forth interactions that occur between readers/instructors and writers/students about drafted writing. The single downward arrow on the right shows that after the student has published an assigned piece of writing by posting it to the LMS, the instructor then reads the paper. The arrows on the left of the triangle show that the student reads and rereads about the assignment, and then writes and rewrites for the assignment. The bottom arrows show that the instructor writes comments and the student reads those comments. The internal arrows suggest a cyclical, potentially recursive nature to the process.

Although the interactive quality of writing instruction is better addressed in this second diagram, it remains completely linear and does not consider the reciprocity of a complete write–read–write cycle that occurs through

FIGURE 2.2 Communication Triangle with Linear Interactions between Instructor and Student

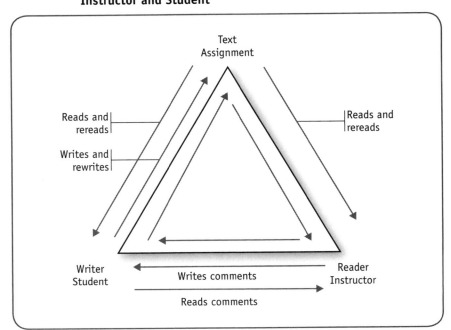

text. Furthermore, it does not address the complications of reading and writing in the online setting.

To this end, Figure 2.3 is an attempt to demonstrate the nonlinearity, reciprocity, and complications of writing an assigned paper for an OWC. As the diagram shows and the following outlines indicate, the write–read–write cycle in OWI is complex. This process is similar in an onsite course except that the intensity of the writing and reading is interrupted by oral communication, changing the dynamic for instructional and interpersonal communication.

In Figure 2.3, the left side considers the steps of writing while the right side considers the steps of reading. Although students typically write and instructors typically read, because they are communicating textually in the OWI cycle, both are shown as having important writing and reading jobs necessary for understanding one another. The instructor, by the way—while typically the teacher—also may be tutor, peer, or even parent or friend in this write–read–write cycle.

Beginning at the top left of the figure, the instructor, who in this illustration is the teacher, writes an assignment and publishes (or posts) it to the

FIGURE 2.3 Asynchronous OWI Writing Cycle in Which Instructors and Students Both Read and Write

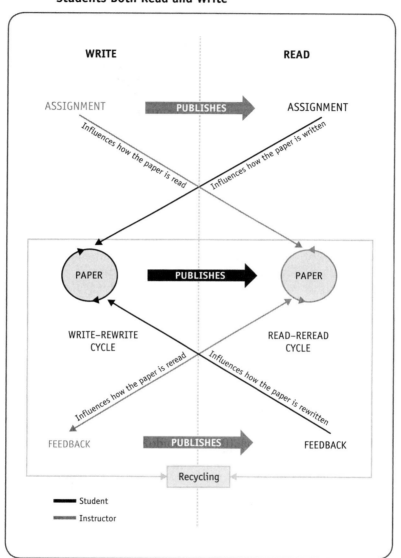

student. As shown by the arrow on the top left that points diagonally toward the lower right side, the assignment influences how the instructor will read the paper later on.

The student receives the published assignment, as shown on the top right, which influences how the paper will be written, as shown by the arrow that starts at the top right and points diagonally toward the lower left side.

At this point, the paper hits a write–rewrite cycle, which is reflected by a solid rectangle. Here, the student writes the paper and publishes it to the instructor, who provides formative feedback and publishes that to the student. If allowed, the student rewrites for more formative feedback and ideally continues to write and rewrite until the paper is due.

Simultaneously, the paper is in a read–reread cycle in that the instructor reads the paper, publishes feedback to the student, who then rereads the paper with that feedback in mind for rewriting. One can assume that the instructor's feedback influences how the paper is rewritten, as shown by the arrow that begins on the bottom right and moves diagonally toward the upper left.

In a slightly more complex way, the paper's text influences the feedback and the feedback influences each writing stage of the paper. This reciprocal relationship is shown by the double-pointed arrow that moves diagonally and recursively from the top right to the bottom left.

The entire write–read–write process is recycled until the paper is considered complete and ready for summative feedback and/or a grade.

Here is another way to understand this reciprocal write/read cycle. Students writing in an OWI setting, as shown in Figure 2.3, engage the following reading and writing work at minimum:

1. Read content and instructions/assignment (sometimes hard to read because instructor's expression is not clear)
2. Write something
   a. Read their own writing
   b. Provide it to outside readers (teacher, tutors, peers)
3. Rewrite based on feedback
4. Reread revised text and edit
5. Publish writing
6. Receive feedback
7. Read and interpret instructor feedback (two different skills)
8. Apply feedback to rewriting (requires cognitive leap or connection depending on how feedback was written
9. Apply feedback to new writing in other assignments (requires still broader cognitive leap or connection)
10. If required, reflect metacognitively about the feedback received from teacher, tutor, or peer, and/or write about the writing decisions one has made

Although this chapter primarily is about student reading needs, it is useful to understand the instructor's job in the context of this same OWI write–read–write cycle. Instructor writing in the OWI setting, as shown above, involves the following reading and writing work at minimum:

1. Writes initial instructions
   a. Teacher: writes (comprehensible) content and instructions
   b. Tutor: reads (and comprehends) teacher assignment/instructions
2. Reads student writing
   a. Interprets the essay and the choices made by the student as text writer in the context of the assignment
3. Writes formative feedback about the writing
   a. Descriptive (what I see)
   b. Instructive (what I would like to see or productive ways to rewrite the next draft)
4. If revision is a possibility, reads the revised writing, evaluates/assesses, and provides feedback
5. At some point, provides summative feedback and/or grade

As we can see, primarily when the instruction is written and not verbalized, many reading (and writing) tasks arise in the OWI setting just for one paper's write–read–write cycle, which is not the only reading task of the composition course by any means.

Add more general reading comprehension to the write–read–write cycle of producing papers, and compounded reading challenges arise. Scholars often claim that students have difficulties comprehending assigned readings (Mayo 2000; Bartholomae and Petrosky 2002). Analytical skills remain necessary for reading texts that will provide models and resources for writing. The issues of student patchwriting and citing sentences rather than content remain. Berrett (2012) quotes Howard and Jamieson as recommending that "students should start writing later, after they are trained to read, analyze, and synthesize their sources, so that they can identify the argument and sort through the evidence" (n.p.).

Special Reading Challenges

Such problems with reading core texts beyond the instructional texts of assignment, student writing, and feedback are not unusual. They can be exacerbated, however, in the text-rich online setting for students who have special reading challenges like dyslexia and multilingual backgrounds. Reading is the primary impediment for OWI students with either of these common challenges, which are presented here as emblematic of a broader range of reading challenges.

Dyslexic students struggle with one of many different types of learning challenges. Wolf (2007) examines dyslexia and how it affects the reading brain, describing the dyslexic brain as the sign of other brain elements and talents — not as a normal versus abnormal brain, but as a common versus uncommon brain. Her examination has potential benefit not only for those who study dyslexia but also for those who want to understand the uncommon brain in an online setting. In OWI, students' differences tend to show up in their writing because it is the primary medium for communication; indeed, teachers may have a minimal picture of students' reading skills. Wolf notes that English is especially difficult to decode when various forms of dyslexia are involved, which is not surprising given that English, like French, is a more difficult language for the so-called normal reader to process (152, 191). When decoding already is challenging and students are in an OWC where accurate and quick decoding is crucial for nearly all aspects of the course, one can expect that reading is, indeed, the primary challenge for OWI students with any learning disability. According to Dunn (1995):

> What is suggested is the importance of both explicit, multisensory teaching methods and engaging, student-centered texts to the learning of LD students. Simply exposing students to "great works" or to provocative political essays and providing opportunities for them to write will likely not be enough for LD students to develop sophisticated written discourse. On the other hand, structured grammar and spelling exercises not connected to anything meaningful in the students' lives are likely to be a waste of everyone's time. Joey learns, and probably LD college students learn, when multisensory links and a high interest in the subject combine. (95)

In a primarily text-rich OWI setting, if students have unreported learning disabilities, a major source of miscommunication and poor learning can emerge. Even when students have reported their disabilities, OWI teachers may be unprepared to help these students in an online setting. Even onsite, it is common for English instructors to recommend that students with disabilities go to their designated disabilities office for help (Oswal 2015; Oswal and Hewett 2013). Clearly, teachers need to be educated in ways to address the uncommon brain of students who struggle to make meaning from the words that comprise their instruction. There are a variety of compensatory measures that can help students with learning challenges. The end of this chapter provides some that may help all OWI students because the nontransparent online setting masks disabilities and equalizes all students struggling with lack of reading fluency.

Multilingual students also face reading challenges because they are second- or third-language learners (Miller-Cochran 2015). Such students "do not process English phonemes in the same way," and their difficulties may stem either from learning standard English alone or from a learning disability in addition to their multilingual issues (Wolf 2007, 194). Add to these concerns the challenges of working in different modalities in the digital setting, and reading difficulties become tough to parse, diagnose, and address. Intervention becomes necessary, but what kind of intervention should we provide? Typical OWI instructors have not learned reading instruction strategies beyond a possible focus on close reading (tested through quizzes of detail knowledge), and the strategies that they do know probably have been learned outside the digital media required in OWI.

Let us look at the problem more specifically through one multilingual student's issues. "Mihyun" was one of Alan Hirvela's (2005) multilingual undergraduate students in an online course. Hirvela indicates that finding, selecting, and using research sources can challenge English language learners who may have learned such skills in generic courses for multilingual learners:

> Here we see a reminder of the importance of critical thinking in the composing process, especially as regards the retrieval, evaluation, and appropriation of electronic source texts. That is, to complete these assignments successfully, Mihyun had to make careful judgments of which sources to use and how to use them. These were not minor operations; they necessitated sophisticated levels of engagement with the sources themselves and the tasks they were linked to. (351)

Mihyun, the student to whom Hirvela refers, did not have the confidence even to patchwrite when she tried to write a researched essay; instead, she used a solid cut-and-paste strategy without attribution for source use. Having read what she believed were the best words for explaining a concept, she could not accept her own more limited vocabulary as useful (347). Despite having "been taught about summarizing, synthesizing, citation practices, and working with electronic sources in her ESL writing courses, . . . she still struggled with her use of these practices and texts outside those courses" (353). Interestingly, this student did begin to write more of her own text when the assignment more robustly required student input into a problem and where the reading lent itself to background context and not to a particular solution (347).

The use of hyperlinks and the practice of screen reading also emerged as problematic for this multilingual student. Hyperlinks take readers to information in a nonlinear manner, making it "safe to say that reading electronic texts in cyberspace is not like reading the linear documents that tend to comprise the world of print texts" (Hirvela 2005, 341). Interestingly, the higher the level of thinking asked of the student, the less she was able to do her reading on screen; instead, she printed out entire articles and highlighted them as she read (346) — much like the native English-speaking students in Haas' (1996) study. Hirvela's point is that multilingual students need explicit reading and source citation instruction in all their disciplinary classes that require reading and writing—not just in an introductory English language learning-focused writing course.

In OWCs, students' linguistic and other backgrounds are less apparent, meaning that multilingual students, for example, may be hidden by the online setting—as are many students with physical and learning disabilities and socioeconomic challenges. One cannot count on an unusual name to signal that the student might have a multilingual background, for example. My experiences tutoring and coaching Asian students reveals that it is not uncommon for them to take on more American-sounding names (e.g., Max, Robin, and Jennifer) as their school identities. As Xu and Jaggars (2013) indicate, reading challenges for some students can affect all students in the class, and if they are not addressed by informed teachers, those with reading challenges can lower the potential for everyone's success (24).

TO WANT TO READ

Undoubtedly, reading in OWCs is hard work, likely harder than but certainly different from the various reading tasks in traditional onsite writing courses. Beyond skill issues, however, the need for college students to work on their reading is a point of contention between contemporary teachers and their students in terms of attentiveness and motivation.

Recall that Nathan (2005) studied students by inserting herself into a freshman year and learning from her new peers. To limit their workloads, Nathan finds that students—a category into which she fit her own behavior of that year—"restrict the amount of time and effort one spends on a course by doing no more than is necessary" (119). Such restriction requires decisions about attendance, doing a course's readings at any given time, and in general how much effort to spend on any assignment. As a student, this professor who regularly had published and met all of her academic obligations found herself "pick[ing] and choos[ing], often relegating textbook reading to cram sessions during exam time, sometimes skipping readings altogether. On papers, I cut my normal multiple revision process to just one draft and then a final paper. Even so, by pure standards I was practically a drudge" (122). She continues: "Most commonly, students simply don't do the required reading for class. I'm not kidding. In certain classes the professor would be lucky if one third of the students read the materials at a level of basic comprehension" (122).

Although it is a bitter pill to swallow, almost any anecdotal discussion in a professional online forum or at the faculty lunch table would support Nathan's contention that students do not read their assignments sufficiently to talk or write about them. In fact, Nathan realized that the anthropology courses she taught as a professor were but "one of the many balls being juggled in the time management challenge faced by each student"; her students simply chose what to do and what to let go (136). That realization led her to change her teaching style and assignments.

Nathan learned that for students to read the assigned material, they needed such motivation as whether there would be a test or quiz on the material, whether the material was directly relevant to other homework, and whether the material would be discussed in class such that each student would have to participate in some specific, required way (138; see also Warnock 2009, 64–66). Students' decisions to complete only work that will be assessed, for instance, are connected to the evolving roles of today's students in an economy where many balance part- or full-time work, heavy course loads (in order to graduate sooner or incur less debt, potentially failing some courses as a result), family and home life, and other relationships. While explicit relevance is important (Bunn 2013), apparently, simply being able to answer a teacher's question or participate in a discussion would not fit that last category for too many students. Subsequently, Nathan's advice to other educators is to ensure that any reading be assigned only when it has "direct and immediate" use in the coursework and is justified in such a way that students can understand its priority in their time management decisions (138). This advice strips away the added reading that professors might assign to broaden the students' general knowledge beyond what a lecture could cover. In an OWC or onsite writing course, it suggests that all reading should have intimate connections to required writing even if the writing is low stakes in nature.

That splash of cold water must be considered in light of Bartholomae and Petrosky's (2002) belief that student readers need to be active readers, willing to interpret what they read. When the motivation for completing an assignment is based on juggling various professors' syllabi, students may leave the reading out of their relatively few weekly study hours. If they find a text to be difficult as well, they may walk away feeling like a failure. Still, as Bartholomae and Petrosky tell any students who are willing to invest the time to read their anthology's introduction, just because a text is difficult does not mean that the reader has failed the job of reading. Sadly, many student readers simply quit difficult readings believing that they are incapable of addressing the task—and some may have had this belief since the fourth-grade shift from learning to read to reading to learn. Bartholomae and Petrosky find that when their students have difficulty, they are "confronting the experience of reading, in other words, but they were taking the problems of reading—problems all readers face—and concluding that there was nothing for them to do but give up" (vi).

Teaching students to reread is one helpful approach. While teachers may understand that frustration with challenging readings is common, students may not know that they are having a normal experience. Getting students to understand this fact is a challenge we can address with explicit instruction in rereading. In a way, contemporary students are frustrated with knowledge, skills, or abilities that are not readily accessible. Such rusty or inexpert skills seem logical given a propensity to do little reading for classes when many activities compete for students' time. According to Bartholomae and Petrosky, "our students need to learn that there is something they can do once they have first read through a complicated text; successful reading is not just a matter of 'getting' an essay the first time" (vi). The authors assert that working hard with a piece of reading leads to owning the text's meaning as something totally one's own. Indeed, they make an excellent point by comparing the work of the reader to the work of a writer. We teach our students to rewrite, to revise; similarly, we need to teach them to reread. Rereading is not a sign of failure but rather the natural work of a reader who is integrating the reading into his understanding of the world. Bartholomae and Petrosky suggest that asking a series of questions regarding a reading makes "the work of rereading" real in a respectful manner (vii).

Motivation and Skillful Reading

Given the reading-intensive nature of OWI, it is crucial for students to learn strategies that address both motivation and skills. Contemporary students may have too little patience or time for the hard work of reading, leading to complaints of boredom with difficult texts. According to Bartholomae and Petrosky: "College students want to believe that they can strike out on their own, make their mark, do something they have never done before. They want to be experts, not just hear from them. This is the great pleasure, as well as the great challenge, of undergraduate instruction" (ix). Indeed, this message connects with Levine and Dean's (2012) belief that students want to be seen as experts and often do not understand that becoming experts requires effort. Wolf (2007) explains how much work the brain must do in reading and how it rewires itself neurologically to develop expertise. To get to this point of expertness, however, students have to fit schoolwork into their busy schedules and fight the apparent "boredom" of studying, reading, and writing. These are issues of attentiveness and motivation. As discussed in Chapter 1, students often claim boredom when they feel unmotivated. Yet, such boredom has a genuine place in education if only we can teach students to harness it to their benefit. Boredom's job is to mark the point where things become hard and thinking must change, signaling a need for different strategies or levels of effort. Students need to learn what is stopping them from learning, from taking the next necessary step. Is it their reading abilities? Is it the intellectual or emotional challenge of new material? Is it fear of being wrong? Is it simply laziness?

In studying how professors read in this digital age, Jennifer Howard (2012) claims that the distractions of the busy world and the many distractions inherent to reading in a college setting indicate that reading shorter texts is easier and/or better for students. She compares professors, who often balance multiple tasks, with students who may balance multiple jobs in order to go to college. If professors find themselves changing their reading habits to shorter texts, doesn't that make sense for students, too? Alice Horning (1978) noted well before the digital age that students who have difficulty with certain types of academic texts often do not have any difficulty with texts that interest them in other ways such as reading about automobiles, photography, or some other hobby. Educators Michael Smith and Jeffrey D. Wilhelm (2002), authors of *Reading Don't Fix No Chevys: Literacy in the Lives of Young Men*, would agree that teachers should engage students in reading at the point of their interests. The ability to hook one's interest in a subject to reading is a positive aspect of student reading skill. Yet, it also is an indicator of the critical nature of attentiveness and motivation in completing assigned reading of any nature.

Becoming a "Good Enough" Reader

Bartholomae and Petrosky (2002) suggest that by not providing a single *correct* reading of a text, instructors encourage students to learn and think for themselves. They note that such teachers will need "to be comfortable turning the essays [articles to read] over to the students, even with the knowledge that they will not do immediately on their own what professionals could do — at least not completely, or with the same grace and authority" (ix). This advice is sensible yet challenging to enact. Teachers of reading and writing typically have high levels of skills in these areas and need to give up control of what they consider to be a *good* reading to accept instead a *good enough* reading. In the same way that teachers do not need to be experts in everything, neither do students.

The related questions for this book, however, are the following: How do we help students to achieve a good enough reading of a text — particularly in an online setting — given that students have to read so many different things in order to learn what they need to know? In fact, how do we help students learn to reread when we do not physically see them to know that they are not reading well to begin with or that they are not learning what they can from a text? We are left most often with only the essay or a discussion post as proof of reading attentiveness and skill.

As a corrective measure, James Lang (2012), author of "The Benefits of Making It Harder to Learn," recommends that teachers should make it harder to learn rather than easier. Lang cites a study where researchers considered ease of learning and material retention. In this study, students who read texts with challenging fonts — in other words, uncommonly used fonts — appeared to learn the material better (as evidenced by their memory of it) than those students who read the same material in traditional or conventional fonts. The researchers concluded that introducing cognitive dysfluency into a learning situation may increase retention and understanding because it challenges the learner to work harder. Lang likens this kind of learning to the difference between driving on autopilot to an American grocery store and driving on a different side of the road to the grocery in England. The idea is to "push students out of autopilot," and this strategy translates practically to providing students course material in strange fonts, using stem sentences, and leaving logical gaps in the material for them to find and resolve, as with cloze exercises.

Lang stresses that the creation of "desirable difficulties" also must account for keeping students motivated. Some example strategies he gleaned from other teachers when he put the question out to a group include asking "students to process or translate course material using unusual rhetorical or expressive modes" (such as a text message, e-mail, or blog), requiring "students to argue on behalf of unfamiliar positions," asking "students to find or identify mistakes" (some of which would have been seeded by the professor), and planning "for failure" in settings where students typically are used to being asked to be successful. These kinds of strategies for reading and writing can turn students' thinking upside down and shake up rote, automatic responses to an assignment or material. This concept is much like the dealing with the attention blindness that Davidson (2012) describes. By taking the blinders off and changing the picture to something unexpected, we may find students learning differently.

The online setting, which by its text-rich nature makes the work of reading and writing more challenging, seems an ideal place to enact desirable difficulties. Certainly, OWI's primarily asynchronous nature remains a different learning environment in formal school settings from recreational ones. Using computers, reading digitally, and composing onscreen still are sufficiently different from what many students have encountered in lower school settings that it can be off-putting initially. Discomfort used wrongly may further disadvantage marginalized students. However, any sense of discomfort used appropriately can disrupt old behaviors in positive ways and allow teachers to convey new thinking about reading (and writing) through strategies and practical experiences. Providing students with carefully placed and outlined "desirable difficulties" may be used to the advantage of reading and writing as opposed to the potential disadvantage of having students feel too comfortable in the online setting.

ACCESSIBILITY CONCERNS

The CCCC OWI Committee (2013) believes that the overarching principle for teaching writing online is inclusivity and accessibility for all students. This principle was developed to guide the other fourteen OWI Principles and all the effective practices that educators might advance (see Hewett "Grounding Principles of OWI" 2015). Outside of LMS technology, about which teachers typically have little choice, the first place where access issues emerge is in the textual presentation of instructional writing. We know that some students are nonfluent readers because they have particular disabilities, others because they are multilingual learners who may have too little textual history with English, and still others because their socioeconomic or home backgrounds may not have encouraged reading. In the spirit of that position regarding inclusivity and access, Part Two's reading activities and Part Three's writing activities are designed to broaden access to students with physical and learning challenges as well as to multilingual students and those from varying socioeconomic backgrounds. This guidance suggests that (1) students of all learning types are assisted through a wide variety of accessible lessons and that (2) we must remain vigilant to inclusivity by preparing alternative methods for engaging a lesson.

What Is Access?

For the purposes of this book, access has two meanings. The first meaning of access is needs-based access, comprising all digital-era nontraditional students—young and older—described in Chapter 1. Students with permanent physical disabilities and learning challenges wake up with them day after day. Unlike people with such disabilities as a broken hand or impaired thinking from illness or grief, their problems are not curable with time, recommendations, or solutions. Similarly, unlike our typical goals for helping students to develop reading and writing fluency, where improvement will come with time and stay with them for a lifetime, the physical or learning disability remains. Students with ADHD will have it tomorrow and the next day and the next day. For blind students, the next day will bring the same multitude of challenges in a text-rich world that they faced the day before. For students with dyslexia, text will still jump around in their brain the next day, sometimes making sense and other times not. Students with an audio processing disorder will have thinking difficulties every time they are asked to meet in a live, voice-based peer group—whether they meet the next day or the day after that.

Some institutions will require that students with disabilities report those challenges to an office of disabilities services. Without such a report or registration, teachers may not be held accountable for providing special access to these students. For example, a student who has not reported to the office of disabilities services or who has not met the requirements of particular documentation may not be eligible for such accommodations as increased time to take tests or a learning assistant's presence in the classroom. Students with disabilities learn coping mechanisms for their problems, and they have to concentrate on employing those strategies in order to function in college-level courses. Although one might stop at the legal threshold for meeting such requirements, we can choose to not make their problems worse by becoming knowledgeable teachers who provide reasonable alternatives in our OWCs. If we develop our classes with inclusion and access in mind at every step, we still may need to provide special accommodation for particular students, but we will have developed a more ethically and morally inclusive setting overall.

As we know, some students will never let us know they are having problems. Therefore, students should be considered proactively, not retroactively, when developing OWI-based reading and writing assignments. With regard to digital-era technology, all students have some learning weaknesses and strengths to which we should be responsive. Given that we do not always know who would benefit from a particular type of accommodation and that students do not always self-disclose their special needs, it behooves online writing instructors always to provide accessible written instructions and to allow all students to respond in accessible ways. Students of all ages have different learning preferences at various times, especially with respect to digital technology. Some always may prefer text while others sometimes may prefer text and other times audio or video. When we routinely teach using a variety or combination of text/audio/video, students are more likely to have their individual learning needs met in the OWC. Even with these media variations, the course likely will remain text-rich, requiring students to read a great deal. The combination of text-based and multimodal lessons in Part Two has been developed to improve the potential to reach students of all learning types and needs.

In order to support success with these multimodal lessons, transcripts for audio or video lessons, for example, should be included as a matter of course because some students are more text-oriented learners while others are more visual learners. Transcripts easily can be provided if the lesson is developed first in text and then read into the audio/video software. Such transcripts can substitute for closed captioning provided that hearing-impaired students are receiving the same information in the transcript that is delivered in the audio portion of the video. However, where technological access is challenging, as discussed below, teachers may need to adapt the lesson to a common modality that all students can use.

A second meaning of access regards the physical or financial availability of the technology needed to participate in the class. Although we can agree that students need to have reasonable access to technology, financial and logistical exigencies may prevent this imperative from becoming a reality. Institutions will have different policies regarding who is responsible for providing the access for completing coursework. To provide access consideration from a teaching perspective, for example, if a reading lesson in this book suggests that students collaborate through audio/video and the course LMS does not include such technology, teachers who want to use the lesson as developed must enable students (through clear instructions) to use a free platform like Skype or ooVoo. However, these platforms may not work with some students' hardware or they may lead to an unacceptably high learning curve for particular students. The problem then rests with the teacher to find a creative solution (although enlisting the student as a partner in developing an answer is a useful approach). To this end, teachers can — and possibly should — reconfigure the lesson to be something that individual students can complete outside of a cooperative group. In any case, because some students may be using older technology that does not have a camera or voice option, attention to access means the instructor must provide an option for participation outside of the preferred method for the lesson.

A special kind of case arises with the remarkable number of students who are attempting their OWCs through mobile phone and tablet (sans keyboard) technology. In doing so, they may experience themselves as limited in typing capabilities or spatially challenged in rereading their own text, as Haas' (1996) findings suggest. There is gray area in terms of how to accommodate these students, particularly if there is no institutional policy about student access to technology. If their own mobile technologies interfere with the necessary learning, which is possible given the length of texts that are read and written in any writing-focused course, students can be encouraged to borrow more standard devices (Rodrigo 2015). Most institutions provide computer labs for students who can come to campus. Yet, for OWI students who are geographically distributed in other parts of the state or world — or who simply do not have transportation — other accommodations may need to be considered. Soldiers, for example, are severely limited by their duty station — occasionally a war zone — in terms of technology access (Gos 2015). As well, many working students find themselves on business trips during their courses, leaving them working with sometimes spotty Internet connections and reliant on cellular technology. Often a phone call, IM chat, or other interpersonal communication medium like WebEx or Skype can help both to clarify what is possible for students in such cases and to discuss the likely impediments and solutions for meeting course outcomes — provided that the communications technology does not introduce yet another financial or technological impediment.[2] Compromise and creative thinking often can resolve such problems.

At any rate, in a course where writing instruction is the primary objective, teaching new technology should not be prioritized over course goals of

---

[2]Although some might think that using the phone is anachronistic or inappropriate given the OWI setting, it remains the simplest means of connecting with students in that it does not require accepting plug-ins and the like. WebEx, for example, has become a familiar synchronous digital meeting space, but many schools do not provide WebEx-like technology for writing courses, which is why OWI typically is asynchronous. Switching modality from asynchronous to synchronous technology can change the entire dynamic for the student who needs connection with the teacher. Getting off the computer and onto the phone can help both parties.

teaching reading and writing, as OWI Principle 2 suggests (CCCC OWI Committee 2013, 11; Hewett 2015; Warnock 2015), even when digital rhetorical awareness also is part of the course goals (DePew 2015). To this end, it is helpful to use the course LMS and to provide information through any additional technology only if necessary and in as transparent a way as possible. Finally, it is useful to know that however much information we provide to students through such media as podcasts, YouTube, and other audio/video technology, not all students will avail themselves of these lessons or extra information. Research shows that students may elect to watch part or none of such video in keeping with their learning preferences or perceived needs (Green, Pinder-Grover, and Millunchick 2012). That does not mean that students should not complete their assignments; it simply means that they may not avail themselves of the entire lesson just as they may not read content or other lesson material carefully or at all. This is a "leading a horse to water" case; we simply cannot make all the students drink thirstily of what we conscientiously have provided. However, when teachers provide adequate access and instruction, these student decisions reflect their learning choices, which may or may not be helpful to them and do not reflect on the teacher.[3] Students will make their own learning decisions for which they ultimately must take responsibility.

Why Writing Teachers Need to Pay Attention to Access

To put a finer point on this issue of access, while the CCCC OWI Committee (2013) has no regulatory authority and has taken only a moral and ethical stance on access, the United States has taken a legal and regulatory stance on access through the ADA and the Section 508 policies. In light of the CCCC position statement (2013), OWI and other writing teachers would do well to rethink the ADA's requirements for equal access as an opportunity to improve writing teaching and learning for everyone. Typically, the information technology (IT) departments of higher education institutions are tasked with the purchase of accessible hardware and software and for general institutional compliance with the ADA, leaving little for teachers to consider. In fact, using the institution's LMS for onsite courses or OWCs may make providing accessible courses somewhat easier. First, the LMS will have been vetted by the IT department for general accessibility and compatibility with screen readers and the like. Where students need additional assistance, the office of disabilities and the IT department will

---

[3]Katie Green, Tershia Pinder-Grover, and Joanna Mirecki Millunchick (2012), in studying how first-year engineering students used screen casting, urge teachers not to worry about whether students actually watched the screen cast because using screen casting technology for their courses can help students to master material and promote self-efficacy more generally (217, 233–34).

have developed specific ways to assist students. Second, when the LMS is the portal for uploading any lessons that use different media, students do not need access to sites outside the LMS. In theory, then, using the LMS alone — however imperfect for all teaching scenarios — enables all students to take advantage of the teacher's uses of multimodal lessons and multiple media that may speak to their various learning styles and preferences.

Teachers understandably worry about how considering and enabling access will cost them in time and energy, perhaps even thinking that they should avoid OWI because of such costs. Their concern is well-founded because there are, indeed, costs in terms of time and energy to developing accessible materials. Yet, these costs can be mitigated with teacher training, thoughtful planning, and reusable lessons. Excellent resources for such training can be obtained through Sloan Consortium workshops on the ADA and accommodations, as well as through the federal and state governments and, likely, through one's own IT department or distance learning office. Sherryl Burgstahler and Rebecca Cory's (2008) principles of universal design assist in thinking about how to provide access efficiently; using these principles of universal design "reduces, but does not eliminate, the need for accommodations for students with disabilities" (24–25; see also Breuch 2015). Among the example effective practices the CCCC OWI Committee (2013) offered for providing inclusivity and access in OWI are that teachers should "determine their uses of modality and media based not only on their pedagogical goals but also on their students' likely strengths and access" (9), "provide students with reasonable alternate means outside the LMS for conferencing or meeting for office hours" (9), and "offer instructional materials in more than one medium" (10). Professional development training and consistently thoughtful uses of modalities and media regarding both expected learning outcomes and students' learning needs can help to mitigate time and energy costs in providing accessible OWI lessons.

Practical Strategies for Promoting Inclusivity and Accessibility in OWI

The following are practical ways to use technology and inclusive techniques when attending to a student audience with a wide variety of reading skills, abilities, and disabilities. These example strategies apply both to the reading-focused lessons presented in Part Two and to the writing-focused tips presented in Part Three:

- Obtain training by the institutional IT department to learn how to use available technology in accessible ways.
- Obtain training by the institutional office of disabilities to learn how to assist students with diverse or multiple special needs and when to guide them to that office for assistance.

- Use audio/video lessons to vary the instructional media in online settings. When teaching through such media, provide a text-based transcript of the lesson. To provide a transcript quickly and easily, write the script before recording. It is alright to deviate slightly from the script in a spontaneous comment during recording. Students with audio or audio/visual access difficulties, to include deaf and blind students as well as those with limited technological access, will benefit from the text all the same. Such technology as Camtasia or Dragon NaturallySpeaking can help with this work. Writing Program Administrators (WPAs) or other administrators might purchase a software license for their writing instructors, both onsite and online.

- When providing images, graphics, or video online, add an explanatory caption and/or descriptive transcript, as well as the general connections you would like students to make from the viewing and/or reading.

- When commenting on writing or developing a lesson for students on revision, be aware that vision-impaired students who use screen readers, for example, may not be able to read marginal comments. Ask them about this capability. Many will be able to read tracked changes, but ask about this as well. For classes that include these students, require that all students insert their peer-response comments in brackets [ ], which makes them accessible to everyone.

- Along these lines, certain colors will be unreadable for students with color blindness. Because color use is important to formatting wisely in online settings, it can help all students to know which colors work and which do not. It should not be a privacy problem to ask students about this issue in a general post to the class. Some may reveal (privately or publicly) that they have difficulty distinguishing between red and green while others may have difficulty distinguishing between blue and yellow, for example. Differences between purple and blue also can be hard to see. Allow students to tell you which colors work best, and avoid the colors that do not work. (On a different note, many writing teachers routinely avoid red because it potentially carries negative affective meaning for students; there is no harm in following this general proscription.)

- Be flexible. At times, it may be helpful to allow students with certain kinds of writing disorders to read their responses into an audio recorder and link the file to their posting. In a text-rich environment, such students may find they need a break on the writing of smaller tasks (e.g., written journals or peer response) in order to focus on the more important writing ones (e.g., graded essays, multiple required drafts, or written class discussions).

- When asking students to post photos or scans of their texts or other work, avoid giving grades or extra credit; alternatively, provide different ways for students without access to complete the project successfully.

Students who do not have the appropriate technology may need to use a work-around, and they should not be penalized for not having access to such technology in a writing class no matter how useful it may be to the work. The focus in the writing class is always the writing regardless of how valuable other media may be. Pedagogy should trump technology, as OWI Principle 2 clearly indicate (CCCC OWI Committee 2013).

- Encourage students who may benefit (including slow typists) to experiment with voice recognition software like Dragon NaturallySpeaking. This kind of software, although not free, may help students with writing block, as well the students with a wide variance of reading and writing fluency and comfort levels. Such encouragement is not to say that teachers should not expect a more standard final text-based document, but only to enable students through the processes of writing more flexibly.

- Always use an accessible PDF file when providing PDF-based text for students to read. To learn how to make accessible PDF files, consult your version of Adobe or Google "accessible PDF file." This kind of file should be readable by a blind individual's screen reader.

- Select texts (i.e., articles, textbooks, blogs, and websites) for their functional readability. For example, texts should have adequate headers/footers, headings/subheadings, and font quality and size for readers of all college ages.

- Select readings that are appropriate to the college course level. Incorporate into the writing assignments such learning activities as those presented in Part Two to assist readers who are having difficulty with those readings. Giving either the entire class or individual students such access to additional materials will enable them to choose whether to help themselves become stronger readers in the context of this writing class. Teachers do not need to assign themselves more work in this area although they should feel free to work individually with students online just as they would in an onsite setting. Additionally, teachers do not need to grade or evaluate all assignments in order to use them purposefully with students.

- Encourage writing genres that meet your institution's writing course requirements, but if the technology is available to all students and if the course goals permit, stretch those genres to include digital venues like blogs, collaborative texts through wikis, and hypertext writing that takes advantage of a less linear writing presentation.

EDUCATORS' RESPONSIBILITIES

Reading is a critical literacy in OWI that can be made more difficult (and, conversely, more interesting) by digital media. To teach students to read better — an acknowledged part of teaching writing — will require a consciously focused attention to problems that may arise online (Council of Writing 2011, 10). Maclellan (1997) rightly emphasizes the need for students to get involved in their reading:

> If reading is to continue as a medium of instruction in higher education, it must be pursued intentionally by students. This means that students recognise [*sic*] that learning will only happen with effort on the part of each individual reader and is not a natural consequence of carrying out particular reading activities. The effort is concerned to transform extant knowledge into some desired, not-yet-attained knowledge and may involve several intermediate transformations. In appreciating that desired learning requires active, cognitive processing, students recognise [*sic*] that learning is inherently problematic. This is not to say that the learning from text need necessarily be painful or difficult, just that it is not guaranteed. (285–86)

Claims of boredom or lack of time are insufficient to convincingly argue that contemporary undergraduates cannot make changes in their reading strategies to strengthen their literacy skills. Although the online setting provides significant challenges for students of various backgrounds, its rich, text-intensive nature can be helpful to them as the world becomes increasingly digital.

Whether they are helping students with a basic reading issue or deliberately using desirable difficulties, at a minimum, educators need to teach students practical ways to read and make use of their reading in a text-based setting. A necessary first step is to acknowledge overtly that reading can be hard work and that such effort is necessary to an education. Learning to self-engage and wanting to reach deep to find one's own motivation are crucial to reading for college generally and for OWI specifically.

Part Two of this book, "Reading to Learn," provides practical strategies for overtly teaching students reading skills in fully online and hybrid OWI settings. These same strategies can be engaged in various other settings to include onsite classes where digital technologies are available.

3

Practical Considerations for Teaching Reading Strategies

OH, I KNEW THAT!

When I left high school for college, I naturally had a lot to learn. Like many future educators, I soaked up those lessons and loved college. I left with my bachelor's degree in four years with highest honors in two majors; in the final two years, I added a secondary-level education minor. The next fall, having gotten married and relocated from the East Coast to my husband's U.S. Army post on the Kansas prairie, I immediately began graduate school.

When I started the master's program, I handwrote my first paper and experienced an exquisite embarrassment as I saw other students turn in neatly typed pages. I went to the professor and apologized, giving the mostly true excuse that I had just moved and had not yet unpacked my typewriter. He looked at me and sardonically advised me to open my boxes and get myself in order. In all honesty, despite being an experienced and successful student, I actually had forgotten that I needed to type my work—it never crossed my mind, despite having typed numerous papers for four years. The new realities of marriage, moving, the military life, and an advanced educational level had disrupted my thinking as a student, causing me to forget some of what I knew. I relearned quickly. This embarrassment got my full attention.

Entering college from high school (or after years in the workplace) provides a similar kind of disruption for our students. All learners can benefit from being reminded of what they learned before or what they need to know now in a new context or setting. They must remember what they have forgotten and learn new strategies for making what they do know work in the present situation. Particularly the younger nontraditional students introduced in Chapter 1 may forget—or may not know at all—to read deeply and to think about their reading in the context of their writing, especially when their new college lives disrupt their old ways of looking at the world and at their education.

So it is with many students in OWI. When students choose the online educational environment for writing instruction, their understanding of writing instruction from the perspective of high school student or of employee must change. Likewise, their understanding of digital tools must change from the perspective of using them for social networking to using them for educational purposes. When these students receive educational content and instructions almost completely via text, they also may need to be reminded about some of the basics of reading consciously and thoughtfully, especially at this time when digital experiences reshape reading.

Thirteen years after having completed the master's program and having recently left military life, I entered a Ph.D. program and my learning/student self was shaken once again. This time, I found myself completely out of sync with the vocabulary of rhetoric and composition's theoretical and historical readings. I had to learn how to read at a new level, whereas some of my younger peers who had gone straight through school already understood the vocabulary and the contexts in which it was used. People much younger than me talked about the readings with such fluency that I felt foolish and lost. Had I become as dumb as I felt? Despite having taught writing for years, I had missed much in the professional literature. In essence, I had to relearn how to read purposefully. One professor's exercises helped me a great deal. She assigned a one-page, ungraded response paper for each article and book read. In these response papers, she freed me to flounder and struggle my way through new meaning in academic writings. With a simple "grade" of a check minus ($\sqrt{-}$), check ($\sqrt{}$), or check plus ($\sqrt{+}$), she provided a safe, concrete way for me to relearn and learn. In addition, by listening to other students read their response papers or talk about the texts, I had the peer-based opportunity to test my own thinking and to see where it came up short and where I had found a different meaning. Indeed, I realized quickly that I understood the scholarly content differently because my life and teaching experiences diverged from the school-based ones of my youngest peers. Despite my rusty literacy skills, I recovered quickly and used my adult learning strengths to read and learn deeply. In a few months, my insights added to those of my younger peers.

This experience is much like those of the adult nontraditional students who have spent years in the workforce. While their life and work experiences certainly count, they have to open themselves to new or changed levels of reading with strange vocabulary that can be off-putting. In doing so, they may experience moments of feeling stupid or not up to the task at hand. When OWI is added to the mix, any work they have done digitally can help with the educational transition, but the context of performance, grades, and exercises that often have little real-world transfer again will be disruptive. These students will need some kind and thoughtful assistance in realizing their current abilities, stretching themselves in new ones, and learning how to hold their own cognitively and affect-wise in this setting.

LITERACY STRATEGIES

All of the literacy skills that are treated as comprehension themes in Part Two are needed at one time or another to help students read better in OWI settings. Undoubtedly, they also help students in traditional settings. Some of the themes are ones that students learned — or should have learned — in elementary school. The majority are ones that students may need to be reminded that they know. The movement from an analog educational setting to a digital one provides a helpful cognitive disruption that students can use to anchor old and new literacy skills. Such cognitive disruption will be hard to face at first, causing some students to want to quit when the reading and writing begin to get tough, as Bartholomae and Petrosky (2002) suggest happens. Teachers would do well to reach out to those students using other media like e-mail, IM chat, video chat, and the phone, so long as the venue does not require downloading new software. We should encourage students by overtly explaining that reading and writing are hard work for everyone and that their thinking can be jarred by the online setting. Practice, rereading, and continued self-engagement will help them to move beyond feeling of being incapable or of boredom so that they can succeed (Wolf 2007; Bartholomae and Petrosky 2002).

Recognizing that it may be more difficult to predict which students have challenges with particular reading skills in OWI, in addition to the ethical imperatives of inclusivity and accessibility, Part Two provides multiple methods to present those strategies in an online setting. There is some redundancy as well as choice built in to these chapters because redundancy as reinforcement is especially possible using digital tools and especially necessary for accessible lessons (see Warnock 2009, 56–57, for example).

The comprehension themes in this book have emerged in part from Tanny McGregor's (2007) *Comprehension Connections: Bridges to Strategic Reading*. Such themes are commonly taught in elementary school by teachers whose specialty is reading. By reiterating and supporting the skills that we learned in the earliest of our reading experiences, we take advantage of the cognitive disruptions that college and OWI as different learning environments naturally provide. Dunn (1995) suggests that "college teachers can adapt whatever ideas they can glean from creative elementary teachers who attempt to help their students find alternate paths to learning when conventional neurological paths might be somehow blocked, impeded, or otherwise occupied" (77). Such adaptations make use of already created neurological pathways and work to develop new ones with respect to college-level work in the online setting.

Elementary school children learn — consciously or unconsciously — about the following comprehension themes, using them to become more intentionally thoughtful readers. Comprehension themes need to be taught explicitly, particularly with respect to reading content material. In this book, these themes are considered reminders of what our students once learned and now need to reconsider in a new context:

- Metacognition
- Schema
- Inference
- Questioning
- Relevance
- Visualizing
- Analyzing
- Synthesizing

Chapters 4 through 11 address these comprehension themes in the above cited order, providing specific activities that OWI instructors can use and adapt for fully online and hybrid OWCs. They also can adapt these activities for synchronous or asynchronous settings — using only the core ideas to rework them for a different modality. Specific readings and activities can be swapped or changed entirely to meet the needs of particular student populations or institutional preferences.

Interestingly, some elementary school reading lessons skip analysis as a literacy strategy or comprehension theme (see McGregor 2007, for example). Analysis — taking ideas and argument apart to find their meaning — is crucial to being able to synthesize — pulling disparate ideas and arguments together from various sources to create new meaning. Since analysis is so central to critical thinking and to the kinds of writing that undergraduates are expected to do, it needs to be addressed with reading in mind for college students.

TEACHING READING OVERTLY

Using Multiple Senses

The chapters that follow suggest various kinds of direct instruction and cueing that offer students "the opportunity to use their other senses as a kind of backup system" (Dunn 1995, 77). The idea here is that one may need to engage multiple senses in reading and writing at any level. Learning writing in an online setting sets up cognitive disruption that can interrupt learning because of the unfamiliar need to work in a text-rich setting and to mediate the learning through technology; at the same time, such learning can use that disruption to stimulate the mind to new levels of cognition. According to the Council of Writing (2011): "While many students have opportunities to practice composing in electronic environments, explicit and intentional instruction focusing on the use and implications of writing and reading using electronic technologies will contribute to students' abilities to use them effectively" (10; see also DePew 2015).

OWI lends itself beautifully to such learning opportunities because it provides multiple media and modalities that can be used very deliberately in an online writing context. Furthermore, OWI enables a kind of educational plasticity in the affordances of images, voice, and video in conjunction with text. To this end, at some point, college educators should expand the concept of reading beyond text, while simultaneously focusing on and improving text comprehension. There is an elegant complexity in reading for the online environment that finds completion in the subsequent complexity of using writing to teach about writing itself.

Direct instruction through the senses also can come in the form of "deliberate actions" that encourage learning. Such actions can be "underlining words, taking notes, summarizing the reading material and answering questions," but are always intentional and represent a somewhat conscious choice (Maclellan 1997, 280). Maclellan (1997) stresses that students need to be given activities that will help them in their reading. Teachers can provide abundant activities while remembering that the learners will choose the ones that they will use—hopefully after having tried the suggested activity first. In keeping with adult learning theory and the understanding that many college-level OWI students have adolegogical traits, students will choose the strategies that best address their goals and will disregard others. However, the strategies they choose "will determine whether the learner selects the appropriate information to attend to, organizes the information into meaningful units, and/or makes connections between the new information and what he/she already knows" (280).

Explicit Reading Strategies

Within the eight comprehension themes taught in Chapters 4 though 11, five explicit reading strategies are engaged:

1. rehearsal (e.g., mimicry and practice),
2. organization (e.g., outlining, inferential thinking, and analysis),
3. collaboration (i.e., as a means of talking through readings and trying out strategies),
4. metacognition (e.g., self-reflection at all levels of reading), and
5. affect (i.e., learning reading survival strategies, time management, and ways to enjoy reading).

The first three explicit strategies are cognitive approaches while the last two address the learner's self-management of his or her learning (281). Maclellan indicates that these strategies interact "particularly in students who are aware of themselves as learners; are aware of, and use, various strategies discussed here; recognize the demands of different kinds of academic tasks; and have sufficient content/domain knowledge such that they can actually engage in some thinking" (282). In other words, the students that Maclellan describes are functioning as we would want mature adult learners to do. For this growth to andragogy to happen, however, students need to be consciously aware of their goal, equally aware of the reading strategies that can help them, and resolved that the goal is important enough to take the time to implement them. The activities in Part Two can assist with developing such conscious awareness.

Active Reading Cues

Teachers want students to read actively and consciously. Reading remains a challenge for college students and teachers because, as Adler-Kassner and Estrem (2007) indicate, even though critical reading often is called for in writing program guidelines, it is neither explained nor taught in any clear and strategic manner. They caution against common practices that require students to be passive readers or enable them not to read at all, such as Nathan (2005) describes in her book about returning to college. Such practices include asking questions to which we know the answer (in other words, rhetorical and yes/no or closed-ended questions) and elaborating on what students say rather than asking someone else to do that for them (Adler-Kassner and Estrem 2007, 39). These practices allow teachers to fill the silence that often occurs when students fail to complete their readings for class. In an online setting, unless the class is held onsite or synchronously online via video, such a silence not only is notable through the lack of writing in response to a discussion prompt but also through students' vapid (e.g., "Really? I thought so, too.") and often praise-based (e.g., "Great comment, John.") responses that fail to interrogate the reading or what a classmate has said. There can be no doubt of a "critical need for composition instructors to define carefully how we want students to be as readers, and why, within the framework of reading and writing in our classes, programs, and profession, participating in these ways is important for them as readers and writers" (39; see also Warnock 2009).

Practice-Based Reading

Practice-based reading strategies encourage readers to look at language as "a system that contains and generates meaning, while at the same time users employ that system based upon their understandings of the contexts where it is used" (Adler-Kassner and Estrem, 42). Adler-Kassner and Estrem recommend that teachers engage practice-based reading, where:

> readers think carefully about the elements sponsorship associated with their reading. Where do they read? How do they do it? What captures and does not capture his or her attention? What structures, genres, and/or ideas are privileged here, and why are they privileged? How have the reader's experiences contributed to his or her interaction with these practices? How are these interactions with, and genres of, reading perceived by the outside audiences, and why? This kind of reflexive reading can help readers begin to articulate their own reading processes, become attuned to areas where successful reading practices can be emulated and less successful ones improved, and consider the consequences of engaging in various genres of reading in various contexts. (43)

Such practice-based reading resembles the engaged metacognitive reading outlined by McGregor (2007) and Maclellan (1997) in terms of the active role readers must take "in analyzing both the context for [their] reading and the activity itself" (Adler-Kassner and Estrem 2007, 43).

Engaging muscle memory is an example of a practice-based reading strategy that can help readers and writers who struggle. Using varied media—to include suggesting that students skywrite or gesture as they read or click the mouse on different lines or parts of the screen for screen reading—can stimulate muscle memory, which helps students who have various reading challenges or even a general dislike of reading. Such activities are not as far out as they may sound for students at the college level; after all, it is the kinesthetic effect of muscle memory that enables people to remember how to spell when typing on the keyboard (Dunn 1995, 78). Similarly, we can ask students to read their work aloud, recording it if they have the tools or to read to us over free software like Skype. Such methods assist learning or linguistically challenged students, as well as contemporary digital-era undergraduates with recalling how to read well in an online college writing course.

Multiple and Varied Reading Exercises

In short, multiple and varied reading methods are necessary for students in an OWC because their learning styles are masked by the online setting. No one teaching philosophy or method will address all the students in a course, so teachers must be both flexible and generous with providing learning opportunities that speak to different senses, needs, and learning speeds. The exercises in this part of the book encourage the use of various media and sensory learning. Among these are the following techniques:

- Multimedia
  - Use of synchronous and asynchronous chat

- Use of audio recordings of teachers and students reading
- Use of audio/video recordings of teachers and students both reading and writing
- Use of voice recognition software for struggling, disabled, and blocked writers
- Multiple writing platforms and genres
  - Journals for private and semiprivate writing (when between student and teacher)
  - Blogs for public writing of a semifinished or substantive nature
  - Wikis for public, collaborative writing
  - Discussion posts for public comments and communications of a relatively unfinished or shorter nature
  - Chat for brief exchanges about the course or writing
  - Whiteboards or PowerPoint for symbolic forms like Venn diagrams, mind maps, charts, sketches, art or visual presentations, outlines, and the like
  - Assignments for essay or other writing that will be assessed formally
- Multiple approaches
  - Working on reading by focusing on difficult or problematic moments in the text[1]
  - Reading thoughtfully by extending and testing the methods of analysis in various authors' works
  - Rereading a text
  - Reusing a text for an extended piece of writing or for multiple writings, perhaps from different perspectives
  - Practicing critical reading through trying that style in one's own writing, a form of conscious mimicry[2]
  - Individual reading-to-writing practice
  - Collaborative/small group reading practice
- Local- and global-focused exercises
  - Stem sentences for completion[3]
  - Thinking stems[4]

---

[1]See Bartholomae and Petrosky (2002, vii–viii) for some of the reading approaches listed here.
[2]See Mayo (2000, 75).
[3]See Horning (1978) for the predictive value of stem sentences.
[4]See McGregor (2007) for thinking stems.

- Cloze exercises
- Replacing headings and paragraphing
- Explaining reasoning behind reading or writing decisions
- Self-reflection

All of these methods are considered first in the context of content-focused reading in OWI settings. A variety of different techniques for using the primary strategy for different reading purposes are infused in each chapter, such as cloze or fill-in-the-blank exercises, stem sentences, multimedia, using different modalities, and rereading.

TEACHING READING IN AN OWI SETTING

Writing instruction minimally involves teachers' efforts in developing coursework, teaching writing lessons, reading drafts and final essays, and providing formative and summative feedback. All too often, there are many more students in the class than the 15 to 20 recommended by the CCCC Committee for Principles and Standards for the Postsecondary Teaching of Writing (1989) and (2009), both of which are confirmed by the OWI Committee's position statement (2013). This suggested workload is reasonable and avoids overwhelming writing teachers with essay review both in and out of class.

OWI teachers do all the work of onsite teachers plus they read and respond to written questions, e-mails, and discussion posts. They do not have as clear a distinction between what they are to do "in" and "out" of class because most of the time, writing classes are taught asynchronously, which gives the appearance of all the work happening outside the class. Because OWI carries a heavy literacy load, online writing teachers may express concern when they are given teaching suggestions that can lead to additional work. Part Two's eight literacy comprehension themes and their corresponding lessons may inspire some apprehensiveness along those lines.

Apprehensions that people have shared include the following administrative and institutional concerns:

- The writing program provides prescribed, predeveloped courses.
- On a quarter system, the term is shortened to six to eight weeks from a standard twelve to fourteen weeks.
- Teachers receive little or no professional development or training in OWI.
- Teachers who do not want to teach online are given no choice in the matter.
- Part-time faculty are inadequately compensated for their work.

- Teacher effectiveness assessments are based on retention and students' end-of-term evaluations, both of which may be low.
- Too many students are enrolled in the course because many drop out; when students drop out, they are counted against teachers where retention is valued.
- Students are unprepared for
  - reading online,
  - the level of the writing course, and/or
  - the expectations of an OWC.

These concerns can be addressed to varying degrees by sharing the OWI Committee's position statement (2013) with WPAs and administrators and asking for the fair treatment these principles advocate.

There are other teaching-related concerns that cannot be addressed at the administrative and institutional levels. These apprehensions reflect a sense from OWI instructors that they already have too much work and not enough time, and are doing too much for students. These concerns speak to a broader need to understand the OWC as one that requires great interactivity between teachers and students so that it can meet individual students at their points of need.

In an onsite setting, as this book reflects, writing teachers meet their students face-to-face for approximately three hours per week (even in some hybrid online courses). They get to talk orally in class and out of class (i.e., in hallways, during office hours, and at essay conferences). These onsite meeting hours typically are not used by teachers for the time-intensive tasks of reading and responding to student essay drafts but for another level of teaching. The approximately three hours per week that onsite teachers work directly with their students (office hours notwithstanding) are missed in the online setting, where some teachers teach only through their responses to essay drafts.

Nonetheless, these three hours—hours that I am using here merely for illustration purposes as teachers may spend many more hours outside of reading and responding to essays—exist to be used online through written communications with students: responding to e-mails, reading and responding briefly to journal entries, and prompting/responding to discussion posts. They also may involve announcements and written encouragement to the entire class, as well as new written content or brief assignments that teach students what their writing or questions reveal they need just in time. These tasks are part and parcel of OWI—not adjuncts to it that require extra time on the part of the teacher.

The point is that if a writing teacher can add any amount of reading instruction and connect it reasonably to the writing instruction of the OWC, doing so is perfectly within the scope of the job. While it may not be possible to teach more than a few of the reading lessons offered as examples in Part Two, any of that work is a legitimate use of the OWI teacher's time and any of it may help students improve their college reading skills to the benefit of their writing. The strategies in the chapters that follow have been written with issues of apprehension and time in mind. For example, adding a reading lesson to an OWC requires no additional training because the concepts and lessons are fully explained for teachers and students. Additionally, these lessons do not need to be graded and require minimal response from teachers.

Justifying this use of time and finding time to teach reading are, of course, two different things. To carve out time from the three or more hours one allots to each course per week, there are some short cuts that will help students and will not cause great time disruption:

- Ask students to reflect on what they have learned in a lesson through a private journal entry (i.e., visible only to student and teacher). Respond to the journal entry with one to three sentences at most. Your response may ask students to follow up, which many of them will do because they tend to miss having more personal interaction with the teacher about their reading and writing challenges. A quick read and brief response need take no more than two minutes per student—if that—but the rewards are great in that this work establishes an understanding that the teacher will be reading what the student is assigned to do and that he or she cares on an interpersonal level. This kind of journal response can be used weekly or biweekly or several times within a single major writing assignment, but it should be done often enough to establish a pattern that students can anticipate.

- Write ideas out before doing any audio-/videotaping to make providing a transcript or outline as a substitute for more technologically sophisticated closed captioning more efficient. Make a habit of providing some text to accompany any images or videos (including YouTube links); similarly, provide images to accompany text whenever possible.

- Learn other skills necessary for equal access and learning accommodations before the semester and use these skills for every OWC to assist all students and to keep the skills sharp.

- Even though group work can be difficult to manage and contentious for students, try one or two group sessions with a reading lesson in mind. Students may not like what they are being asked to do, but they still can be asked to do it. Make the job reasonable in length, clear in expected outcomes, and connected in some way to the course's writing goals. Give students sufficient time to complete the peer response or talk cycle, typically at least five days. To make the group work more efficient, develop a pattern in your OWC that requires students to have checked into and used the LMS at least twice a week (e.g., Sunday and Wednesday) if not more often.

- Respond to students and prompt them to higher levels of discussion about any of these lessons, but beware of doing the work for them. Your requirement to write should be much less than their need to write in any written assignment.

- Schedule lessons that require your response around the essay write–read–write cycle so that you are not overwhelmed with other reading and writing during essay draft work.

- Remember that your responses to student writing in class discussions and journals are primary teaching methods for OWI; they are your conferences with them (Hewett, *Online Writing*, 2015). Reject the idea that reading or other lessons are busywork for you or the students. When you teach in OWI, you read and write rather than talk. Well-written lessons, as described in Part Three, are your job as an OWI teacher.

- Reinforce with your students that they cannot skip these or any other lessons (unless you have built into the syllabus a choice to pick and choose their work) as a mere adjunct to their formal essays. Reading and writing lessons simply are not busywork. They are OWI in practice.

Remember that the more we practice reading and writing skills for OWI classes, the faster and more efficient we can become while maintaining effectiveness. For more practical ideas on how to manage OWI teaching and to make it work well, refer to my book *The Online Writing Conference: A Guide for Teachers and Tutors* (2015) and Warnock's *Online Writing Instruction: How and Why* (2009).

TEACHING READING COLLABORATIVELY

A final practical strategy to consider in teaching students to read to learn is collaborative group work. Collaborative learning through group-based reading, writing, or feedback workshops is a deeply honored teaching and learning strategy in the rhetoric and composition field, and it takes direct advantage of the OWI's capability to engage social construction through technology. As a practice, collaborative learning in writing instruction stems from Lev Vygotsky's (1962) work and was advocated by Kenneth Bruffee (1984, 1993). Collaborative learning is expressed through online (Hewett and Ehmann 2004) and onsite peer tutoring (Howard 2001), class discussion (now sometimes called a "flipped classroom" where students are asked to teach each other), peer response group work, and collaborative writing projects. The underlying belief is that just as people learn language in social settings, so students can learn writing from each other as a contained social group. Particularly when more nontraditional adult students entered college in the 1970s, as Howard (2001) indicates, the traditional "individualistic" learning style needed to be changed to incorporate peer-to-peer work (54). Composition theory stressed that writing classrooms should become more peer-centered and less teacher-centered. OWI supports such peer-centered work through any LMS where the entire class sees a discussion thread or small groups can be configured to limit interactions to those in the group.

Collaboration is used multiple times in Chapters 4 through 11 as a suggested setup for reading lessons. However, while collaboration is a natural fit for OWI, it is a challenging concept to enact practically. This next section considers some of the key issues for assigning collaborative or group-based lessons to OWI students, particularly in fully online (although also in some hybrid) settings.

Collaborative Writing in OWI

Collaborative writing in OWI involves software that enables unified communication among group members. One of the benefits of using the LMS is that it typically facilitates group work and group sharing of ideas through written discussions, helping to create what teachers hope is a sense of community in the distributed classroom. As Part One indicates, OWI students certainly need to have some sense of cooperative learning in order to encourage each other as they read for class. Indeed, they will be reading both their own writing and the writing of other students as well as content and written instructions for the course. In doing so, students will have opportunities to teach each other what they are learning and to share with each other both their original and not-so-original ideas. The opportunity simply to talk to each other, whether by voice or text, not only humanizes the OWC but helps students to locate themselves on a learning spectrum.

Technologically, unified communications software integrates a number of synchronous technologies like IM chat, video/voice conferencing, interactive whiteboards, and data and document sharing for joint revision, as well as asynchronous technologies for e-mail, single-authored document development, and other uses. When offered together in an LMS or other groupware, these tools suggest that working on reading, writing, or revision in a team setting is considered natural. Indeed, according to Jukes et al. (2010), "The digital generation accepts the idea of working with people online as completely normal" (106). Contemporary students are said to be group-learning focused, and comfortable with social networking, collaborating, and sharing answers and content (Levine and Dean 2012, 166).

Yet, as with other uses of digital tools, undergraduate students need to learn to interact online for structured purposes other than social and informal learning, such as the experiential knowledge that gaming is said to engender. Collaboration is necessary for students to be "equipped for knowledge-age work" (Burnett and Roberts 2005, 55). To this end, Jukes et al. (2010) recommend that teachers "plan joint work, to negotiate the distribution of work between group members, and to resolve conflicts" (109). They further suggest shifting instruction to project-based learning from instruction (82); this is a strategy that college-level writing teachers already have employed for years in their portfolio, service learning, and critical, real-life approaches to writing.

Nonetheless, group or team writing assignments in college often are unsuccessful. To some degree, this failing may relate to questions of multitasking and boredom discussed in Chapter 1. What students do with groups of people for fun is not necessarily what they must do for school. School is always school no matter what educators do to make it look like outside life or the business world. Students who are not willing to engage fully with projects for the sake of what they can learn may not choose to power through the challenges involved in negotiating problems with peers. Students do not necessarily share the same goals with one another, and they sometimes do not share the teacher's goals. Their sense of what collaborative work should look like often differs from the teacher's vision. OWI teachers often are frustrated by the high dropout rate students have — not necessarily dropping out from class, but from their group work — where one or two students are left to complete the work.

In the preface to *Team Writing: A Guide to Working in Groups,* Joanna Wolfe (2010) indicates that she studied student teams in technical writing and engineering courses where collaborative writing is regularly expected. Many of the students expressed anger and resentment because they did not feel they had the power to change the team's writing when they saw that it needed to be changed. The instructors did not seem to be aware of their students' feelings. Wolfe explains that "students needed guidance and structure, which instructors were unaware they had to explicitly provide" (v). The key to this information is that students need explicit education in what they can do, what they cannot do, what they should do, and how they can work together on group writing to the best advantage. This is not information that students necessarily own when entering any course. Therefore, if students are exposed to collaborative writing in their college writing courses, they need to learn how to do it in carefully considered and overt ways.

Such explicit teaching relies on a definition of collaboration that the instructor is comfortable with. For writing, Wolfe outlines three settings for collaboration:

1. In an interactive group setting, the entire group talks together with one or two people acting as scribes for the writing. They can do this work face-to-face or synchronously online through audio/video or IM chat.

2. In a divided setting, the group divides the document into sections, and each person takes a section. This work is asynchronous in that the group is not working together and people likely are writing at dif-

ferent times, so it can be accomplished onsite or online. In a college setting, the writing typically appears to have been quilted together and reveals the individual voice of each writer in the sections. Sometimes the students' schedules do not allow for time for a completely edited document. Divided group writing probably is the most common collaborative form in a school-based online setting.

3. In a layered setting, every group member can have more than one particular role, and typically one member works on the document at a time. It is layered in that each individual's contribution to the document is developed on top of another's writing on top of yet another's writing (6); everyone is cowriter and coeditor. Layered collaboration can occur asynchronously onsite or online using various media or even synchronously through software that enables two or more people to work on a document simultaneously. It is the most challenging type of collaborative writing to do because it requires giving up individual authorship in favor of a group voice. It also requires the additional effort of blending voices and, hopefully, perfecting text at some level.

To be able to collaborate in writing is a trickier skill than one might expect. It requires confidence in one's writing ability, a willingness to share ideas and authorship, and an understanding of how to negotiate meaning among multiple writers. Moreover, it requires explicit permission to blend authorship, which is something not often found in college, where fears of plagiarism abound.

Interestingly, such collaboration can be difficult for college teachers both to do and to teach. In my own experience writing and editing with scholars, the idea of authorial ownership tends to get in the way of shared authorship. For example, in preparation of the book *Virtual Collaborative Writing in the Workplace: Computer-Mediated Communication Technologies and Processes* (Hewett and Robidoux 2010), educators who evinced a solid interest in collaborative writing agreed to co-revise and coedit chapters in a layered manner using a wiki that enabled a record of changes. My coeditor and I found that the writers provided some comments to one another but failed to make any textual changes. When asked about this practice, they indicated a discomfort with multiple authorship and a desire to preserve authorial ownership despite their theoretical beliefs in collaborative writing.

In a similar way, students struggle with layered collaboration, but for different reasons (Wolfe 2010, 9). The parameters of plagiarism are unclear in academic settings. Even though collaboration among writers is a well-known business writing strategy (Lunsford and Ede 2012), the notion of sharing authorship in student work is handled irregularly and even fearfully. Sadly, even the use of a tutor's assistance can be construed as an opportunity for plagiarism (Hewett 2015; Spiegelman 1998, 2000). Recently, Harvard University has been in the news for directing its professors to "set out carefully in writing and at the outset of a course or course assignment the extent of permissible student collaboration in the preparation of papers, computer programs, or examinations" (Landergan 2013, n.p.). In nonwriting courses, students are allowed to discuss problems, but they are instructed to "work through the problem yourself and ensure that any answers you submit for evaluation are the result of your own efforts." Another Harvard professor wrote in her syllabus that "any written work should be 'the result of your own thinking, writing, and research, and must reflect your own ideas about and approach to the topic'" (Landergan 2013, n.p.). In this environment, students must let the professor know if they receive help with their writing.

It would be absurd to excoriate any professor or policy that asks for individual work on an individualized project; however, it seems equally absurd to allow students to exchange ideas but not use them if the ideas are not the result of their own efforts. This tension can be untenable. Ideas, once shared, become group property, so to speak. It is impossible to unsay an idea and to return to earlier thinking not influenced by those ideas, and it is unfair to ask this of students. In any collaborative setting, ideas are shared both in discussion and writing. How can students who are given permission to discuss problems together—a social construction learning strategy—guarantee the written results are their ideas alone? Wolfe (2010) aptly states that "co-writing and collaborating give students opportunities to share expertise, learn from others' mistakes as well as successes, and—most importantly—solidify what they have learned by teaching it to others" (5). What students can learn to do is to credit fellow students for the inception of particular ideas—if, in doing so, they are not penalized for not doing all of the thinking themselves. For this remedy to work and to foster genuine collaboration among students, teachers must understand the nature of collaboration in relation to plagiarism and then be clear about how collaboration is to be assessed.

Until there is clarity about the nature of collaboration, authorial ownership, and plagiarism in academic settings, students will receive mixed messages that interfere with their abilities to collaborate genuinely in OWI. All undergraduate students need this kind of work. Indeed, because they do their work in a technologically distributed setting, OWI instructors are perfectly poised to teach students new ways to position themselves as individual and collaborative authors that include giving each other both feedback and revision strategies through such direct methods as tracking changes.

Collaborative Reading in OWI

Similarly, collaborative reading can help students develop literacy skills. To use it well, however, one must set reasonable expectations for students and for any collaborative approaches to literacy strategies in OWI.

Reading typically is an individual process — or, at least it has been whenever people do not read aloud in class. Likely, many students have not read cooperatively — in a group or aloud to a group — since grade school. For some students, reading aloud has been a rare experience. Individualized reading is an example of how a concentrated individual focus might cause a sort of tunnel vision or attention blindness.

In OWI, where much of the work is asynchronous, cooperative reading typically does not happen although group discussion of individual readings is a popular written task. Reading collaboratively is an activity that can take advantage of one of the digital era's changes where the actual process of thinking and doing has become more important than the product: "synthesizing the vast and diverse forms of information, contributing and commenting, customizing, and remixing" (Davidson 2012, 17). These processes are in sync with new ways of looking at the world with the ubiquitous nature of the words *context, global, cross-cultural, multidisciplinary*, and *distributed* (18).

Useful OWI reading lessons that involve collaboration may benefit from the following principles of cooperative learning:

- positive interdependence,
- individual accountability,
- promoting interaction,
- team skills, and
- group processing (Belfer and Wakkary 2005, 36).[5]

These skills, the linchpins to which contemporary composition teachers connect their instruction, are challenging to engage in any writing course, but they are harder to use in an online setting because of the high possibility that students simply will not show up to talk or read synchronously or to post their work asynchronously. Students may feel uncomfortable even e-mailing their classmates, and it is common, in my experience, for those who have e-mailed a group member not to receive a response.

Practically speaking, collaborative reading ought to be a synchronous activity, although asynchronous distribution of recorded oral reading can substitute. Where instructors find collaborative reading activities in Part Two, they should consider their students' access needs first and address group modality (i.e., asynchronous or synchronous) and media (i.e., text, IM chat, voice, video, and the like) second. All of the exercises can be adapted to include or remove collaboration from the strategy as presented.

---

[5]Originally cited in David W. Johnson, Robert T. Johnson, and Edythe Johnson Holubec (1993).

Problems with Collaboration in OWI

The first problem to consider with collaboration in online settings is that students will have a challenging time getting together for group meetings. Students have difficulty meeting synchronously for any part of the activity when they are geographically distributed in different time zones and have different school and work schedules. They struggle especially when classes meet asynchronously and there is no single time and day of the week devoted to the course. Indeed, some institutions will not allow teachers to require students to meet outside of class even though in OWI almost all activities occur outside the bounds of a particular class period. Some students also will object to collaborative groups because of past, failed experiences where they were left as the responsible student in the project.

An obvious instructional option is to reject uses of collaborative reading and writing in one's OWC. However, there are advantages to keeping the collaborative exercise in place, not the least of which is the students' abilities to teach each other materials that they are finding difficult to read and write on their own. As Jacobs and Hundley (2010) assert:

> Because learning to work interdependently in collaborative ways is an instructional objective in many courses, simply avoiding student group work is not a feasible solution. Nor can and should faculty be expected to micromanage every student interaction, dispute, misunderstanding, or hurt feeling. Practical suggestions for such cases might include clear performance expectations of students, the ability to evaluate and provide feedback on student-partner performance early and often, structuring graded assignments in such a way that does not disproportionately disadvantage a high-performing individual who ends up with poor-performing or "social loafing" student colleagues, and a willingness for the instructor to listen and intervene in group dynamic issues when warranted. (61)

To address useful collaborative experiences and to make them fair to students whose group members simply do not care to do the work or respond in a timely manner, it seems best to use small rather than large groups and to make group work short, pointed, and relatively low stakes grade-wise. It is not necessary to grade—or even to respond to—every action taken in an OWC although the archival nature of interactions makes this possible (and tempting). Karen Belfer and Ron Wakkary (2005) indicate that designing, implementing, and assessing collaborative learning usefully may mean requiring group members to assess the group and themselves individually. It also can mean having the students develop their own collaborative learning scenarios. Such actions can inspire the uninspired to join in by encouraging them to buy into the activity.

OBJECTIONS TO NOTIONS OF COMMUNITY It may be helpful to remember that what we want to occur in OWI may not happen as planned. Recall that contemporary students are people of various ages who have a wide range of technological sophistication and an equally wide range of time and energy to commit to their studies. Understanding these core characteristics can help teachers determine what they believe to be reasonable collaboration requirements and lessons.

The focus on building community in the classroom is what Nathan (2005), citing the French anthropologist Herve Varenne, indicates is "the shared American ideal of community: a place of equality, informality, intimacy, and reciprocity" (93). This powerful and principled view impels teachers in many disciplines — not just the writing classroom — to ask for students to be orally responsive to each other and to connect other students' ideas to their own rather than simply to provide their own ideas alone. For example, Warnock (2009) saw the OWC as a having a "humanistic potential" through a writing course's focus on interaction "beyond content delivery." OWI:

> allow[s] students to build a community through electronic means. Perhaps for some — but not all! — such a community will never wholly replace the interactions of an onsite class, but for students whose options are limited, these electronic communities can build the social and professional connections that constitute some of education's real value. (xix–xx)

Sadly, this oft-cited view seems to be overly optimistic as it played out in Nathan's (2005) experiences and as it plays out in many writing classrooms. While we certainly see discussion writing in OWI that seems reciprocal, for example, a genuine intimacy in which the students see each other as equals deserving of their time may not be possible for many students or even reasonable to ask of them.

In her book, Nathan discusses communities, providing some insight into group work. As she explains, community building is a popular buzz phrase in college circles, particularly among composition teachers. Nathan's fellow students indicated that they were interested in community building, but what they really meant was the community of their personal networks of friends (55). I think these networks are like small families that students develop in their college years, to some degree taking the place of their nuclear families from whom younger students in particular are becoming more independent. These "small, ego-centered groups that were the backbone of most students' social experience in the university" were where Nathan's student peers chose to place any extra energy they had after work and school (55). This scenario seems completely normal in that any one of us only has so much time and energy to go around; at some point, we choose to spend any so-called downtime with our family and our closest friends.

Thus, in an academic setting, given the dual responsibilities of paid labor and schoolwork that most students shoulder, it seems reasonable — not comfortable, satisfying, or even good for learning, but reasonable — to expect that some students will give as little time as they possibly can to their so-called class communities. For OWI, this expectation means that teachers and students most likely are on different pages of the time management calendar regarding how much energy should be given to group discussions or other community-building classwork. For example, in order to encourage response in OWI discussions, teachers frequently advise requiring of each student a set number of responses per posted discussion. Such a requirement stems from practicality in an environment where if they do not have to respond to one another, many students will not respond at all. Without further requirement that the responses be substantive, thoughtful, and directly related to the previous response, the dialogue quickly devolves into clichéd, contentless talk ("Yep, me, too!" or "Well said, Joe!"). In Nathan's experience, "ideas are rarely debated, and even more rarely evaluated. Most [face-to-face] classroom discussion, when it does occur, could be described as a sequential expression of opinion, spurred directly by a question or scenario devised by the teacher, which is subject to little or no commentary" (2005, 95). We might liken such discussion to the divided collaborative writing style discussed earlier. Such sequential discussion certainly is found online as well.

PRACTICAL STRATEGIES FOR COOPERATIVE WORK If we take the view that students need cooperative writing work in OWI—a view that has great merit—then we must think carefully about the times, ways, and reasons for using groups so they are employed wisely given students' needs and propensities. When building groups for collaborative reading or writing projects in OWI:

- Use regular, small groups of two to four students where they can learn each other's schedules and communication preferences. If possible, keep these groups stable throughout the term, but be willing to change them quickly if some group members drop out of class (or out of sight, not posting required work for more than one week), when the group members indicate they have reached an impasse, and after the teacher has attempted to intervene. Instruct students on how to be welcoming of new group members when such changes occur.

- Use groups for the talking that does not otherwise occur in OWI. Remember that such written talk also may be occurring as side chat through the LMS's IM chat feature or outside the LMS through Skype or Facebook, which can be a good thing for helping students to cohere into a functional online class.

- Make some or all of the group work ungraded or otherwise low-stakes work, but be sure that it has a clear purpose for students who are asked to do it and that they have some tangible requirement for completing it. Reject any busywork developed merely for the sake of having a cooperative group.

- Connect the assignment directly to the reading or writing lesson to be learned. Using open-ended discussion questions or closed-ended quizzes that students have to answer (but that teachers do not necessarily have to grade) is one way to keep students engaged.
- Set reasonable and clear parameters for responsiveness, but have realistic expectations that some students will be more socially oriented learners and more responsible group members than others. Decide how you will address the unresponsive groups members to include, if possible, communicating with them individually.
- Provide a way for students with nonresponsive group members to complete their work satisfactorily.

Reading to Learn

HOW TO USE PART TWO: READING THOUSANDS OF WORDS A DAY

The comprehension themes in Part Two primarily address reading for content, which provides conceptual knowledge, research resources, and discussion material for writing. Each chapter in Part Two is modeled on problem-centered instruction. Each includes an explanation of the primary comprehension theme to be considered (what it is), a rationale for addressing it (why it is important), and a sample lesson for the online setting (how to teach it), as well as a rationale for connecting reading to writing in OWI. The how-to-teach exercises are focused on content reading strategies. These lessons are expanded in Part Three as more explicit exercises for instructors on how to write lessons for students; models include lessons for students regarding instructional language. The ways that teachers write lessons about reading content, writing-focused content, assignments, feedback, and interpersonal communications all are crucial to students' abilities to read to learn.

Each chapter in Part Two concludes with a self-contained, reading-focused, writing-anchored exercise. These exercises use concrete explanations, sensory experiences, and visual imagery that can make abstractions come alive. These concrete experiences include teacher modeling tips and guided practice that students can do alone or with others. Because they typically lack the shared face time found in synchronous settings, getting students to engage actively in learning can be challenging online; to that end, instructors should freely adapt these suggested exercises in ways that they believe will make them more lively, engaging, or specific to their course focus and student population — age, level, genre, and employment goals.

Some of these exercises suggest using public writing in the LMS discussion forum. I identify these as "discussion posts" or "whole-class" writing exercises; some of these exercises may work in a wiki-like setting where all students can build a text together. If you believe that the students will not benefit from a group setting, these exercises easily can be adapted to an individual lesson where group discussion is unnecessary. For individual posts, I use the term *journal* to indicate writing that is seen only by the writer and the teacher.

Similarly, to appeal to students with different learning styles and abilities, these exercises have been written to engage various affordances of an LMS and the unique modalities and media uses of OWI. Where using audio/video, phone, IM chat, or other media is not possible or could pose an impediment to students with limited access, these exercises can be adapted to make more use of text or other LMS-friendly venues. In cases where the selected reading is not interesting to teachers or may be inappropriate for the class, the lesson can be adapted to use different authors or even different types of readings and/or follow-up prompts.

The lessons are envisioned primarily as assistive literacy lessons that can be adapted and more deeply connected to existing writing assignments in an OWC that acknowledges the critical importance of reading at all levels. Thus, the lessons are scaffolded, yet easily adaptable to an individual instructor's needs. Since reading and writing are so intimately related, these reading assignments easily fit within most writing assignments, providing materials for discussion posts or early drafts, for instance. There is no need, in other words, to drop a favorite reading or writing assignment from a course in order to incorporate any of the selected reading comprehension themes. For specific examples regarding how to incorporate these lessons into your writing course, see the two sample assignments, which are linked and scaffolded, in Appendix B. Read together, these two assignments demonstrate how you can select comprehension themes and activities from Part Two and adapt them as seems most helpful toward teaching your course's desired writing skills.

Finally, quoted statements like those found at the beginning of each chapter in Part Two can be used to teach the eight comprehension themes (metacognition, schema, inference, questioning, relevance, visualizing, analyzing, and synthesizing). Possible student tasks for these quotes include, but are not limited to the following:

- Share your thoughts in a discussion forum about one or more of the [metacognition or other themed] quotes. What does it mean with regard to [comprehension theme]?
- Write about [comprehension theme] using one or more of these quotes in a journal or other informal, low-stakes writing assignment.
- Create a meme using one of these quotes either partially or in full. A meme would use an image (e.g., drawing, photograph, or symbol) to transmit a principle or key idea to the culture at large. Share the meme through

the Internet or mobile phone technology using Facebook or other social media. After twenty-four hours, report in a discussion or journal entry the kinds of responses you received. Do you think it should go viral? Why or why not?

For additional suggestions for quotes to prompt student writing, see Appendix A.

To anchor a lesson, mention and/or directly use the concept in a related or future writing assignment. For each of the lessons, make adaptations or provide necessary explanations to connect the selected lessons to the concepts, content, and needs of your own writing course. Students especially will want to know how a particular reading skill will help them with their writing in the context of the required assignments for your course.

These lessons do not need to be graded by the teacher. Answer keys (to a cloze exercise, for example) can be posted to the class after a few days with students then being asked to remark about their success in a discussion forum. Additionally, lesson responses can be self-assessed with a student journal entry, for example. Therefore, teachers need only read the entries and respond with one to three sentences. Such personal contact about any literacy lesson assures students that the lesson is not merely busywork; they can see that the teacher reads and cares about what they are experiencing. Minimal, yet personalized response sets boundaries that ease the instructor literacy load. Although occasionally such contact can lead to recursive discussion in journal entries, teachers would do well to see this ongoing conversation as a positive occurrence that connects a student more deeply to the class and to reading and writing overall.

These comprehension themes and literacy lessons are informed by the theoretical material in Part One and supported by ideas offered from a wide variety of professionals in literacy and composition instruction. Where individuals can be cited in traditional scholarship, an internal citation cross-references the sources found in the References section at the end of the book. Where the origin of the material is not a published source, the original source is cited by a footnote with appreciation for assistance in this project.

4

Using Metacognition for Reading

To read without reflecting is like eating without digesting.
— Edmund Burke

WHAT IS METACOGNITION AND WHY IS IT IMPORTANT?

Metacognition is defined here as thinking about our thinking or awareness of our thoughts. Being metacognitive has to do with noticing our thinking and then naming it as what we do (McGregor 2007, 11). Being consciously metacognitive has to do with deciding to notice our thinking and naming what we notice as metacognition. The goal of this chapter is to teach or remind students about this concept and to help them to use metacognition consciously.

Students will know what we are talking about when we describe metacognition because they think metacognitively all the time. They may not, however, have had this skill named before or they may not remember the name. There can be a relief in learning that almost everyone has the capacity to be metacognitive. Indeed, it is this capacity that presumably separates humans from other animals. Once named, we can work with such thinking together, using metacognition for coursework as well as for understanding how people communicate with others.

Metacognition is a necessary part of reading genuinely, of taking in what is being presented in the text and thinking about how it relates to one's current knowledge — or extant conceptual knowledge, as Maclellan called it (1997, 279). We use metacognition when we are consciously aware of what we are reading and think about the reading as we read. Such awareness can be stimulated by annotating a text, for example.

Without this awareness, we can read in an unthinking manner, simply running our eyes over the pages, seeing and decoding the words, yet not considering them for deeper meaning or integrating them into our personal knowledge base. In fact, our minds may be somewhere else entirely, reviewing a recent phone conversation or thinking about a movie seen the night before. This kind of distracted reading often is called *fake reading* because the words on the page are acknowledged but not considered or digested. *Real reading* is not happening.

All of us can fake read. Many of us learned to do it as a method of self-protection in elementary school when called upon to read a passage aloud in class. If, for example, a student reads a passage aloud and is actually thinking about how he sounds to his classmates, he is fake reading. His mind is not connected to the words and their meaning—only to his self-awareness of their sound. His action could be seen as protection against looking and feeling stupid or awkward while enduring the potential embarrassment of reading incorrectly in front of the class.

Another time students fake read is when they are called upon to read aloud and are awakened from a daydream. They realize they have not been paying attention to the previous students' readings or to class in general. The startled attention to the reading would include gathering their thoughts, wondering what they had missed, and feeling left behind—any of these conditions would lead to reading the words but not the meaning behind them. People who are really good at fake reading can fool listeners into thinking that they are excellent readers because the text sounds "right" or "good." However, if asked to explain what they just read, their responses reveal a shallow understanding of the text's meaning.

In later years, students might fake read even when reading silently. This is a dutiful sort of reading: the chapter is assigned and they need to get it done. So, they allot a half hour to the task and read the words, but all the while they are thinking of the next task or hurrying to finish before leaving for a paid job. Few words may penetrate the brain to create a lasting impression in such cases.

Or, perhaps, as when I first read Cicero as a young graduate student, one might read while nodding off in a pervasive sleepiness that begs the eyes to close. The self-protection of such reading is in getting through the task while not challenging the reader to focus on new, difficult vocabulary or to rethink the ideas involved. In fact, to be quite honest, if I do not have my own good reason for reading certain philosophers now—like some passage I want to find or a thought I want to understand better—I find myself drifting off. This is an example of an adolegogical learning process in which the learner might do what she is asked to do out of obedience to the task but not engage in it fully because she does not have a personal connection or understanding of how or why the task can benefit her.

As the examples above demonstrate, fake reading can be a self-protective action, a bad habit, or a way to feel as if one has addressed the task without really doing so, thus removing pressure from the assignment. It seems likely that most students are aware that such fake reading is not helpful in college-level work, but they may not be fully aware that they are doing it. Real reading certainly takes significantly more time than fake reading, and it requires a higher level of concentration and cognition. And, as explained earlier, the contexts in which the contemporary student operates may not easily allow for the necessary amount of undivided, sustained attention for real reading. If a student is running between class and workplace, stuffing homework into a few minutes here and there, fake reading serves a purpose albeit one that is unhelpful for college success.

Regardless of students' reasons for attending college and the conditions under which they do so, they need to understand that assigned readings are intended — in a good-faith sort of way — to build knowledge, enhance understanding, and challenge thinking. Fake reading cannot engage any of those goals. Once they understand this reality, some students will be inspired to change their reading strategies. Consciously employed metacognition can help.

HOW DOES METACOGNITIVE READING HELP WITH WRITING?

Students will want to know how these metacognition-focused reading lessons help them with their writing. Because metacognition is a primary reading skill, it helps writers in both online and onsite settings. Reading metacognitively can help writers in several ways:

1. Recall that reading from digital devices, to include computer screens, has its own challenges that students need to be aware of and that a lesson in metacognition may assist them with developing that awareness. How they think about writing when they read it onscreen can help them to consider how their readers — teachers and peers, for example — may read their own writing onscreen. In turn, such knowledge opens the opportunity to talk about textual presentation.

2. The understanding of metacognitive reading can help students to write differently or better in an online setting because they can learn to apply a similar self-conscious focus about how they write with handwriting versus typed text.

3. A more consciously metacognitive reader is likely to understand assigned readings and content materials better, providing the student with more and better fodder for online (written) discussions and other low-stakes writing.

4. Readers who use their metacognition will be able to make better choices of source material for researched writing.

5. Students who read metacognitively also can learn to apply that same reading skill to reviews of their own and peers' writing, making them better self- and peer reviewers overall.

HOW CAN WE TEACH METACOGNITION IN ONLINE SETTINGS?

Focused lessons about metacognition can help students to see their reading efforts differently. In most OWI settings, we are unable to see our students face-to-face so we cannot exhibit a variety of facial expressions to indicate fake reading or lack of engagement with the text. Therefore, teachers need to be creative in demonstrating metacognition. Metacognition is one of those cognitively abstract ideas that may not be conveyed easily to students through reading alone, given that the students likely are not consciously metacognitive readers in the first place. Therefore, they first need to have a concrete image for and experience with metacognition as a named skill. Such concrete images and actions will provide experiential learning that helps a lesson to stick. Concreteness in an OWI setting may be achieved best through images. Although pictures may work, providing a lesson through audio/video likely will be received better for this setting because teachers can combine images with an audible explanation of how they represent metacognition. Once teachers provide basic examples and explanation, they can ask students to provide additional examples through text, images, or audio/video.

Students also need the time to talk about what they are seeing and learning about metacognition. In an onsite or hybrid classroom setting, such talk can happen in class, face-to-face. In a fully online setting, this talk needs to happen through synchronous video, text-based synchronous chat, or asynchronous IM chat. Most often in OWI, it happens asynchronously and typically in a discussion board, also called a message board. Prompts include: "Read XYZ article. When you read it, what are you thinking about? This is your thinking about your thinking." Or "Look at XYZ advertisement. What do you think about when you view it? What do the advertisers want you to think about? How does *your thinking* differ from *their purpose* for you?"

An issue that might arise in an OWC, whether synchronous or asynchronous, is that students might find it challenging to use writing to describe what they are thinking about an object, image, or reading. Doing so requires meta-talk. For example, in Maryland's Annapolis Harbor at the City Dock, there is a bronze set of four life-sized statues; the main statue is of Alex

Haley reading a book to three unnamed children who, in rapt attention, sit and lay at his feet. Students should be given access to one to three images from different camera perspectives. They will know what they see and may think they are supposed to describe it. Description is a fairly straightforward task that students have learned a lot about in their school years. Metacognitive thinking is not about description, however. To gauge their own thinking about the statue set—to think about what their brains are thinking about what the statue set means—is more difficult to convey in words. To this end, students might benefit from a teacher's model:

> I know that Alex Haley wrote *Roots* about his ancestor Kunta Kinte who was actually sold in Annapolis, Maryland. When I see these statues, I think about how real slavery was for Haley. Then I think that any one of the shoppers at the City Dock could have been slaves or buyers at an auction two hundred years ago. I also think about how much the movie *Roots* did for me in making Kunta Kinte seem real.

Students can be encouraged to see that the teacher's thinking jumps about, wanders a bit, but does not digress from the primary subject of the statues into something completely different like his favorite ice cream flavor. Aside from a model, teachers might provide students with metacognition sentence stems such as:

- I'm thinking _____.
- I'm noticing _____.
- I'm wondering _____.
- I'm seeing _____.
- I'm feeling _____.
- I'm considering _____.
- I'm contemplating _____.
- I'm meditating _____.
- I'm pondering _____.
- I've been thinking about _____ and noticing that _____. This is a new thought because _____.

These types of assistive strategies can help students learn how to express their thinking metacognitively. (For more sentence stems to prompt students' thinking, see Appendix A.)

Finally, students need opportunities to practice this new awareness of metacognition. Such practice may include lessons that do not address reading directly, lessons that involve reading, and such exercises as reflective writing about metacognition and its place in their lives. These lessons should be short and low stakes (unless teachers want to include them as a part of graded work)—requiring a minimum of effort of both teacher and student—and they should enable class interaction whenever possible.

METACOGNITION EXERCISE: ANNOTATION

Fake reading often is connected to the fact that someone other than the reader has set the agenda. One way for students to learn how to set their own agenda is through questioning, a comprehension theme that Chapter 7 addresses. Another way to help students create their own agendas is to teach them to annotate their texts. Annotating texts is like having a conversation with them. This strategy helps students to find what is important in a text and helps them to think metacognitively about what they are learning.

Text annotation is a tactic that serves college students well because they often own the books or print the documents that they are reading. Even rented books, electronic books (e-books), and screen-read articles (e.g., PDF files) can be annotated. Why don't students automatically annotate, then?

First, the admonition to never write in books has been ingrained from an early age. In elementary and secondary public school settings, textbooks typically are borrowed from the school for a semester and used for years by many students until they are discarded for newer books. Hence, when they hit the college level, they may react like one student, who told me she doesn't like to write in her textbooks. In fact, however, she was previously never allowed to write in a book, which makes the taboo all the harder to break. Textbook ownership means that students have a freedom to talk to themselves about the text—to think metacognitively in a concrete way—through annotations. For this freedom to work, they may need to be told frankly they are *allowed* now to write in the texts they own and rent. If they continue to worry about writing in their books, then they might be more open to annotating by using sticky notes, notebooks/steno pads, or light pencil alone. E-books and screen-read files usually have an easy-to-use marginal comments function and/or highlighter; for sight-impaired students who use screen readers, it may be a good idea to talk about the best medium for their reading.

A second reason that students may not annotate their texts is that they are worried about the text's resale value. Here, a candid discussion of which books one might keep or resell is a good idea. In general, students tend to resell books that are not in their major field. We should encourage them to keep writing-focused books and handbooks for when they are writing papers in classes unsupported by writing teachers and for use after graduation in business and professional settings. Some online resources, like Bedford's Writer's Help, allow students to purchase up to four or more years of access; these also have annotation features. Two ways to encourage students to keep certain books are (1) to actually teach them how to use the text and (2) to expect them to use it for and in class. Students who know how to find what they are looking for in a handbook, for example, are more likely to keep it for future reference. At any rate, if students are worried about resale value, they should check with their bookstore about the kinds and amounts of markings the bookstore accepts and work around those limitations.

A third reason that students do not annotate their books is simply that they do not know how. Having not had the opportunity in the past, they need a lesson in how annotation can help them keep the metacognitive conversation going. Even students from private secondary schools where they owned their texts each year may need such lessons.

Students benefit from learning that having purchased a book is one kind of ownership. To understand it and be able to use the text well is an even more important kind of ownership. It means owning the information by knowing where it can be found in the text (using spatial recall, for example) and by having considered its relevance. Annotating what they read leads students to this second kind of ownership!

The following are lessons for building annotation skills that students can use when reading their texts. First, explain to students the concept of metacognition and how annotating texts helps them to think metacognitively about what they read. Then, provide students with annotation strategies, asking them to try out the strategies to find the ones that work best for them. Remind them that text *ownership* involves owning the material by understanding it consciously more than possessing the physical book.

Fake reading often is connected to the fact that someone other than the reader (you!) has set the agenda. One way to learn how to set your own agenda is to annotate your textbooks, handouts, and even electronic texts. Annotating texts is like having a conversation with them. This strategy helps you to find what is important in a text and to think metacognitively about what you are learning.

1. Use a pencil, pen, and/or highlighter tool to respond to the text. Decide on a style that will be helpful to you.

   a. For example, pencil or pen is helpful for asking questions, writing comments, and responding to the author with your own thoughts.

   b. A highlighter is helpful for emphasizing the key words in a sentence or the key sentence in a paragraph. Be careful! A highlighter can be used too much, leaving more text yellow or pink than untouched. It's best to highlight only important ideas that you want to remember. That may mean reading twice or three times to determine importance. It's okay to reread the material, by the way, because it can really help you to understand it better.

   We review determining importance as a literacy strategy in Chapter 8.

c. Having a personal language can be helpful in annotating texts. For example, notes inside brackets [ ] can mean your own thoughts while notes inside parentheses ( ) can mean a summary or restatement of the author's thoughts. Simple markings like checks (√), straight lines (_____ or -------), directional arrows (↔ → ↘ ↗), and question or exclamation marks (? !) can become a personal annotation language that you will recall and understand quickly. Always use the same markings to help you be certain of your own intentions when you reread the material weeks, months, or years later.

2. In a hands-on setting with print text, it can be helpful to draw circles and lines or even Venn diagrams among ideas and concepts. These kinds of annotation allow one to make connections from one idea to another.

3. Write an outline in the beginning or ending of a chapter. A notebook may be helpful for this type of annotation because it can become involved with details. Outline only the main points that you want to remember or reconsider at a later time. Be sure to comment about these points with your own thoughts. What you think about the reading is as important as the reading itself in helping you to learn, retain, and discover.

Demonstrate electronic annotation properties in a voice-assisted video recording. Make it general enough to reuse and use your script as a transcript for students with text-based learning preferences.

4. "Dog-ear" the pages to mark a page you want to find again. Dog-earing means to bend a corner of the page in a flap that looks like a dog's floppy ear. If you don't want to bookmark by creasing the page, buy some removable plastic or paper sticky tabs. Use this strategy to mark a page you want to return to or one that holds a key concept that needs to be connected to other ideas.

5. In a website, e-book, tablet, or PDF document, there are annotation tools, too. These are helpful because it can be very difficult to remember where you read something important in such texts. Most of the time, you can highlight key text with color, use marginal comments to write notes to yourself, and sometimes even draw lines from one part of the text to another. You also can bookmark key pages using the software's commands.

Although you may want to personalize this instruction to the course's specific needs, for the sake of time, there are numerous YouTube videos providing generalized demonstration of annotation strategies.

6. Learn to annotate freely, but thoughtfully. Remember that not everything an author says is worth remembering or

questioning. Not every idea is important or even a good idea. That is why we often must reread a passage to (1) learn the material and then (2) distinguish the important ideas from the less useful ones.

Show online students an example of a well-annotated text such as the one shown in Figure 4.1. Make it large and clear enough to be readable.

FIGURE 4.1 Annotated Text

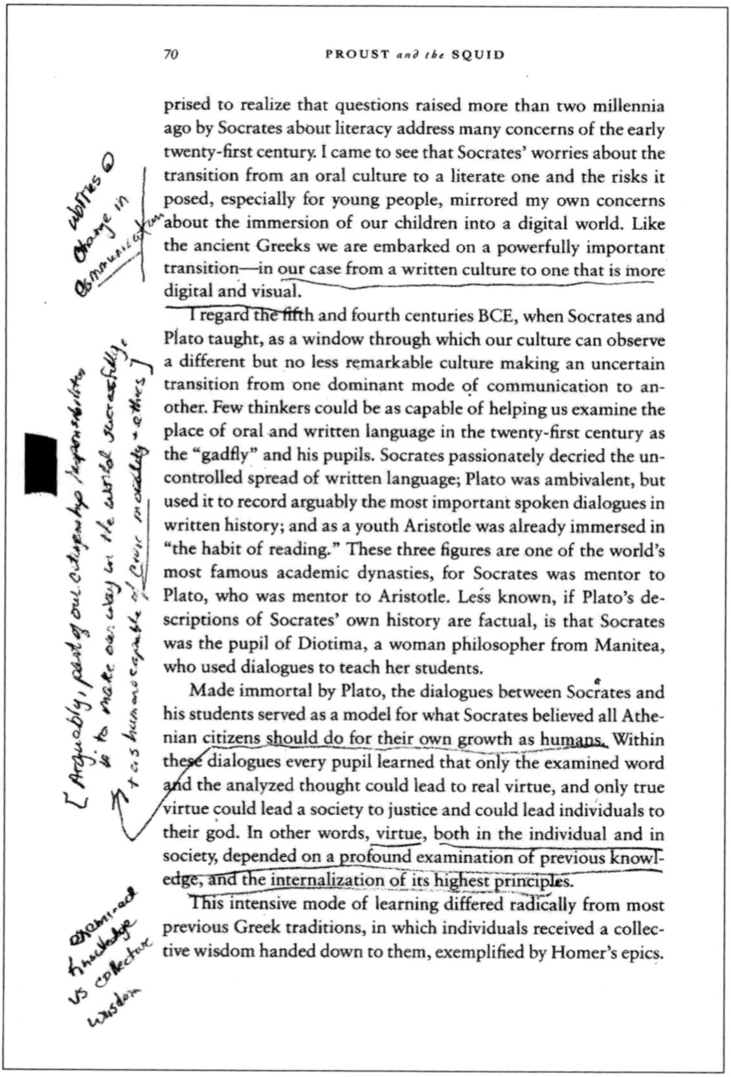

70   PROUST *and the* SQUID

prised to realize that questions raised more than two millennia ago by Socrates about literacy address many concerns of the early twenty-first century. I came to see that Socrates' worries about the transition from an oral culture to a literate one and the risks it posed, especially for young people, mirrored my own concerns about the immersion of our children into a digital world. Like the ancient Greeks we are embarked on a powerfully important transition—in our case from a written culture to one that is more digital and visual.

I regard the fifth and fourth centuries BCE, when Socrates and Plato taught, as a window through which our culture can observe a different but no less remarkable culture making an uncertain transition from one dominant mode of communication to another. Few thinkers could be as capable of helping us examine the place of oral and written language in the twenty-first century as the "gadfly" and his pupils. Socrates passionately decried the uncontrolled spread of written language; Plato was ambivalent, but used it to record arguably the most important spoken dialogues in written history; and as a youth Aristotle was already immersed in "the habit of reading." These three figures are one of the world's most famous academic dynasties, for Socrates was mentor to Plato, who was mentor to Aristotle. Less known, if Plato's descriptions of Socrates' own history are factual, is that Socrates was the pupil of Diotima, a woman philosopher from Manitea, who used dialogues to teach her students.

Made immortal by Plato, the dialogues between Socrates and his students served as a model for what Socrates believed all Athenian citizens should do for their own growth as humans. Within these dialogues every pupil learned that only the examined word and the analyzed thought could lead to real virtue, and only true virtue could lead a society to justice and could lead individuals to their god. In other words, virtue, both in the individual and in society, depended on a profound examination of previous knowledge, and the internalization of its highest principles.

This intensive mode of learning differed radically from most previous Greek traditions, in which individuals received a collective wisdom handed down to them, exemplified by Homer's epics.

The black rectangle on the left side is from a paper sticky tab. Notice that the page is not overly marked but uses lines and symbols, as well as written ideas, to convey what the reader believed was important.

Then, in audio (or text), explain the markings to the class. Read the text where there are underlines and share why it is marked for future reading. Read the marginalia and explain what the thinking is behind that. What does the check mean? The straight line? When students know more about how teachers annotate, they are more likely to imitate our actions.

Ask students to annotate all of their readings or, at the least, to do so regularly. To anchor the lesson, assign a connected journal prompt like the following:

> Evaluate your annotation strategies before and after this lesson about metacognition and annotation. What did you do before? What are you planning to do differently now? In what ways do you see your use of metacognition — thinking about your thinking — changed by these annotation strategies?

Although students may say that they annotate and ask questions of their texts, their reading behaviors typically do not show such attention. To anchor a behavior change, ask students who have the appropriate technology (e.g., a scanner or camera) to post a clear image of one of their annotated text pages and a brief explanation of why they marked the text as they did.

5

Using Schema for Reading

A good book should leave you . . . slightly exhausted at the end. You live
several lives while reading it.
                              —William Styron, interview, *Writers at Work*, 1958

WHAT IS SCHEMA AND WHY IS IT IMPORTANT?

Schema is a word that represents our unique memories, opinions, and background, as well as the extant conceptual knowledge we bring to our learning
and our lives in general. We have a past—a full life—that is as distinctive
as a snowflake is unique. Like all humans, our past experiences help to
define us as the people we are today. Understanding our unique views of the
world enables us to understand others. After all, what are snowflakes but
the distinctive icy crystals that collectively glisten with sunlight and form
a snowy scene that everyone enjoys? So, too, our prior knowledge intensi-
fies our learning and, when shared, changes the learning and worldview of
others. The goal of this chapter is to teach or remind students about this
concept and to help them gain a conscious sense of how to use their schema
in reading college-level texts.

   With respect to reading, everyone has a schema, and that worldview filters everything we read. This unique perspective is one reason that theorists
like Jacques Derrida tell us that no two people read the same text. Truly, my
reading of a text will differ from yours because I cannot help but bring all of
my life's history and my particular thinking behaviors to the project of that
reading. My schema sifts through the text's meaning, helping me to make
that meaning sensible to me. It helps me to move beyond a mere textbase and
into a situational model. You and I can have discussions about a text—for
example, in a book club or professional development meeting—precisely

because we read the book differently based on our backgrounds. Otherwise, there would be nothing to discuss and no fresh ideas to exchange!

Our students, too, have schemas that influence their reading. While their earlier teachers may not have used this word to describe worldview, students likely have discussed how their own lives and background knowledge influence their reading and writing. If not, it is high time they had this discussion in an explicit way that allows them to use their schemas consciously with their reading and writing.

Reading in an online setting is text-rich because everything from instructions to nonfiction articles is provided as text; where there is a lot of text, students may be especially tempted to skip reading in favor of other activities. Therefore, it is especially important to bring their schema to conscious thought. Indeed, the schemas are there anyway, but students may think they are doing something wrong by filtering their reading through their life histories and previously developed knowledge. A lesson on how we can use our schemas purposefully offers students permission to address such reading filters metacognitively. Attending to reading is easier and more pleasurable when we have explicit permission to use our personal-background thinking in the process.

For students who have andragogical or mixed adolegogical learning characteristics, learning to use one's schema is especially important. Students need to find relevant connections between their life experiences and the educational material they are learning. Sometimes they need help in making this effort clear and conscious. An understanding that one's schema filters all that we read, learn, write, and do can provide the spark to ignite the making of connections that are necessary in college reading and writing courses.

HOW DOES READING WITH SCHEMA AWARENESS HELP WITH WRITING?

As with metacognition, students will want to know how these schema-focused reading lessons help them with their writing. Schema, because it is part of one's experiential, background-based thinking, is necessary to reading fluency in both online and onsite settings. Reading with one's schema in mind can help writers in several ways:

1. As with metacognition, reading from digital devices, including computer screens, has its own challenges of which students need to be aware and with which a lesson in reading with one's schema in mind may assist. For example, students may need to consider how they learned to read—whether using a child's computerized toy, a tablet, a book, or all of these. Such knowledge can lead to a self-assessment of whether they

are better (or merely different) readers from hard copy text or on screen. When applied to writing, these considerations influence students' abilities to read their own writing differently, to choose media deliberately for reading, and to use metacognitive awareness.

2. When people use their schema to read, they consciously connect what they are reading with their own lives. In particular for adult students, who are said to learn best when they bring their experiences to the table, knowing this about good readers will help them to make thoughtful connections with the texts they are writing in either the online or onsite setting.

3. When students see how their own schema influences their reading, they can be taught to see that readers of their essays likely will read the writing through the lens of their personal schemas and not through the student writers' schemas. As such, students can understand better both the notion of audience awareness and the vagaries of how different people may respond to their written essays.

4. Students can use an understanding of schema awareness to influence their own audiences' schemas through audience analysis and write their essays with real readers in mind.

5. Students can become more aware of how their schemas affect their writing as well as their reading, allowing them to make more thoughtful choices about their own purposes, topics, selected content, point of view, and the like.

HOW CAN WE TEACH ABOUT USING SCHEMA IN ONLINE SETTINGS?

Teaching about schema, like teaching about metacognition, is a process primarily of reminding students of what they already do when they read: they always apply their prior knowledge and personal experiences to their reading. However, they may not do so consciously. If they do so consciously, they may not know that this is a process they use naturally and one they should use when reading—that using one's schema is a good reading strategy. In other words, students may need to be told that they have permission and freedom to employ their schema in their reading because that quality gives them ownership of their own reading.

To get to this point, however, students will need to see schema as a concrete thing, not an abstraction. The lesson in this chapter is developed to help with this need. All of the conditions inherent in a primarily asynchronous OWI setting can make learning about schema both harder (i.e., students and teacher do not meet face-to-face to enable expressions to convey meaning) and easier (i.e., multiple media can be used to develop a sense of concreteness around the abstraction that is schema—text, still images, audio/video). Teachers need to take advantage of any affordances the LMS provides in terms of dialogue potential through discussion posts and wikis, as well as opportunities for teachers and students to post multimedia files that express and illustrate schema.

Models of using schema when reading are appropriate for helping to get the message that we do not—we cannot—read without our schemas interacting with the text. In addition to the exercise presented below, teachers can develop an example of their own schema usage. They also can ask students to read a common short story and take notes about where and how their schemas inform them about the characters' actions and in visualizing scenery, for example. Everyone, including the teacher, can compare their experiences in an online discussion session.

SCHEMA EXERCISE: CONNECTING YOUR WORLD AND THE READING LIFE

Because schema exercises naturally involve some personal revelation about one's life and worldview, it is helpful to make these activities low stakes to encourage self-exploration and moderate, appropriate self-revelation.

One definition of schema is "the organized pattern of thought." Another is "the thinking that comprises (makes up) our own worldview—our background experiences, opinions, and knowledge." Our schema is the context of who we are; all we have learned in the past; our families and family structures; and our experiences of fun, tragedy, success, and so on. Your schema is different from mine. We each bring our own schema to our reading and writing in any class and at every moment. We can't help it. That's what humans do!

Explain the concept of schema to students. Here is one possible explanation.

Our schemas make up a map or web of our lives. To better understand yourself as a reader or writer, think about your learning schema. We all have one although each is different.

Provide students with a schema drawing of your own or use the schema provided in Figure 5.1.

Figure 5.1 is an example of one person's learning schema from grades kindergarten through six. What did Beth say she learned from drawing her early school experience schema?

FIGURE 5.1 Beth's Learning Schema (Elementary School)

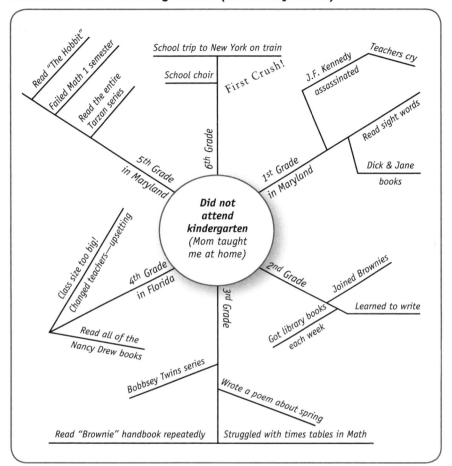

First, she saw a connection between her early reading
experiences and her interests. She grew up when reading was
taught in first and second grade. Perhaps you learned to read
in preschool or kindergarten or earlier? After learning from very
simple books (*Dick and Jane*), her class was taken to the library
once a week. One of Beth's favorite books, mentioned in her
schema, was about a little girl who was a Brownie Girl Scout;
the writer was one, too. The Brownies in her class all took turns
taking that book from the library to read. It was their collective
favorite book (with *Misty of Chincoteague* closely following). She
read that Brownie book four times by third grade.

*Lead students
through the schema
drawing so that they
can understand it.
It is common for
readers to see an
illustration and skip
over the details, so
helping students with
the details is a good
idea.*

Later, Beth's schema reconnected her with her first crush
about whom she daydreamed during an elementary class trip to
Washington, DC. She remembers that bus trip in part because she
talked to her teacher about reading J. R. R. Tolkien's *The Hobbit*
on her own since the teacher had been reading it to the class.
The teacher encouraged Beth to give it a go, which she did, and
reading that book later led her to tackle *The Lord of the Rings*
trilogy.

Writing out this schema did more than just take Beth down
memory lane. It gave her a new perspective on her reading
history. For example, she saw how her interests drew her into
reading as with the Brownie book and later reading feasts on
horses and biographies of queens and famous women. She
realized that her early experiences with Tolkien are why she
invites young readers she tutors to read such fantasies for a
taste of genuinely original writing. Appreciation for Tolkien later
led Beth to enjoy the *Harry Potter* series by J. K. Rowling and to
share it with others. And she began to see how her schema is
intimately connected to reading from early life.

Ask students to try out a schema drawing. Have them draw a learning schema from their earliest school days using a design style of their
choice. Students can draw this schema online in a whiteboard setting or
with PowerPoint tools, or they can opt for pen and paper. (Remind students
that if they use pen and paper, they should plan to photograph or scan the
drawing—if they have access to these tools—to import it as a file into the
assignment.)

From your experiences, draw new lines that express how your
reading history comes from those experiences. What do the
experiences make you think about? How do they make you feel?
What is the relationship among such experiences, associations,
and your attitudes about reading today? Your attitudes about
writing? Your attitudes about college overall? How do they
connect to your choice to be in an online writing class—if they
do at all?

Your drawing is a concrete depiction of some part of your
educational past and learning schema. Name your drawing. Is it

a wheel? A web? Some other object? (Beth sees hers as a web, for example.)

To anchor your learning, share your schema in your small discussion group and write a discussion comment about what you've learned about how your background knowledge influences your reading. Respond to other students' schemas and comments with any associations or connections you see with yourself.

If students indicate in discussion or journal posts that they have not learned anything from the exercise, provide them with challenging questions as responses to their discussion posts. For example, in response to "Knowing these things about myself doesn't do anything for my reading," ask "When did you first learn to read? What was your interest in books or stories then? Make direct connections with your childhood topics of interest and your current major in school or your favorite reading material now. Write at least five sentences in response to my questions." Notice that the last two sentences are commands, not questions. Sometimes students dismiss questions — even genuine ones — as unimportant, as Part Three of this book explains. To the degree that any teacher can require better thinking from a student, a switch from questions to more directive language can help. For sight-impaired students or for any students who do not have the technology to share their schemas developed at home, ask for a written or orally recorded schema.

6

Using Inference for Reading

More people are reading more words from more screens every day. It's not going to be long before the majority of text people read is in a digital format.

—Cory Doctorow

WHAT IS INFERENCE AND WHY IS IT IMPORTANT?

Inference is a skill that relies a lot on educated guessing. An educated guess usually is based on our schema and, hopefully, lots of good reading. We infer when we use the clues in a text to guess such things as what motivates characters' actions and the emotions of the writer. Inference is related to prediction; we can predict what we will read next and then learn from the text whether that prediction is correct. The abilities to infer and predict regarding a text are grounded in strong reading skills, but also in a conscious awareness that we *can* guess and that we automatically *do* guess about what we are reading. The goal of this chapter is to teach or remind students about inference and how to use it more consciously because it is useful far beyond anticipating what happens in a storybook.

Inference is part of the basic nature of reading. There is more than meets the eye, so to speak, in any written text. There are layers of meaning in any text. When students first learned about inference, their teachers may have called the textual hints that lead to accurate and educated guesses *context clues*. Inferential skills enable us to combine the small bits of a story or article for the purposes of making good guesses at the broader meaning of the piece. In essence, inference uses our own schema (i.e., our individual intellectual and experiential background) plus the context clues in the reading to help us make educated guesses.

Inference works best when readers can make solid guesses based on what they know and what they believe is plausible. Inference is a skill that was taught early in readers' lives. It does not matter whether the text is a fictional story about which they might determine the reasons for characters' actions or a nonfiction essay for which they must reason out the main point or guess at the author's purposes for addressing an issue in a particular way. Because students have learned about inference at least once, it can be retaught or brought to conscious mind, and inference skills can be strengthened in online writing course settings.

We seek conceptual knowledge beyond content knowledge alone. Using inference well can help students to develop a stronger situation model regarding what they are reading.

Inferential thinking is more than just predicting a story's ending. It is important because inference helps to keep readers interested in and engaged with the text. As Part One shows, getting students interested and keeping them engaged with their readings for a writing class is challenging. There are so many competing interests that students will choose over doing their reading.

Inferential reading especially challenges weak readers who read word-by-word rather than in chunks of text and in paragraphs. The more slowly one decodes, the more the meaning of the combined words loses over the challenge of understanding each word separately. Online students who might have the most difficulty with inferential reading are those with very basic (often called "developmental") reading skills, students with learning challenges like dyslexia and other reading processing disorders, and multilingual learners. Although OWI teachers cannot focus solely on inference for these students alone, addressing this literacy skill can help all readers.

HOW DOES INFERENTIAL READING HELP WITH WRITING?

As with other comprehension themes, students need to be told (or to learn through experience) how these inference-focused reading lessons help them with their writing. Although the writing tools and genres may change in online settings (e.g., web pages and blogs are common genres in online settings), moving between the online or onsite settings using inference should be fairly straightforward. Reading inferentially can help writers in several ways:

1. In online settings particularly, where whole-class and peer group discussions as well as interactions with the teacher happen through text and without the benefit of body language, participants will need to use

inferential skills to read and decode written messages. Stronger inferential skills may help readers and writers to avoid misunderstandings. Conversely, when writers learn how to read inferentially with purpose, they can be taught to apply that same level of purpose to their writing in the online environment.

2. Reading inferentially will help students when they need to work with challenging texts that will become discussion material for the class or source material for an essay. When they learn to look for context clues to help them understand a writer's primary point, they will be able to annotate more thoughtfully and then recall the major points more quickly.

3. With the ability to read inferentially, student writers can use knowledge transfer to understand an important need for evidence in their writing, which is to help their readers infer meaning. A conscious use of evidence in expository and argumentative writing is necessary for both convincing and persuasive writing.

4. Inferential reading is a skill that student readers need to bring to their peer group readings of their classmates' essays. Conscious knowledge of how to make inferences will help them to determine whether their classmates need to add such context clues to their own writing and will give students the vocabulary to talk to their peers about it.

HOW CAN WE TEACH INFERENCE IN ONLINE SETTINGS?

It can be challenging to get students to recall what they already know about inferential reading and to understand how to apply it in the increasingly challenging college-level texts they must read. One of the most important ways that we can encourage such thinking is to define inference and demonstrate that they infer from their own knowledge all the time. Adolescent and adult students would do well to make connections between what they already do and what they can do more purposefully.

Concrete examples can help students to recall what they learned long ago as a literacy skill but use daily as a functional skill. For example, I can explain through writing or an audio file that when I hear a woman walking behind me in the city, her high heels clicking on the sidewalk, I infer that she probably does not have to walk too far.

The evidence (high-heeled shoes) + My educated guess from my background (walking in heels for any distance causes painful feet) = A likely result (the wearer probably walks only a short distance in the heels)

Here is another concrete example of inferential thinking. If someone looks for evidence about pets in my home, she probably would find it to be pet friendly, even a bit overboard: there are two dog beds in each major room, toys in each room plus a filled toy basket in the pantry, two sets of filled dog dishes, and two dogs sleeping on the sofa. The evidence indicates I have two dogs, each with its own place to sleep and toys to play with. Additionally, despite having their own beds, they choose the sofa for napping and apparently are allowed to do so. The observer's schema would tell her that well-cared-for pets often are catered to. The inference would be that I treat my two dogs very well.

One of the benefits of teaching online is the plethora of examples one easily can find and link to from the Internet. Both teachers and students can look for such evidence of inferential thinking online and link to them for the class to see and discuss in relation to their writing or to writing more generally. Facebook memes and brief videos found on YouTube and other outlets make excellent media for examining inference. Search for images and videos that tell stories where viewers are encouraged to guess what will happen and may find themselves guessing wrong. For example, videos of dogs or cats or other animals playing rough may be cute and aww-inducing, but typically, a video that begins with cute will end with cute. On the other hand, a video that seeks to startle viewers or to persuade them in some way may begin with a story and end unexpectedly. Commercials intended for initial airing at Super Bowl games are among these. Viewers must use inferential thinking to see how the creators got from the beginning to the ending in any logical manner. Movies, while much longer, similarly can be literal no-brainers or intellectual puzzles that require inference to understand the story from beginning to end. For example, *Free Willy* (and *Free Willy 2, 3,* and *4*) are in the no-brainer category because their very titles indicate that the desired outcome of a free whale will occur. However entertaining, the *Karate Kid* movies similarly use a packaged plot type that easily can be guessed—there's a lonely teen in need of a parent figure, a bully or set of bullies, a teacher of karate, hard work, and a showdown in which the teen wins the fight and experiences self-respect. Some movies, on the other hand, challenge viewers to use all of their comprehension skills, with inference among them, to follow the plot and to try to figure out how they might end. Examples include *Being John Malkovitch*, *Requiem for a Dream*, *The Matrix*, *A Beautiful Mind*, *Inception*, and *Cloud Atlas*.

Finally, it is important to help students with inference by moving from audio/video examples back to reading itself. Teachers should demonstrate how course texts guide readers to educated guesses about meaning. To many students, reading page upon page of solid text unbroken by pictures and other images is daunting—even impossible—work. Thus, it is helpful to show them how the text (if well written) will guide them to good guesses through the uses of signposts like headings, subheadings, and transitions. In doing so, to get through the daunting material, students may need to learn such skills as purposeful skimming (looking for context clues in headings and boxed material) and rereading, as discussed in Part One. Using inference is a way of reading between the lines. After gaining confidence with well-written texts, students will become more adept at inferentially reading poorly developed texts — of which they will read many in their postsecondary education.

INFERENCE EXERCISE: USING TEXTUAL AIDS IN READING

College texts that inform by providing information can be challenging to read. As mentioned above, lengthy, plain text can be daunting. Some readers see such text as hard work they do not want to undertake. Others are somewhat overwhelmed by what they imagine they should learn from such text. Many students have had the unfortunate experience of only being asked to memorize content for their courses rather than to use it for thinking fodder or research material. When reading is hard, students may express that it is boring. Any of these experiences can lead students to choose not to read assigned texts. While perhaps understandable, refusal to read is not an acceptable response to college reading assignments.

We can help students by showing them how to infer what a text is about and asking them to annotate the most important issues that the text raises (see Chapter 4's OWI metacognition exercise to help students with annotation skills). Textual signals that help readers infer meaning include the following:

- Chapter titles
- Abstracts
- Key word lists
- Headings and subheadings
- Chapter outlines
- Paragraphing
- Formatting styles

In a traditional text, chapter titles reveal the text's primary focus. Abstracts provide a brief synopsis of its key points. Key word lists provide terms that can help in future library and Internet content searches, but they also can be read as vocabulary to be defined by the reader. Headings and subheadings lead the reader through the text and, if compiled in an outline form, they comprise a literal outline of the chapter or text. Sometimes, authors build knowledge redundancy by also offering a chapter outline in the beginning or ending of a text. Paragraphing, signaled by indentation, is perhaps the most powerful indicator of meaning in that most often paragraphs denote connected ideas or meaning chunks. Font variations and other formatting also signal that the author is stressing certain pieces of information over others.

These visible signals are incorporated to help readers move through challenging texts with confidence. We can remind students about these textual signs, which they have learned to use in earlier school years. However, the increased use of the Internet and thoughtfully constructed web pages provides another kind of text with different textual signs that students need to learn to read. They may need overt lessons in inferential reading for web-based texts because the sheer linearity of the text is missing from linked pages, or nodes, where readers can hop and skip through the text using unique organizational schemes that differ from the set organization of a traditional text. Here there still may be titles, abstracts, key word lists, headings and subheadings, outlines, paragraphs, and formatting signals. However, hyperlinks within the texts often take readers to new subject nodes, where the topic has changed and the reading mind must adjust quickly. The nature of inferential reading changes in this case. Additionally, paragraphs often are separated differently in that web-based paragraphs tend to be shorter with fewer sentences and literally are chunked in smaller bits for screen review. Many do not use traditional indentation but rely on line spacing to indicate paragraph change. Practically speaking, web-based paragraphs enable more white space for screen reading.

One way to teach students how these textual tools help them to infer meaning in readings — even those difficult readings where the text looks overwhelming — is to create dysfluency by removing the textual signals. This practice also is called providing "desirable difficulty," where students can learn from the challenges presented to them (Bartholomae and Petrosky 2002).

1. Provide students with a digital file of a text that is not from a textbook or reader that they are reading; for example, it can be one that will be useful in an upcoming essay assignment. Remove the title, head, and subheads so that students have only the main text. Try not to leave any sign of where these signals would go. To do so, I recommend choosing a text of no more than two to three typed, single-spaced pages. Copy and paste the text from an original digital copy (include the author so that you have provided some attribution) and then remove the textual signals. Alternatively, use voice recognition software like Dragon NaturallySpeaking and dictate the text to your word processing program without including those signals.

   [**Variation:** List the textual signals you have removed at the bottom of the text, encouraging students to place them where they believe the signals meaningfully belong.]

2. Ask students to read the article and, either in synchronous groups (if possible) or individually, to give the text a title based on its meaning and insert headings and subheadings where appropriate. Have them use marginal comments or brackets in the text at the points of insertion to explain why they made the choices they did. The written part of this exercise requires them to articulate how they inferred where and what these textual signals should be, potentially leading to deeper understanding.

3. Ask students also to write a paragraph or two about what they have learned. For example, prompt them to discuss the usefulness of this exercise for understanding how they individually (as opposed to any group work) infer meaning in a text. Self-reflective writing helps to anchor the lesson, so do not accept "I didn't learn anything" as a response. Your prompts can connect it to a problem or challenge that will be introduced in an upcoming essay assignment.

4. Discuss the exercise in small groups or as a class. Have students share their documents in a common folder or venue for public viewing.

As an additional or alternative assignment (best used after the previous one is completed), provide students with another, shorter text — maybe two typed pages maximum. This time, remove the title, heads, subheads, paragraph signals, and any special formatting. The text should be all one paragraph. Ask students to find appropriate paragraph breaks and to explain in marginal comments or brackets why and how they selected those breaks. Their responses should help them to discuss how they inferred the paragraph breaks from content (text) plus evidence (schema) to equal their educated guesses (inference) of the text's overall meaning.

7

Questioning the Reading

Digital television, satellite radio, videogames, iPods—so much media. Do books even matter anymore?

—Mo Rocca

WHAT IS QUESTIONING AND WHY IS IT IMPORTANT?

Questioning indicates curiosity about something. Encouraging questioning is one of the primary ways of helping students learn to be interested in what they are reading and in keeping their focus and alertness attuned to reading. As reading becomes more challenging, the questions become more vital. For students who have specific kinds of reading challenges like dyslexia, asking and answering questions can help them to gain confidence in their ability to find meaning in words. The goal of this chapter is to teach or remind all students about this concept and to help them gain a conscious sense of how to use questioning when reading college-level texts.

The "Into the Book" project, developed by the Wisconsin Educational Communications Board, is designed to help teachers and students work with the various literacy strategies of reading. The project sets goals for elementary student reading that certainly are helpful in college and beyond. Students need to be reminded of the early skills they learned and that using those skills is not a sign of weakness in college but of strength, confidence, and thoughtfulness. Using them purposefully is a sign of a mature, metacognitively aware adult learner. The following questioning goals were adapted from the "Into the Book" project:

- Generate questions about the text, which provides a purpose for reading and enhances understanding (asking *what?*).

- Generate questions before, during, and after reading (asking *when?*).
- Question for a variety of purposes (asking *why?*):
  - clarifying meaning,
  - speculating about text,
  - determining author's style, intent, content or format,
  - focusing attention on specific components of the text,
  - locating a specific answer, and
  - reflecting on ideas inspired by the text.
- Use the text and prior knowledge to generate questions that provide a purpose for reading and enhance interaction with the text (asking *how?*).
- Generate questions for a variety of purposes to include answers that are in the text, inferred from the text, and beyond the text (asking *where?*, *who?*, *when?*, and other pertinent questions).

These questioning goals remain useful for students in OWCs because they so often complete (or fail to complete) their reading outside the context of an onsite meeting where questions and answers include vocal inflection and facial expression. They need to learn how to ask and answer questions for themselves with confidence that having questions is a sign of reading vitality and not reading stupidity.

Sadly, education has beaten the curiosity out of a lot of students, who seem to see their coursework as something to be endured in the name of gaining a degree (see Rose 2012, for example). Rather than entering into each course with a curious nature, they enter in dread of the requirements: How much reading will there be? How much writing? How many quizzes and tests? When is everything due? Is the teacher hard or easy?

The educational system has played strongly into this mind-set with endless, and often meaningless, evaluations of student knowledge — merely at the level of recall. Teachers, too, get caught in this web, being asked to teach to a test in order to keep their students, institutions, and themselves at the top of assessment-based categories.

At the college level, we must relearn how to welcome and reinforce questions as a form of curiosity about learning. Students must relearn how to ask the questions in a safe environment where fear of looking dumb or going off topic is needless. Indeed, many times, the questions we ask are more meaningful for learning and for life than their answers. In an online setting, teaching this reality is important to help students find the willpower and confidence to engage — often feeling alone — the challenging reading they are given.

Questioning as a literacy skill means that students know they can and should ask questions of texts before, during, and after reading. Their answers to their own questions might differ from those of their teachers, but as writing teachers, we know that students need to explore material before they can engage it for writing purposes. It is particularly in questioning that we see the innately entwined nature of reading and writing.

HOW DOES ASKING QUESTIONS OF READING HELP WITH WRITING?

Students will want to know how a question-focused reading lesson helps them with their writing in either the online or onsite setting. As with the other comprehension themes in Part Two, some of the reading and writing skills are similar regardless of the learning environment. However, there are cases where the digital venue offers different challenges for students. Reading with active questioning can help writers in several ways:

1. Asking questions of materials found on the Internet is critical to stronger student writing because many students only engage Internet-based searches (ignoring brick-and-mortar libraries) for their researched writing. Particular questions to ask include: When was this material written? Who is the author (or sponsor) of the material? Where is the author (or sponsor) located? What makes the author (or sponsor) authoritative in this area? Why should I believe this material over something else? How is this material potentially useful to my thinking and writing? How could it mislead me or other readers?

2. Asking questions of a reading is a way—quite frankly—to stay fully awake and critically conscious when tackling difficult reading or meeting a challenging time schedule, as many OWI students do. Paying closer attention to the reading by writing out questions, annotating the book or file, and internally building a case for the text's value through questioning can help students use the reading thoughtfully as source material in their writing.

3. When students learn to ask questions of reading material, they can be asked to consider their own essays (and those of their peers) as reading material, too. The change of perspective enables them to ask questions of writing more objectively. In an online setting, they can use brackets [ ] or marginal comments (e.g., the Comment function in Microsoft Word) to ask these questions. Such questioning as a practice makes them better peer readers in terms of their ability to write out the questions and concerns they have of peers' drafted writing.

HOW CAN WE TEACH QUESTIONING IN ONLINE SETTINGS?

Focused lessons that include questioning skills can help students to understand that asking questions is a positive thing—even (or especially) in college. When students fear that their questions reveal ignorance, they often are reluctant to ask them of the reading or of the teacher. Indeed, online writing instructors have shared anecdotally that their students seem reluctant to send them questions through e-mail or chat about what they find confusing. This experience actually is contrary to online teachers' fears that they will receive endless e-mailed questions day and night. It is possible that the very exercise of putting the question into writing might solidify a sense that they should know the answer and are revealing a weakness to the teacher. Some online writing students either will muddle through a misunderstood assignment or not complete the assignment before risking asking a question. Teachers can help by checking in with students who seem lost through a shared journal (private to student and teacher), e-mail or phone conferences, IM chats, and teaching them through such methods that asking questions is not only acceptable but expected.

Teachers must be explicit about asking students to say that a reading or an assignment is confusing. It may help to model asking a question and getting a response through a course frequently asked questions (FAQ) wiki or a questions-only discussion forum devoted explicitly to a challenging reading. Inviting students to add questions and answers to the wiki can relieve anxieties and engage them in active questioning.

In an OWC, students need specific opportunities to see others asking questions that may be difficult to answer. For example, as indicated above, teachers can encourage endless question asking without feeling compelled to answer all the questions by asking students to post any questions they have during the term to the LMS and, if they want, to respond to each other's questions. In OWI, peer group work can help students see that they are not alone. An exercise like a question-asking contest can engage them in the process. Then, students need the time to talk about what they are wondering and the possible answers to their questions. In a traditional or hybrid classroom setting, such talk can happen in class, face-to-face. In an online setting, this talk needs to happen through synchronous video and/or text-based synchronous or asynchronous chat—with ample time for students to log in and contribute. Additionally, in online settings, if students read from the screen rather than hard copy, they should be taught annotation tools for documents and PDFs, for example.

Finally, students need opportunities to practice questioning as a particular skill. Since asking good questions can be more important than getting good answers in terms of research and learning in college-level courses, question-asking practice may include lessons that do not address reading directly; some that involve reading; and metacognitive, self-reflective writing about asking questions and its place in their lives and schema. These lessons should be short, focused, and low stakes, and they should enable class interaction whenever possible.

QUESTIONING EXERCISE: ASKING QUESTIONS

Students can have difficulty retaining their curiosity in educational settings where assessment is valued more than critical thinking. Some might argue that students have not learned to question adequately. This simple exercise is designed to remind them of the basics of asking good questions that can lead to deeper knowledge and to satisfying curiosity. Since this exercise is for writing students, it is about writing in general, but it requires effort on your part as teacher to take the learning to the next level, which is to read answers to the questions while modeling good writing. As Part Three stresses, remember that your job as teacher in an OWI class is to be as interactive as possible in helping students develop such skills. You might estimate that your writing part of this exercise will take about two to three hours.

In a discussion prompt, tell students to ask you questions about your life as a writer. Keeping the question area narrow should produce both better questions and a reasonable amount. Coach students to keep asking questions until they have covered the area well. For example, you might begin with sample questions for them:

1. When did Professor Smith first start to like writing?
2. What is the worst writing grade she ever received?
3. What kind of writing does she like the most? The least?

When they have asked all kinds of questions, in a brief (300–500 word) response, answer as many questions as you are able or willing to do, and post your response to the discussion forum. This teacher writing provides an opportunity for students to see you write informally (something they need to see often) and also to satisfy their curiosity about you. When you have finished, provide students with the following questioning thinking stems and ask them to use a few of these stem sentences to write back to you using the discussion space for the entire class's benefit. Continue the discussion with personal or general responses to students' posts until their interest wanes or as long as you believe the exercise is worthwhile.

Questioning Thinking Stems

1. I wonder _____.
2. What if _____?

3. Why _____?

4. I don't understand _____.

5. It confuses me _____.

6. How could _____?

7. At first I wondered _____, and then I thought _____. What did I learn?

8. What is _____? Why is _____ that way? How do we know _____?

Explain to students that they can use these thinking stems as sentence starters whenever they are working to absorb the content or meaning from new ideas. Provide them with other opportunities to use such stem sentences as idea starters so they can see that some of our best ideas are expressed simply. Remind students that questioning is always critical both to learning and reading. We never grow out of our need to ask good questions.

8

Finding the Relevance

Someday you will be old enough to start reading fairy tales again.

—C. S. Lewis

WHAT IS RELEVANCE AND WHY IS IT IMPORTANT?

Relevance in reading is about determining what is important in a text. Particularly when students are reading nonfiction for college courses, they need to be able to find the most important ideas and move beyond the least important ones. Not knowing how to determine relevance can lead students to highlight everything they read, which is a waste of their time and may result in giving up on the reading. The goal of this chapter is to teach or remind students about this concept and to help them gain a conscious sense of how to determine relevant passages when reading college-level texts.

Life is full of details. Many of them are extraneous. Those of us who multitask regularly know that; much of what we do is of little importance and more quickly accomplished if given total attention. Details can get in the way of clarity when we are immersed in them.

McGregor (2007), for example, recounts the story of the first time her daughter went to the circus; the child stared in amazement at the three primary rings and everything happening on the periphery of those rings. She needed her parents' help to distinguish the most important acts from the merely entertaining ones. While experienced circus-goers have learned that the most exciting acts occur in the center ring, new circus fans may not know how or where to focus their attention. Like readers, they have to learn this skill.

Web pages, the Internet, TV, news programs, commercials, and advertisements are all like the circus. In everyday life, it is difficult, yet valuable, to determine what is important to pay attention to and what is not. One of the ways to discern relevance is to look for distractors that sidetrack us from the important issues. Political speeches and advertisements are good places for finding such diversions. In *Now You See It: How the Brain Science of Attention Will Transform the Way We Live, Work, and Learn,* Davidson (2012) analyzes a television commercial for an antidepressant to illustrate how to locate distractors. She demonstrates how the distractors—such as images of children swinging or people having a birthday dinner—keep viewers from taking in the gravity of the medication's side effects (30).

In reading, as in everyday life, we must learn to distinguish what is relevant from the distraction. Distractors are the opposite of relevant factors; authors may employ distractors to change our focus. However, in most texts, authors do not employ distractors (at least not intentionally). Instead, they attempt to enhance the text's primary meaning for us through supportive details; textual signs like titles, headings, and formatting; and references to authority. As with the circus, students need to learn or relearn how to find the most important parts to remember.

College-level reading can overwhelm students, particularly the busy students who comprise most OWCs. They must dig through the distractors of their daily lives and make the time to do the reading. Sadly, as Nathan (2005) indicates and our own anecdotal experiences may support, too many students do not make their reading—maybe especially in writing classes—a priority. They may not believe the reading is sufficiently connected to the writing assignments or to their goals for completing the course. It is our job to select readings purposefully and to explain—even demonstrate visually or orally—why and how they are, indeed, critical to the course goals. Just as important, we need to remind and reteach students how to accomplish the task so the readings support knowledge that is useful to their thinking, discussion, and researched writing needs.

Without knowing how to determine what is important versus what is supportive or supplementary in a reading, it is common for students who do annotate their texts to do so poorly or to annotate everything. We need to help students separate the wheat from the chaff, or as McGregor (2007) says, to "separate the fact from the fluff" (80). The reality is that pleasure reading or self-assigned reading is different from college-assigned reading. If we want students to get something out of their school reading, we need to teach (and reteach) them how to do it. Then, they need to find their own best strategies and practice them. In short:

- If we read for everything, we get bogged down in the unimportant.
- If we read for nothing, we get little value from the reading.

How do we avoid these problems?

- We must learn to read for the heart of the matter, for the issues of critical importance.
- We must be able to distinguish helpful supportive detail from distractors.

HOW DOES READING FOR RELEVANCE HELP WITH WRITING?

Students will want to know how these relevance-focused reading lessons help them with their writing in either the online or onsite setting. Reading for relevance can help writers in several ways:

1. Reading for relevance from a computer screen can help students who are seeking supportive material for their papers. With care, the copy-and-paste feature of most word processing programs enables great accuracy of quotation. This advantage easily is countered, however, by the many ways that students may forget or choose not to cite their sources, making it a patchwork of other people's words. Screen reading for relevance should be taught with care.

2. Reading for relevance is particularly helpful when students need to work with challenging texts that will be discussion material for the class or source material for an essay. Many students will abandon a difficult text and not be able to apply it to writing. Searching for important ideas will open up the text and make it possible to understand and recall the major points for use with writing.

3. Reading for relevance also is important for helping students figure out their tasks and the level of importance (and time) each task might take when they read an assignment. As instructors, it can be helpful to share how long it takes us to do the same readings and suggest that they increase that time by 50 percent, which provides them with a more realistic time frame.

4. Learning to skim read while finding important points will help students complete not only more reading for research but also reading in other disciplinary subjects.

5. Finding relevance in texts can help students find similar points of importance in their peer group readings of their classmates' essays. Conscious knowledge of how to find relevance will help them to determine whether their classmates (and themselves) have answered the "so what" question often articulated in composition assignments.

HOW CAN WE TEACH FINDING RELEVANCE IN ONLINE SETTINGS?

To teach finding relevance, we need to identify various terms for students. They have heard these terms before in early reading instruction and in high school reading and writing instruction. In keeping with the theme of reminding students of what they already know, we should put these terms into new perspective for college reading and writing.

It is useful to acknowledge that professors in college courses typically assign more reading than is possible to read deeply and with continued focus. For example, as an undergraduate, I took a four-week winter reading course where the professor assigned one detective novel for each day of the course, weekends included. There was a close-reading quiz for each of the twenty-eight books. It was crazy, awful reading, and I read faster and with less genuine comprehension than ever in my life—but I passed the darned quizzes. A day or two later, I remembered little from each book. There were too many texts, and the reading, which should have been pleasurable, ran together. It felt too rushed and dense. I hated the course, and the experience could have put me off literature forever.

Typical college reading assignments can feel this dense and never ending. By itself, this is not a bad thing. It is simply a reality in that not everything with which students should be acquainted can be said in a lecture or learned experientially, so they must read about it. At the same time, it is important to remember that many OWI students receive all of their instructions, content, and typical reading materials textually—for reading consumption alone—without teachers' voice or oral discussions, making their reading load heavier. But it also is a reality that college-level reading cannot be consumed as a whole although students may, indeed, try. The adage about eating an elephant sandwich one bite at a time holds here. Sometimes we need to put the reading down, mull over the message, and return to it later. Other times, however, we simply need to skim the material. To this end, students need to learn how to skim and when to do so; they also need to be given the overt message that skim reading is a helpful and appropriate strategy at times.

To skim well while still determining importance means understanding what to look for. As noted in the Chapter 6 discussion of inferential skills, students can use textual signals like titles, headings, and formatting to help them determine importance. In addition, they should consciously use the following:

- Context: Knowing what the text is supposed to be about can help in skim reading to determine importance. Reading titles, abstracts, and annotated bibliographies can help.
- Main ideas: Knowing where to look for main ideas in a text helps one to read more purposefully and quickly. Such places typically are in the:

- Abstract
- First and/or last sentence of the introduction section or paragraph
- First and/or last sentence of the conclusion section or paragraph
- Transitional sentences between sections or paragraphs
- Redundant content or repetitive phrases
- Objectives/goals: These often are like the main ideas but not always. The objectives of the piece often are represented by first-person I-statements from the author(s) or third-person statements with the words *goal, purpose,* or *aim* in the sentence.
  - I propose to demonstrate _____.
  - I believe that _____.
  - We argue here that _____.
  - The goal of this research is to _____.
- Signposts: These are the kinds of objective-signaling statements used as examples above, but they also include:
  - Section headings
  - Call-outs or boxed material that repeats or summarizes points
  - Arrows or other symbols
  - Highlighted material or materials shown with varying fonts and colors
- On the Web, these kinds of signposts may be clickable links and tabs across the top or down the side of the page.

When seeking relevance, college students also need to know that sometimes a particular text is not relevant to what they are seeking, as with a research project. Research (literally, search again) means culling through a number of texts, discarding some, and reading more deeply into others. Student writers, however, may believe that there must be something of relevance in each selected text and then try to make the text fit into the paper being developed. Students should be informed that it is okay to abandon a book or text that is not revealing a clear connection to what they are researching. It also is okay, once the main idea and helpful supportive details have been found, to quit reading. In other words, one does not need to read every word of every selected text or use every selected text for the writing.

Along these lines, reading for relevance in an online setting—in other words, reading from the screen—can be challenging. For example, as discussed in the Introduction, many people multitask at the computer, which divides their attention. Distractors seem to be everywhere, and the ability to open multiple windows makes the situation worse. Helping students to realize they need to maintain focus when searching for relevant material online is crucial. Tips for students include closing unnecessary windows and IM chats, setting a timer for when e-mail might be checked, and putting one's phone in silent mode.

In an online setting, teaching these skills may rely on audio/video lectures because they are not as easily explained in writing alone. Video actually should demonstrate skimming a text that everyone has access to. Although it will not be possible to demonstrate how the eyes focus when the brain reads, it may be helpful to give students a short lesson on saccades, fixations, and regressions, as described in Chapter 2. Knowing that neurological science can track eye movement with reading can help students to understand better what happens when their eyes move across the page and to discover whether they are fast or slow readers and full-text or skim readers. To that end, a lesson might define these terms, say a little about the science, and then directly connect eye movement with the process of skimming.

Video also can be used to show teachers' highlighted examples of what they learned when skimming the article. This type of modeling, a teaching strategy recommended in Part Three, requires that teachers actually do the same work they ask of students and to be able to demonstrate and explain it for students. We should tell them the rationale for our responses. When talking to students about what we find to be main ideas, for example, we should ask them to do the same work. Providing the rationale for their answers helps them to anchor what they are saying in the real activity and helps them to be purposefully metacognitive. What is important for elementary school readers is even more important for college-level readers: "Kids should know that all words, sentences, or paragraphs are not created equal. Some carry more weight than others" (McGregor 2007, 77).

Of course, attention to access means that audio/video always should be accompanied by a written transcript for students with audio processing disorders, those who are visually challenged, and those who learn better through text.

Additionally, students need opportunities to practice reading where they can share what they have learned about finding relevance and skimming and then figure out how they need to repeat those actions or do them differently in the future.

RELEVANCE EXERCISE: SKIM READING FOR RELEVANCE

Choose a lengthy text that you plan to have students read for the course. To help them be prepared for more reading in your class and others, preferably make it a nonfiction piece. *Make certain that all students have a copy of the text, and ask them to read it before viewing or beginning the following lesson.* Although a synchronous meeting may be helpful for encouraging students' questions, this exercise can be taught asynchronously by providing a question area in the discussion forum or another page in the LMS, such as a wiki, where all students can write and see what has been written by others.

If you do this exercise synchronously by voice, be prepared to provide a brief transcript for visually impaired and audio-processing-challenged students. If you use IM chat, plan to transfer the chat to a word processed document and clean it up (i.e., simply delete times of posting and extraneous material, as well as providing minimal sentence markers like capitalization and periods) for screen reader access.

Example essays include:

- "Is Google Making Us Stupid?" by Nicholas Carr
- "The Ends of the World as We Know Them" by Jared Diamond
- "The English-Only Movement: Can America Proscribe Language with a Clear Conscience?" by Jake Jamieson

Articles such as these have specific points to make, but the points are not always made in a direct manner. So, while students can, indeed, find main ideas and use signposts to help guide their reading, these texts reflect how challenging nonfiction reading can be. Such types of articles provide good opportunities for modeling reading for relevance and for the skill of skim reading given that they reflect the kind of nonfiction reading students receive as research for writing and as content for other courses.

If you have learned enough about it, teach students a little about how the brain works in terms of forming neural pathways when reading. Use relevant material from Chapter 2 to discuss how the eye uses saccades, fixations, and regressions when reading. Provide students with this explanation or one like it, and contextualize new vocabulary:

1. Saccades are the flicks of our eyes as they move over the text.

2. Fixations are our eyes' moments of focused attention on the text.

3. Regressions are when our eyes return to text previously scanned.

Ask students questions that help them to understand the nature of saccades, fixations, and regressions in relation to their own reading experiences:

Do you remember when you were learning to read and your eyes fixated, or rested, on words or phrases as you tried to sound them out? As you became a more experienced reader, your eyes probably began to flick over (saccades) certain common words or phrases and then they settled (fixated) on the newer, less familiar material. When you were aware that you had missed something important, your eyes moved back (regressed) to previous text. Doing so filled in the cognitive (mental) gap and connected what you missed or misunderstood to what you were reading.

Interestingly, fixations reveal where we spend most of our reading time. Typically, we fixate on content words (nouns) and skip (use saccade) function words like articles (i.e., *a, an, the*) and prepositions (e.g., *for, and, nor, but, or, yet, so*). Fixations help us to determine the most important information in the text. When we predict (infer) that a text will reveal something particular and there is a mismatch between what we thought we would find and what we actually found, we usually reread the text, perhaps fixating on other passages, to learn where the prediction failed.

Engage students' interest on a metacognitive level that involves their schema about their own reading experiences. For example, ask them to figure out when their own eyes flick, fixate, or regress on the selected reading material. We may not always notice when our eyes are making these movements — they are so fast and natural to the reading process. With encouragement, students may determine some fixations and regressions, considering the rest to be saccades. Then, ask students why they think (engaging metacognition) they used particular strategies with various parts of the reading. Ask them to be specific when discussing where and when they realized they used particular eye movements. Finally, ask them whether they think their eye motions have been similar in past readings (engaging schema).

Explain that finding what is relevant in a text has to do with knowing that not all information — and not all paragraphs or sentences that contain information — have equal importance. That is why sometimes it is okay to skim reading material (use saccades). If we are looking for a particular concept, for example, we can skim over material that does not deal with that concept and focus (fixate) on relevant material. If we do not understand the material in light of reading further, we may need to return (regress) to earlier passages.

Students may be concerned that they are somehow reading wrongly or deficiently. They will benefit from learning that saccades, fixations, and regressions are perfectly natural and that each reader uses these eye movements naturally and, possibly, uniquely.

Follow up this lesson with an online discussion prompt like the following:

We have discussed our reading of this text in terms of skim reading. We have shared information about our eye movement in reading: where we flick or move our eyes quickly, where we pause, and where we return to reread. Then, we connected our eye movements to finding the main ideas of the text and the most important supporting details. In effect, we have learned one way to understand skim reading.

1. Reread XYZ article. You may skim read or read more slowly — whatever works best for you as a reader.

2. Find the main idea(s) and the important supporting details.

3. Write a one-page single-spaced journal entry (about 200 words).

First describe the main idea(s) and supporting detail of what you read. Support your response with details from the article. Second, use some of the following thinking stems to consider this part of your response:

Relevance Thinking Stems

- What's important here is _____.
- What matters to me is _____.
- One thing we should notice is _____.
- I want to remember _____.
- It's interesting that _____.
- When I read _____, it didn't seem too important, but _____ changed my mind/made me think _____.
- The relevance of _____ is that _____.

Describe what you noticed about your own habits regarding saccades, fixations, and regressions as you read. How does this experience help you to understand how to find relevance through skimming college-level reading?

Post the journal entry in the appropriate journal assignment in the LMS.

Variation 1: Scan or photograph how you have annotated the article, and then write about it or provide an audio file in which you describe your reading process using the questions provided above. Alternatively, make a video of about five minutes to provide the detail requested in this exercise. If you use the audio/visual media of a video, show how you have annotated your article to reflect the main idea and important supporting details. For example, you can hold the document to the video camera and point to places where you have found your eyes tend to fixate or regress. Explain why you think you read as you do. The video does not need to be perfect, but it should be as well conceived as a one-page journal paper for my reading would be. Post the video in the appropriate journal assignment in the LMS.

Variation 2: Reread the exercise written above. *Do not do the exercise.* For this task, focus instead on the instructions (not the content) for the exercise. The goal is to read for relevance in assignment instructions.

- If you were going to complete the exercise, what would you do first? Second? Last?
- Which ones are the most important parts of the task? How do you know?
- How do these instructions help you to know what to do?
- How could they be written or presented differently (or better) to help you know what to do?

Write your responses in one or two paragraphs using complete sentences. Post your response as a journal entry.

9

Visualizing a Text

TV. If kids are entertained by two letters, imagine the fun they'll have with twenty-six. Open your child's imagination. Open a book.

—Author Unknown

WHAT IS VISUALIZING AND WHY IS IT IMPORTANT?

Visualizing a text is a literacy skill that brings the reading to life through the mental and sensory images that we imagine as we read. It helps us to create a situation model, as discussed in Chapter 2, and find meaning in layers of text beyond mere content recall. Students learned this skill early in elementary school as they listened to their teachers reading and then described what they heard in discussion. Sometimes they were asked to draw or paint their perceptions of the texts they had just heard. The goal of this chapter is to teach or remind students about this concept and to help them gain a conscious sense of how visualizing helps them to understand and retain the material in college-level texts.

Visualizing what we read helps with recall. When we apply our senses—imagining the feel, sight, sound, taste, and speech involved in a text or passage—our ability to remember it is enhanced. Visualization actively involves our schema because our background knowledge is directly related to the mental pictures we conjure in relation to what we read. Visualization also uses metacognitive thought by virtue of thinking about what we have read to enliven and personalize the connections between readers and text.

College-level reading topics often seem dry. At times, the texts that students are given to read are poorly written, making a challenging subject also a difficult read. Sometimes, the subjects are not of great interest to students who have not yet learned that boredom likely is a sign of their lack of engagement rather than a problem inherent to a subject or discipline. Students badly need to be reminded that their engagement with a text is their responsibility and that it is a reasonable part of college-level learning. Visualizing is a pleasant, yet mentally stimulating, activity that students can use to engage with what they are reading and to learn something from it.

HOW DOES READING TO VISUALIZE HELP WITH WRITING?

Students will want to know how these visualization-focused reading lessons help them with their writing. In both the online and onsite settings, texts often evoke images for readers to help them engage with the topic. Both college-level textbooks and general web pages often have pictures. Scholarly academic papers, however, may not provide such visual stimulation. In this case, readers often have to provide their own mental images to increase their interest in sometimes dry material and to help the reading stick. Reading for visualization can help writers in several ways:

1. Visualization helps to anchor a challenging nonfiction reading in the same way it can implant fiction in one's mind. This literacy skill can help students manage readings for their researched essays if they use visualization to help them draft. For example, for a writing assignment, they can visualize how they would organize various research materials in support of a series of reasons and details—numbering them or using another organizational scheme.

2. In Part Two's lessons, students have learned about metacognition, schema, and asking questions among other literacy skills. The act of visualizing also can be used purposefully to help students write expository and argumentative essays. The success of such essays depends on more than having a strong thesis. It also depends on writing about or with details, which is a practice that may be hard for many students. Often, they think in detail but do not share those details in writing, possibly because they presume subconsciously that the reader already can see what is in their minds. Writers of all levels are guilty of this thinking. These lessons in visualization can help them to develop descriptive details in their writing.

3. Visualizing what is described in texts can help students in their peer group readings of their classmates' essays. Asking students to look for the details that bring the essay to life can help them become more aware of the imagery that even nonfiction relies on to explain, seek conviction, or persuade.

HOW CAN WE TEACH VISUALIZING A TEXT IN ONLINE SETTINGS?

Students will be most familiar with visualizing a text's meaning from fiction. Narratives lend themselves to engaging the imagination and leading to individualized perspectives of what an action or activity might look or smell like. Students began reading, of course, with fiction and a plethora of pictures. Nonfiction, which is what students primarily will read in college, is not so easy to imagine. To this end, we can teach students how nonfiction can be equally evocative of our schemas and imaginations.

Using unfamiliar short essays, song lyrics, and quotations, students can be shown the connection between themselves and the texts and that such connections are similar to the ones they more automatically make with fiction. In some ways, the great variety of images and videos available on the Internet may interfere with students' uses of their own visualization abilities. For example, when we do not know much about a topic or what a particular object looks like, a quick Internet search is a common way to find multiple photos or true-to-life drawings; I used to have to go to another book—the encyclopedia—for that kind of information. Many popular songs are performed to highly choreographed videos, connecting—locking in—particular images with that song that did not belong previously in the listener's personal schema. Our imaginations are, in some ways, underused by virtue of digital technology and artists' desires to show us their own visions.

In the online educational setting, this chapter's exercise can be done through text alone, which may inspire imaginative visualizations if teachers make that a goal of the exercise. The added feature of a teacher's voice or video presence also can remind students of their earliest experiences learning visualization in a reading circle. Reminding them overtly that they have learned (and, therefore, now own) this skill can help them to see the value of visualization in their current reading.

VISUALIZATION EXERCISE: USING A CLOZE PROCEDURE TO EVOKE IMAGES

Cloze exercises most often are used as a way to assess reading skills at various levels. Students may remember them from earlier years. However, a cloze format can be used as a way to help students practice visualization. It is up to the teacher to help students make this connection rather than expecting that simply doing the exercise will make the point.

It is not necessary for you as teacher to read all of the students' cloze exercises or to grade them in any way. You can simply check to see whether they are completed if you want that information for class participation purposes. You can choose to ask students to formally post the exercise to you or the class (or not to post it at all) before looking at the linked key. Ask them to assess their own success, and have them write briefly to you about what they did well and what they missed. Ask them to speculate why they had problems and to explain what they think they can do about it with future challenging readings. (Hint: if you use the word *speculate*, define it in the text in parentheses or surrounded by commas, as I have modeled throughout these exercises. It is especially important that students have clear and comprehensible guidance in instructional texts.)

If students find this exercise more difficult than expected, their challenges may indicate that they need more work on reading strategies than they may have guessed.

A prompt for a cloze exercise might look like the following:

Let's look at how and why visualization is an important reading skill for college-level nonfiction reading. There will be many times in difficult readings that you will not know the exact meaning of words, but you will find that you understand the gist of the words or the passage overall. Similarly, even though you never may have seen a picture or movie of something, you can envision it anyway — from the descriptive adjectives and nouns and from the motion implied by adverbs and verbs. Moreover, you often have memories deep in your schema that help with visualization.

Read the following text about Tai Chi. Right away, you will notice the gaps where words have been removed. Nope. You are not back in elementary school! This kind of exercise, called a "cloze procedure," is designed to help you think about the description of Tai Chi and how it is built through words — to visualize the movements and challenges of Tai Chi as you find the missing words, which are provided below the text in no particular order.

To complete the exercise, you will have to use your schema and inferential skills to think between the lines. But you also will need to visualize what is being described to find the correct words to fill in the blanks.

After you have completed this part of the exercise, read beneath the passage for additional instructions.

I started to train in Tai Chi ten years ago because I liked the way people could move slowly, gracefully, and _____ through the forms. The _____ beauty of the forms was a fairly

superficial reason for joining a class that teaches _____,
but it was enough to get me interested. I only really learned
about its _____ benefits when I began _____ in Tai Chi
and Qi Gong with an experienced, highly skilled martial arts
master. During my years here, I have grown stronger and more
_____. My chronic pain condition is still _____ and painful,
but I do not feel like I'm at its _____. I have new choices in
how I can deal with both pain and difficult times. However,
even though there are many health benefits to practicing Tai
Chi and Qi Gong, I don't do this martial arts _____ only to
be healthy. I do it because Tai Chi and Qi Gong support my
spiritual practices of striving for a _____ life where loving
others is of _____ importance.

Both the martial arts and my _____ practices ask me to be
more _____. I think this means that I should be fully aware
of where I am, who I am with, and what I am doing so that
I am actually giving my _____ attention and not just going
through the motions. It's so easy to just go through the paces
and do too many things because our society _____ us that
the more we can do — and the more tasks we complete — the
more _____ we are. But that's a false idea of success.
Instead, I'm learning to give my attention fully to whatever
I'm doing — one thing at a time — which means that I'm
living more in the _____ moment and not in the future or the
past. Mindfulness assists with living a balanced life because
it helps me to be neither too high nor too low _____, neither
too busy nor too lazy _____, and neither too closed nor too
bare spiritually.

Tai Chi, Qi Gong, and my spirituality all stress the need to
open one's heart to people around us. They teach that _____
ourselves and others is a way to connect with a greater love.
To enable this love, both Tai Chi and Qi Gong are teaching me
how to develop my energy and to use it for my own benefit.
That might seem like a _____ goal, but actually, increasing
our own energy is critical to being able to love others. If
you're not familiar with the concept, think of _____ as the
vigor and life-supporting force that surrounds us. Some
people call it the aura surrounding our bodies and _____
us to all living things. Some people can actually see energy

as colors; often we can feel energy as a warm force like two magnets _____ each other. We can develop energy with deep _____ exercises practiced with physical _____. In those exercises, our minds should be focused on that _____ and nothing else. Building my energy has not been at all easy for me. When I first started to train, my energy level had _____ out, as anyone who is aware of energy could have seen and felt. Now, I have much more energy — enough to feel the _____ of my body — but I have a lot of room for growth. Ultimately, by building my energy more fully, I can help others without _____ my own strength and health. To me, that means I can live a fuller life.

The first degree _____ belt means that I have learned to surrender some of my own _____ and hardness, learning more compassion and kindness to myself and others. It means that I am no longer just a beginner and that I have enough experience to not only "practice" Tai Chi and Qi Gong but to actually "_____" them.

selfish	flow	repelling
flexible	paramount	poses
warmth	teaches	health
spiritual	practice	energy
meditatively	depleting	loving
bottomed	mercy	do
breathing	emotionally	balanced
present	sheer	connecting
physically	chronic	stubbornness
training	fullest	successful
black	mindful	experience

Now that you have completed the exercise, check your answers with the original text. How did you do? Were there words that you could not place?

One object of a cloze exercise is to help you see how you know which words likely fit a context even when you don't know their meaning — in other words, sometimes when you cannot give a dictionary definition, you still can use the words correctly. You gave yourself hints by recognizing adjectives and adverbs, for example, and put those words next to nouns and verbs.

Similarly, you found nouns and verbs to put into the passage by virtue of the other words around the blanks.

Variation: Quiz yourself. Without looking at the passage, write everything you remember about it, calling on all of your senses in this memory. Use complete sentences in your writing. You may draft this writing by using pencil/pen and paper or through typing or speech recognition software.

When you are finished, compare what you remembered with the original text. What is similar? Different? Why do you think you remembered as much or as little as you did? Write about this exercise in the appropriate class discussion [or journal] assignment.

> I started to train in Tai Chi ten years ago because I liked the way people could move slowly, gracefully, and meditatively through the forms. The sheer beauty of the forms was a fairly superficial reason for joining a class that teaches flow, but it was enough to get me interested. I only really learned about its health benefits when I began training in Tai Chi and Qi Gong with an experienced, highly skilled martial arts master. During my years here, I have grown stronger and more flexible. My chronic pain condition is still chronic and painful, but I don't feel like I'm at its mercy. I have new choices in how I can deal with both pain and difficult times. However, even though there are many health benefits to practicing Tai Chi and Qi Gong, I don't do this martial arts practice only to be healthy. I do it because Tai Chi and Qi Gong support my spiritual practices of striving for a balanced life where loving others is of paramount importance.
>
> Both the martial arts and my spiritual practices ask me to be more mindful. I think this means that I should be fully aware of where I am, who I am with, and what I am doing so that I am actually giving my fullest attention and not just going through the motions. It's so easy to just go through the paces and do too many things because our society teaches us that the more we can do — and the more tasks we complete — the more successful we are. But that's a false idea of success. Instead, I'm learning to give my attention fully to whatever I'm doing — one thing at a time — which means

Ask students to either draw a picture of their vision of Tai Chi or Qi Gong or find one via Creative Commons or another royalty-free stock photo source that can be copied and pasted legally — with permissions and appropriate attributions. Explain that they do not have to be artists here; if they can't draw at all, have students further describe this martial arts practice in their own words without looking to the Internet for additional descriptions. In a brief discussion post for the whole class, they should upload (and attribute) their selected image and explain how this exercise did (or did not) help to visualize Tai Chi and Qi Gong.

that I'm living more in the present moment and not in the future or the past. Mindfulness assists with living a balanced life because it helps me to be neither too high nor too low emotionally, neither too busy nor too lazy physically, and neither too closed nor too bare spiritually.

Tai Chi, Qi Gong, and my spirituality all stress the need to open one's heart to people around us. They teach that loving ourselves and others is a way to connect with a greater love. To enable this love, both Tai Chi and Qi Gong are teaching me how to develop my energy and to use it for my own benefit. That might seem like a selfish goal, but actually, increasing our own energy is critical to being able to love others. If you're not familiar with the concept, think of energy as the vigor and life-supporting force that surrounds us. Some people call it the aura surrounding our bodies and connecting us to all living things. Some people can actually see energy as colors; often we can feel energy as a warm force like two magnets repelling each other. We can develop energy with deep breathing exercises practiced with physical poses. In those exercises, our minds should be focused on that experience and nothing else. Building my energy has not been at all easy for me. When I first started to train, my energy level had bottomed out, as anyone who is aware of energy could have seen and felt. Now, I have much more energy — enough to feel the warmth of my body — but I have a lot of room for growth. Ultimately, by building my energy more fully, I can help others without depleting my own strength and health. To me, that means I can live a fuller life.

The first degree black belt means that I have learned to surrender some of my own stubbornness and hardness, learning more compassion and kindness to myself and others. It means that I am no longer just a beginner and that I have enough experience to not only "practice" Tai Chi and Qi Gong but to actually "do" them.

10

Analyzing a Text

You must understand the whole of life, not just one little part of it. That is why you must read, that is why you must look at the skies, that is why you must sing, and dance, and write poems, and suffer, and understand, for all that is life.

—Jiddu Krishnamurti

WHAT IS ANALYSIS AND WHY IS IT IMPORTANT?

Analysis provides ways to read and take apart a text in order to develop a situation model or conceptual knowledge base. The ability to analyze what one reads is crucial to finding the author's meaning. It involves breaking down a text or several texts to glean and comprehend that meaning, as well as to relate that meaning to other texts. The goal of this chapter is to teach or remind students about this concept and to help them gain conscious use of analytical skills in order to develop their reading beyond the basics of simply gaining and retaining knowledge.

Analysis often begins with using one's schema although moving beyond schema is important to earning opinions. An earned opinion is supportable by what one has read in addition to one's life experiences. It brings together a number of resources, and it forms the basis for an educated statement about a problem or issue.

Teachers may complain that students bring narrow background knowledge to their writing courses. The opinions that younger college students in particular bring to their readings often are unsupported and many are learned from listening to others rather than through reasoned thinking. As Chapters 1 and 2 explore, such reasons for this problem also may stem from the lack of depth involved in most information searches using the Internet.

Shallow reading often leaves students with little to write about, unsupported opinions, and inability to relate one text to another or to a problem.

At the college level, teachers may frame textual analysis through reading as a way of understanding how to write a text. One certainly can analyze what one reads as a means of building a framework for writing something similar. Indeed, the ancient rhetorical topoi, or common places, enable ways to find one's ideas, develop them with detail, and even organize them for others to read. These topoi include such strategies as description, illustration, definition, cause and effect, comparison and contrast, division and classification, process analysis, and the like. For example, in any particular essay that students write, they can engage extended definition, description, and cause and effect. The writer can set up a problem and examine it through the primary lens of causes and effects; then, she can use definition and description as ways to develop the material. In this case, the cause-and-effect analysis is the primary organizational strategy with the other topoi providing a structure for idea development. These topoi can support exposition and argument in various genres and about a multitude of topics.

When the topoi are viewed as invention, content development, and organizational strategies, they become useful lenses for analyzing how and why authors come to the points they are making and, for readers, they help with comprehending an author's meaning. Other common analytical lenses include looking at a problem and its stated solution(s); finding and examining the support provided for claims; and examining the audience, purpose, and occasion for the text. While this chapter is not about how to write using analytical skills or lenses, any discussion of reading analytically is connected inherently to the written text and the choices its author made.

Analysis is a more advanced reading skill, and it rightly should take its place alongside writing analytically in a college-level writing course. In other words, teaching analytical reading (and writing) is the work of more than one course, and it certainly is the work of more than one or two reading assignments. Given the importance of analysis, the ideas provided in this chapter may seem minimal, but for the overall purposes of this book — to provide a wide range of literacy strategies for OWI — it can be considered only one part of many.

HOW DOES ANALYTICAL READING HELP WITH WRITING?

Students will want to know how these analysis-focused reading lessons help them with their writing in either the online or onsite setting. Of course, analysis is necessary for reading and writing in any environment, with any tools, and for almost any purpose. When reading texts from the Internet particularly, it is important to pay attention to quality; strong analytical reading skills enable students to reject texts that are poorly researched or that will not aid their writing. Reading to analyze can help writers in several ways:

1. Analyzing what one reads is a popular strategy for teaching analytical writing. Such analysis is a helpful way to teach students why writers make particular choices and how to build a similar framework for their own writing. Annotating texts, once again, is a useful tool for marking up the text under analysis.

2. Teaching various methods for analysis — the topoi, in this case — links directly to teaching content development and organization for writing. Even when the writing course is not built rhetorically around the topoi, emphasizing the similarity between reading and writing analytically may help to create the cognitive connection some students need to understand the core connections between reading and writing, thus providing or supporting a lifelong skill.

3. Analyzing how texts are developed can help students in peer group readings of their classmates' essays. To do a good job, they will need to practice the skill of rereading because they cannot do such an analysis on a one-shot read through (although some will try). Asking students to analyze a peer's essay for how the content is developed or how the material is organized can help students become more aware of how people build effective nonfiction that explains, seeks conviction, or persuades.

HOW CAN WE TEACH ANALYZING A TEXT IN ONLINE SETTINGS?

All of the comprehension themes to this point have provided ways to help students learn to analyze and think critically about their reading; these skills were learned in elementary school and many students benefit from reminders about using them consciously in college-level reading. In this section, we look at some of the more sophisticated analytical skills — some of which students may not know well at all. Ideally, every college class would provide students some opportunities to use these analytical skills consciously once they have been identified. It is up to individual teachers to decide how many of these analytical skills they can teach their students during any one online writing course given their other goals and mandated course outcomes.

The first thing that students need to know is what the reading skills are. You do not need to have taught the previous chapters in total or in a scaffolded way — although doing so certainly is possible. Students still will benefit from being reminded even briefly that they learned about metacognition, schema, inference, questioning, finding relevance, and visualizing text a long time ago. A brief definition of each skill and a statement of how each enhances critical reading can help. Each of these skills deepens reading, but each also can be used in analyzing a text or one's response to the text.

Analytical reading skills that students may have learned in later school years include:

- Description
- Illustration
- Definition
- Cause and effect
- Comparison and contrast
- Division and classification
- Process analysis (asking how to do something and/or why something is what it is)
- Looking at a problem and its stated solution(s)
- Finding and examining the support provided for claims
- Examining and explaining the audience, purpose, and occasion

Choose the analytical skills you want to teach, and think about how you might want to approach them in an online setting. Because these skills are sophisticated, they likely need additional explanation, which can be accomplished helpfully through an audio/video medium or through asynchronous text using illustrative examples. Remember that students do not always view entire lessons provided to them on screen, so it will help to tie analysis reading exercises to their writing. In other words, some of these literacy lessons may be more easily constructed as higher-stakes lessons than those in Chapters 4 through 9 because they likely can be connected to particular writing exercises for the course.

ANALYSIS EXERCISE: ANALYZING WITH ORGANIZATIONAL MAPS

An organizational map can help students to understand graphically how we take apart (analyze) and put together (synthesize) readings to come to new understanding. At a minimum, students can develop an outline for the texts although such maps as the following are relatively easy to draw using a word processing program's illustration software. Particularly talented artists might want to use their drawing skills. Students with access difficulties may need to describe their maps through text or orally through audio files.

I use nursery rhymes to develop the following organizational maps. Despite the simplistic nature of the texts, these maps offer a quickly comprehensible way to talk about how the author has organized the material,

FIGURE 10.1 Description

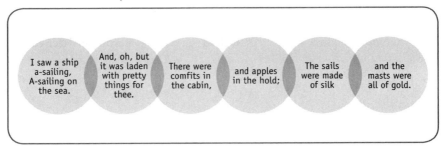

FIGURE 10.2 Cause and Effect

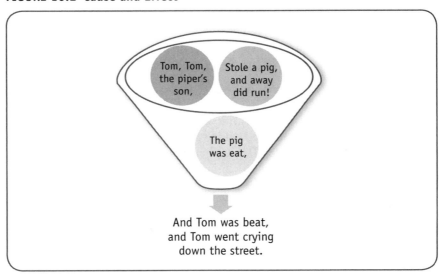

making it easier to understand why this organization works (or does not) for the text.

Provide students with these examples or other, more sophisticated organizational maps for short texts. For the exercise, it is best to provide one or two short texts for students to work with; they can be mildly, but not extremely, challenging. You might provide one fiction and one nonfiction text; the fiction text will be easier to map in some ways. Ask students to work individually to develop an organizational map for each text. They will need to:

- read the text;
- determine the organizational strategy the author has used;

FIGURE 10.3 Chronological Process

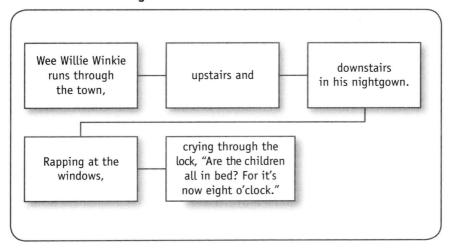

FIGURE 10.4 Cycle Process

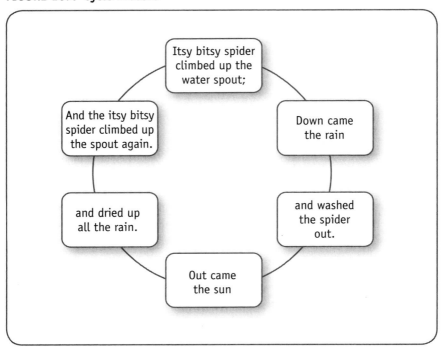

FIGURE 10.5 Classification

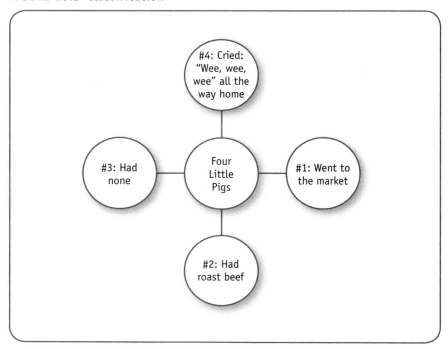

- develop the map (in Microsoft Word and PowerPoint, these maps are available through the Insert tab: Insert → SmartArt → choose a mapping style); and
- in three to four written paragraphs, explain how the organizational strategy works in that text to (1) make a claim/state a thesis and (2) support that claim/thesis.

Ask students to share their maps and explanations in their smaller peer groups to compare their visualization and thinking with their classmates. Give them specific prompts for what you would like them to discuss relative to analytical reading and writing.

[**Variation:** Have students create an organizational map for an essay they wrote for this class earlier in the term. Ask them to post the map and a brief explanation (as indicated by the bullet directions above) in their journal for your review or in their small groups for peer consideration.]

11

Synthesizing

There are different rules for reading, for thinking, and for talking. Writing blends all three of them.

—Mason Cooley

WHAT IS SYNTHESIS AND WHY IS IT IMPORTANT?

Synthesis, like analysis, is a more sophisticated and complex literacy skill that applies both to reading and writing. And, as with analysis, synthesis cannot easily be discussed in a writing class outside the context of both reading and writing. Where analysis breaks down or takes apart ideas and arguments, synthesis combines ideas from various sources to build or form new information and ways of thinking.

The ability to synthesize is an important reading skill, taught from elementary school on, but college students in particular need to learn to use synthesis at a more sophisticated and conscious level in order to develop and use critical thinking, reading, and writing skills. It is at the postsecondary level that we begin to expect truly original thinking from students, but without an awareness of how to synthesize consciously, students may fail to engage this skill. Indeed, without the ability to synthesize, students are left to repeat others' thoughts and cannot claim to be thinking on their own. Synthesis requires that they draw together information from various sources so they can learn, unlearn, and relearn what they think and know about a subject.

Synthesis engages the stronger reading developed by using all of the comprehension themes described in this book. When students use their metacognition and schema reflectively along with their abilities to draw inferences, ask questions, determine relevance, visualize, and analyze, they are ready for the conscious work of synthesizing from their reading. At this point, if they have had an opportunity to work with these reading skills in a scaffolded manner, students should feel empowered to take more responsibility for their reading and how they comprehend it, enabling them to use it for their overall learning and for their writing in particular.

If students cannot synthesize what they read, they certainly cannot use synthesis skills when they write. In both onsite and online writing course settings, students are expected to be able to research and use sources to support claims about issues and ideas. Synthesis of one's reading leads to claims that reflect the student's own thinking and researched writing about those claims that moves beyond patchwriting, or merely plugging in a few words or a sentence from source materials.

HOW DOES READING FOR SYNTHESIS HELP WITH WRITING?

Students will want to know how these synthesis-focused reading lessons help them with their writing in either the online or onsite setting. Reading to synthesize can help writers in several ways:

1. Teaching synthetic reading is a natural fit for any writing instruction that involves critical thinking, higher skill levels, and increased sophistication. Exposition and argumentation are particularly connected to synthesis because they require outside reading as research to develop informed opinions and to support them. When students read to find relevant material for their writing, they then need to learn how to use that material appropriately in their essays. Teaching synthesis with stem sentences, for example, can help students learn how to avoid plagiarism and to use citation correctly.

2. Students often confuse synthesis and summary. Summary is a master writing skill, as discussed in Chapter 1. It can be taught in opposition to synthesis of sources or separately, but using the notion of pulling together various sources to form one's opinion versus explaining what one has read can help students with both writing skills (see Appendix B for example assignments). Similarly, reading to summarize can be contrasted with reading to paraphrase—critical writing skills that students also confuse.

3. Learning to read for synthesis can help students in peer group readings of their classmates' essays. Asking students to look for where their peers have pulled together the thinking of other people to create what seems to be an original perspective can enable them to help their peers better. Learning about synthetic reading also will give them vocabulary for talking with their peers—typically done through written text in

OWI—about what they are reading. Finally, this kind of peer work should help them to become more consciously aware of the need for synthesis in their own essays.

HOW CAN WE TEACH SYNTHESIS IN ONLINE SETTINGS?

In online settings, teaching synthesis is much like teaching other reading comprehension themes. We should take advantage of both asynchronous and synchronous modalities and a variety of media both to teach and to encourage students to work on their synthetic reading.

To synthesize, students should understand the value of rereading; be able to generate meaningful notes, summarize, and paraphrase; and consciously ask questions of a text that they then answer from it (Maclellan 1997, 281).

Completing exercises on synthesis should help students to do the following:

- Read multiple texts on a single subject
- Monitor the reading by consciously holding in the mind what one is reading about that topic
- Write down ideas as they come to mind to make them more concrete—in other words, taking note of one's own thoughts about the readings (metacognition)
- Make connections among the readings and connections with one's prior, current, and possible future thinking
- Draw conclusions
- Share ideas
- Critique ideas based on one's readings

SYNTHESIS EXERCISE: SYNTHESIS AND SUMMARY—DIFFERENT SKILLS

Students have a tendency to mix up the skills of synthesizing and summarizing. We can see this confusion in writing where we ask students to use research to support their claims. Not only do many students provide (generally poor) summaries of what an author has said, but they also may fail to use sources to support new ideas. Looking at this problem from the perspective of reading rather than writing, it seems helpful to encourage students to understand the nature of summary and synthesis as different ways of addressing what they read.

This exercise is intended to convey the differences between summary and synthesis and to provide practice in both skills. While synthesis typically involves reading more than one text, for the purposes of this exercise, I recommend working with just one text. The following example text, "American Idol Worship" by Thomas de Zengotita, provides a way to demonstrate the difference between reading to summarize a text and reading to synthesize and find new ideas. The core exercise directly follows the text.

American Idol Worship

When the ratings numbers came in after last week's Grammy Awards, the news wasn't good for the professionals. A show that features amateurs had attracted a far bigger audience than had the one with the likes of Madonna, Coldplay, and U2. . . . *American Idol* drew almost twice as many viewers as the awards show. What's going on here? Why does this reality show consistently attract the weekly attention of close to 35 million viewers?

It's a nexus of factors shaping the "virtual revolution" unfolding all around us, on so many fronts. Think chat rooms, MySpace .com, blogs, life journals illustrated with photos snapped up by cell phones, flash mobbing, marathon running, focus groups, talk radio, e-mails to new shows, camcorders, sponsored sports teams for tots — and every garage band in town with its own CD. What do all these platforms have in common? They are all devoted to otherwise anonymous people who don't want to be mere spectators. In this virtual revolution, it's not workers against capitalists — that's so 19th century. In our mediated world, it's spectators against celebrities, with spectators demanding a share of the last scarce resource in the overdeveloped world — attention. The *American Idol* format combines essential elements of this revolution.

Have you followed the ruckus over why people don't have heroes anymore — in the old-fashioned statesman, warrior, genius, artist kind of way? People concerned with education are especially alarmed. They invest a lot of energy in trying to rekindle an aura of greatness around the Founding Fathers. But it's hopeless. Ask natural-born citizens of the mediated world who their heroes are, and their answers fall into one of two categories: somebody in their personal lives or performers — above all, pop music performers.

The "everyday hero" answer reflects the virtual revolution, but what about performers? Why are they so important to their fans? Because, in concert especially, these new kinds of heroes create an experience of belonging that their fans would otherwise never know, living as they do in a marketplace of lifestyles that can make one's existence feel optional. That's why there's a religious quality to a concert when the star meets the audience's awesome expectations and creates, in song and persona, a moment in which each individual feels personally understood and, at the same time, fused with other fans in a larger common identity. "Performer heroes" are, in the end, all about us. They don't summon us to serve a cause—other than the one of being who we are. So, naturally, they have been leaders of the virtual revolution. From their perch on high, they make us the focus of attention.

American Idol takes the next step. It unites both aspects of the relationship—in the climactic final rounds, a fan becomes an idol; the ultimate dream of our age comes true before our eyes and in our hearts.

That's mediational magic.

And don't forget the power of music. *American Idol* wouldn't be what it is if, say, amateur actors were auditioning. You can disagree with someone about movie stars and TV shows and still be friends. But you can't be friends with someone who loves the latest boy band, in a totally unironic way, if you are into Gillian Welch. That's because tastes and pop music go right to the core of who you are, with a depth and immediacy no other art form can match. Music takes hold of you on levels deeper than articulated meaning. That's why words, sustained by music, have such power. There is nothing like a song for expressing who we are.

That brings us to the early rounds of *American Idol*, in which contestants are chosen for the final competition in Hollywood. The conventional wisdom is that they are an exercise in public humiliation, long a staple of reality TV. That's not wrong, as far as it goes, but it isn't just any old humiliation exercise—it is the most excruciating form of voluntary personal humiliation the human condition allows for because it involves the most revealing kind of performance there is, this side of pornography. During this phase of the show, the audience, knowing it will eventually fuse in a positive way with a finalist idol, gets to be in the most popular clique on the planet, rendering snarky judgments on one of the most embarrassing pools of losers ever assembled.

American Idol gives you so many ways to feel good about yourself.

No wonder it's a hit. (134–36)

1. Ask students to read the text and to find the thesis and supporting detail.
2. After having provided a lesson about summary writing, ask students to write a sample summary of the text's main points. Remind them that summarizing requires not only condensing the text, but also judging for

importance and organizing for comprehension of the importance. A reader's extant knowledge or schema helps make this level of reading possible (Maclellan 1997, 281).

3. The second part of this exercise is synthesis. Give the students stem sentences like the ones used below to help them synthesize the text to their own purposes.

    a. As _____ says, "_____," which is why XYZ.

    b. People seem to crave the chance to show off their talents even when they don't have any talent. _____ suggests that is because _____.

    c. _____ believes that _____. However, he/she is wrong because XYZ.

4. Explain that the blank parts of the stem sentences represent their uses of the original text (as shown by underlines) and that the rest of the writing (as shown by the XYZ as a fill-in space) represents their own thinking. Fully developed, these sentences represent a synthesis of another person's thinking with their own—leading to entirely new thinking and expression of those thoughts. The stem sentences that are used in this exercise can be a fruitful way to help students begin to work with the text more originally.

5. Require students to share their summaries and their synthesis responses with their small groups or post them to you in a journal or other ungraded response opportunity.

Example Summary:

"American Idol Worship" by Thomas de Zengotita considers the reasons that *American Idol* is such a popular program; it even outpaced the recent Grammy Awards about professional pop stars. Pop music stars have become the new American heroes, and *American Idol* contestants have become the new hero wannabes. They willingly showcase their talents (and lack of talents) while Americans cheer and jeer them, just waiting for the opportunity to be personally touched by the one who will be voted the American Idol. In the meantime, the contestants get a thrill from being judged regarding their popularity and the fans get a vicarious thrill from judging others for popularity. The contestants get attention and the show's fans get satisfaction, leading both to opportunities to feel good about themselves.

    Examples of Synthesis Using Stem Sentences:

    a. As Thomas de Zengotita says, "music takes hold of you on levels deeper than articulated meaning," which is why music seems to have such power over people. Pop musicians are the new American heroes, according to de Zengotita, which makes sense when media of all kinds send that music to our ears at any time of day or night and in any place we might be.

b. People seem to crave the chance to show off their talents even when they don't have any talent. De Zengotita suggests that is because people crave attention. What seems odd and worth exploring further is that people will accept even negative attention like extreme humiliation in their desire to be given their so-called fifteen minutes of fame.

c. De Zengotita believes that the various electronic media that people use give them opportunities to become like celebrities in their power to vote for their American idols. However, he is wrong. People's electronic devices actually trap them into thinking they are more important than they really are. One individual vote would hardly be missed in the grand scheme of American Idol voting. Neither would 5,000 or 10,000 votes be missed.

PART THREE

Writing to Teach

HOW TO USE PART THREE: WRITING THOUSANDS OF WORDS A DAY

Writing strategies for teachers are connected intimately to the reading capabilities of students in online settings. As the Introduction states, the heavily reading- and writing-centric aspects of OWI require that instructors develop different tools, approaches, and working styles; they must train different writing muscles. The goal of Part Three is to to provide teachers with useable writing strategies that meet online writing students' needs, particularly for writing to students about rhetoric and composition.

Literacy Load

Nothing prepares teachers for OWI's heavy literacy load like simply jumping into the pool. The water can be a jarring wake-up for teachers who rely on their students to do most of the writing in their writing course, however. On the contrary, the writing may be more heavily distributed toward OWI teachers, who need to address the writing and written responses of each student. Because of the loss of body/face/voice connections, the vast amount of text in OWCs makes for a rich, but heavy literacy load for students to read — as this book has made clear. However, the sheer amount of additional writing necessary for teachers also is unprecedented when compared with other writing instructional environments. Recall the 30,000 words per term that Warnock (2009) estimates online writing instructors may write during one writing course, for example. Writing is the instructor's primary means of individual and group teaching in OWI.

The number of words we write in OWI may be shocking and worrisome to online writing instructors. However, the amount of text is not nearly as crucial as the quality of the writing we produce. The crucial difference between onsite and online writing instruction — especially in asynchronous settings but also in synchronous ones — is that teachers need to be able to write about writing, do it cogently, and do it repeatedly with similar student writing problems and unique student content and approaches to that content. Students then need to interpret the teacher's messages accurately and do so independently, typically without face-to-face conversations with the teacher. As teachers, we cannot talk our way around a problem, using gestures and facial expressions to pull students along. We need to write as well as textbook authors without the benefits of a publisher's editor. We need to be well-versed in issues of rhetoric and composition and be able to talk about writing to people who have no expertise and lack a common vocabulary about it, and we need to do it primarily with text.

Writing to Teach

Everything written in an OWC should be considered material that is intended to teach students something. Even tone is an instruction; it teaches about uses of emotion and the writer's apparent beliefs about the reader. Hence, we must consider our language and approaches seriously when writing any documents or communications in OWI. As journalist Sydney J. Harris once said, "The two words 'information' and 'communication' are often used interchangeably, but they signify quite different things. Information is giving out; communication is getting through."

We get the message through to students by straightforward language and clarity, a practice I call semantic integrity (Hewett, *Online Writing*, 2015). The easier our messages are to read, the more likely it is that OWI students will learn. Our clarity of writing helps students to make the necessary cognitive leap between what they read about writing and what needs to happen in their own writing to improve it.

By now, it should be clear that students must put more effort into their college-level reading. Students must be reminded about their learned reading skills and encouraged to choose conscious involvement in college reading. Nonetheless, the reading load in OWCs is both heavy (Griffin and Minter 2013) and critical to learning to write with increasingly more mature skills. Teachers have their work cut out for them given that students with all types of learning styles and strengths typically enter these courses through open enrollment. While we cannot choose the online students we will teach nor do the reading for them, we can make their jobs more clear-cut and doable and more accessible overall.

Typically, preparatory classes for teaching college writing focus on rhetoric and composition theory, textual analysis, pedagogical strategies, and meeting course outcomes, but they do not focus on ways that we write for students. That may be because of a tacit belief that if we are good enough writers to get through graduate-level writing, we can figure out how to write well to students. Or, it may be that the ability to write for students simply is a given. Nonetheless, few of us are textbook writers, where clear exposition of rhetoric and composition is expected. Textbook writers also get help from editors because their writing is so crucial to reaching students; teachers do not get this editorial help, and they write relatively quickly under the pressure of their student readers' immediate needs.

Furthermore, many of today's teachers are digital-era immigrants. As such, we have to learn a new style of instructional writing on a conscious level—studying and thinking about and learning the particular differences between the instructional writing we have always done and the instructional writing necessary for a digital age. Older teachers need to think more deeply about these new teaching-through-writing requirements so they can share knowledge with younger teachers educated in this digital age, who already have a different—although possibly unconscious—sense of how to write for students in OWI. We need to learn from each other in conscious ways.

Most important, if they write at all, many composition teachers write scholarly discourse, nonfiction essays, or fiction. They may not consider all of the writing that they do for students to be part of their instructional art. In OWI, however, such writing is the crux of their art. That writing is teaching. And it is teaching to student readers who often read poorly if they choose to read at all. To reach them, we must remember, as Nathaniel Hawthorne once said, that "easy reading is damned hard writing."

The writing that OWI teachers need to provide includes instructional text about writing strategies, feedback, assignments, and interpersonal communication. Chapter 12 provides some general guidelines that can help teachers remember what they know about writing for a student audience and consciously use it in their OWI writing practices. It gives specific examples for writing content about writing, while Chapters 13, 14, and 15 address feedback, writing assignments, and interpersonal communication respectively.

12

Strategies for Writing Instructional Texts

WHAT ARE STRATEGIES FOR WRITING INSTRUCTIONAL TEXTS AND WHY ARE THEY IMPORTANT?

Instructors need solid strategies for writing instructional texts that online writing students will read. OWI teachers, like their onsite counterparts, often need to write content-based materials about rhetoric and composition to help students understand course terminology and writing processes. Although these materials may be provided in a file in the LMS and not as a hard copy handout, this is work that writing instructors have been doing for many years prior to the advent of OWI. However, unlike handouts in an onsite course, to include the onsite portion of a hybrid OWC, such files for a fully online OWC in particular need to be written as stand-alone instruction that students can read, comprehend, and use in support of their writing without the teacher's face-to-face, oral explanation or a live question-and-answer period. What makes this type of instructional text writing special is that it is not merely an adjunct to the teaching—the text *becomes* the teaching.

Similar to having a required textbook for all online courses of that level and type, sometimes OWI teachers are given a course shell into which they can upload original assignments, which is already populated with the course's primary instructional texts. However, teachers may find that students do not understand what they are asked to read or that the written material is not how they would like it to be presented, either of which leaves the teacher to find or write additional text for teaching a point or skill. Another possibility is that the course texts do not offer material relevant to what the class needs at the time, such as material focused on how to write effective peer feedback. In such cases, teachers may opt to write lessons about writing for their students.

COHERENCE IN INSTRUCTIONAL TEXT

Writing instructional text typically is an expository task; the writing explains what something is, why it is that way, and/or how to perform a skill. Students' reading of exposition typically is less skillful than of narrative, as Chapter 2 describes, because of the need for inferential skills. Especially for young or nonfluent readers, inferential reading is accomplished much more easily in a narrative structure than in an expository one (Maclellan 1997; Britton and Gülgöz 1991). Exposition, of course, also happens to be the primary kind of reading that students must address in many college-level courses.

In their study of how to improve instructional text, Bruce K. Britton and Sami Gülgöz (1991) examined how teachers may fail to supply sufficient coherence connections for student readers. They worked from the premise that texts with coherence markers are more learnable for students than are texts where inference is necessary to understand the text. Although students need to use inferential skills consciously in reading, as Chapter 6 indicates, the genre of instructional text is one where needing to infer can interfere with learning the material as the teacher intended it to be presented. Britton and Gülgöz asked:

> What happens when coherence fails to be established because a new sentence does not mention an idea from the previous sentence? In such cases, the human reader may try to make an inference to link the new sentence with some idea from a previous sentence. In other words, the text "calls for" an inference at that point in the text. If the reader succeeds in making a coherence-establishing inference, then coherence is maintained. However, if he or she fails, then coherence is disrupted, that is, the reader's mental representation of the text is not coherent. (329)

Using the Kintsch computer program for their analyses, they found areas where inferences needed to be made, thus indicating possible disruption of coherence for learners using the texts they studied.

In discussing coherence in instructional text, Britton and Gülgöz rely on three principles that are helpful to instructional writing for OWI: (1) repetition, (2) information arrangement, and (3) explicit language.

We already know that placing important documents like the syllabus and assignments in more than one place in the LMS can help students. Redundancy is a good principle for OWI, as described in the OWI position statement's (CCCC Committee for OWI, 2013) Effective Practices 3.6 (13) and 4.6 (15). Britton and Gülgöz's first principle similarly regards repetition of words and terms. They say teachers should "make the learner's job easier by [writing] the sentence so that it repeats, from the previous sentence, the linking word to which it should be linked." A corollary to this principle is that "whenever the same concept appears in the text, the same term should be used for it." Such repetition enables students to see key language in its instructional context more than once, encouraging them to recognize its importance to the lesson. In an oral lesson, teachers likely would do a similar kind of repetition, but in online settings, students' own reading of the text needs to provide that type of idea enforcement.

The second principle regards arrangement of old and new information:

> to make the learner's job easier by arranging the parts of each sentence so that (a) the learner first encounters the old part of the sentence, which specifies where that sentence is to be connected to the rest of his or her mental representation; and (b) the learner next encounters the new part of the sentence, which indicates what new information to add to the previously specified location in his or her own mental representation. (331)

The arrangement of new and old material in contiguous sentences can, like a series of train cars, link crucial material, helping readers to understand that a sentence is intimately connected to what was said in a previous sentence.

The third principle regards using explicit language whenever implicit language could be missed or misunderstood: "to make the learner's job easier by making explicit any important implicit references; that is, when a concept that is needed later is referred to implicitly, refer to it explicitly if the reader may otherwise miss it." Britton and Gülgöz include that principle because they often found "a break in coherence as a result of the later sentence referring explicitly to something that is only implicit in an earlier sentence" (332). In OWI, where students must make a cognitive leap between what has been written regarding a concept and their own writing, implicit language is insufficient. As with reading most textbooks, if the language is not overt about the points to be made — sometimes connected literally by numbers or bullet points — students may miss the message and never even know that they missed the message, particularly given a propensity to read lightly, quickly, partially, or with inattention.

Readers who best are able to make the correct inferences are, not surprisingly, readers with "requisite prior knowledge, working-memory capacity, inference-making ability, metacognitive skills, and state and trait motivation" (341). These are, of course, the traits of fluent readers — traits we hope to instill overtly through the exercises presented in Part Two — yet they are traits too often not found in typical OWI students. The combination of "inference calls and expository instructional text [is] an obstacle placed in the path of the reader. Reducing the call for such inferences will increase the learning of information from instructional text" (342). Britton and Gülgöz's conclusion makes sense given that it is less helpful to avoid assigning expository text to students than it is to provide stronger coherence connections in what we write for them.

Teachers of writing — most of whom know how to write well in a variety of genres and settings — may wonder whether their exposition for students might have similar flaws. In fact, it is more likely than we might think. Britton and Gülgöz provide two primary reasons that teachers might write with poor inferential connections built into their instructional texts. The first reason is the belief that if we use a term more than one time, we should use a different term from the one used first. This belief is an issue of style often called "elegant variation" (340), and it reflects a focus on the language rather than the audience. The second reason is linked to why teachers are paid to do their work: they are experts in their subject matter, which means "their mental structures for the text's subject matter are large, detailed, and highly automatized" (340–41). In other words, teachers automatically skip steps in presenting a concept because they know that concept so well that it might seem apparent to all. I have seen this trait in many dissertation writers, for example, who have come to know a topic deeply and assume their readers know more than they do. Lack of coherence in a dissertation is a flaw that frequently must be addressed before a committee can pass it. When the writer knows more than the reader, who needs the concept to be made explicit, the writer must consciously provide all the needed links. In this way, teachers as writers are much like students as readers: what we know of writing must be put into practice consciously and with intention.

Other flaws that may be problems for instructional text include "absent macrostructure, needless complexity" (Britton and Gülgöz 1991, 342), poorly written headings (or lack thereof), prosaic sentences, overuse of metaphor and other figures of speech, unnecessary symbolic language, jargon, and even a failure to treat the writing like a draft that needs revision. Although it may seem that addressing these issues as flaws is a way of being too easy on students—of doing all the work for them—the instructional writing we do should be as clear to students as possible because it is not their job to infer what we mean when we ask them to do something or when we try to teach them something through text (Hewett, *Online Writing*, 2015). Inference is something they will need as they read for their classes, yet students should not need to employ the same level of inference to interpret our writing to them.

Hence, we see that for instructional expository writing, inferential reading requires coherent writing, while coherence requires repetition, thoughtful arrangement, and explicit language. Read, for example, the following proofreading confidence-building exercise written for students and based in part on how the brain uses saccades, fixations, and regressions. This lesson is based on the fact that conscious proofreading helps writers: "Proofreading, in part, requires that the reader interrupt the normal reading process when making use of saccades. It requires many more fixations per line than readers normally make" (Horning 1978, 267). Taken a step further, proofreading itself can be improved by reading aloud; vocalizing forces us to slow down and fixate on every word and pronounce it, enabling a reader to catch more meaning-interfering errors and local errors. In fact, reading aloud uses more senses (i.e., speech, hearing, seeing, and touch for those who click a mouse, hold a pen, or touch the words with a finger) that help to anchor the text. Unlike fake reading where we read only for the effect of how we sound, paying no attention to metacognition, when proofreading well, we explicitly read every word for how it sounds in the context of other words and whole sentences and paragraphs.

This brief lesson about proofreading was written to demonstrate how to build coherence in a reading lesson for students. The bracketed explanations are meant for teacher-writers, not for student-readers. The coherence connections that make inference easier for students are provided in Chapter 6.

The lesson itself can be adapted and used as a reminder to students in any type of OWC where they need to practice proofreading skills. This lesson uses the concepts of saccades, fixations, and regressions without naming them.

OWI WRITING EXAMPLE 12.1 Proofreading

Proofreading Confidence Builder

Proofreading is an important part of writing for any college course. It is especially important for succeeding in a writing course. When you are working in an online writing course, it can be challenging to get other students to help you with your proofreading. Here are some strategies to improve your proofreading skills and help you confidently judge the readiness of your own writing. **[Note how "proofreading" and "writing course" are repeated. Synonyms like "editing," "checking," or "copy editing" could be used to substitute for "proofreading," but these would introduce unnecessary new terms that might have contested meanings for readers. Where new terms are important, introduce them in an in-text definition.]**

1. Begin proofreading by reading aloud to reinforce the ideas you have written. Reading silently uses only our vision — one of five senses. Reading aloud uses our vision, hearing, and speech — three of the five senses. The more senses we engage, the better we can evaluate our writing.

   a. Reading from the computer screen: Touch the screen with the cursor, and use it to follow your reading slowly — by using the mouse to move the cursor down to each line. To remain completely aware that your goal is to read each word in the document, click the mouse to set the cursor on each line. Now you've added the sense of touch to your vision, hearing, and speech. **[Notice the repetition of "mouse," "senses," and "read/reading aloud"; also, notice the "1" and "a" used to indicate the arrangement of information from old to new.]**

b. Reading from hard copy: Print the document to hard copy. Read it aloud — slowly — with your index finger moving across each line to touch every word or down each line. **[This advice is a repetition of the previous step with the new information of reading from hard copy.]** If you are reading the document onscreen because you cannot print for some reason, you still can read it aloud.

c. For either screen or hard copy reading, **[Again, the type of reading that needs to be done is repeated.]** you can increase the number of senses involved in the proofreading by reading aloud to that person, which includes his or her hearing.

2. Reread what you have read.

a. The first time you read, do it with the content in mind.

b. The second time, read for **g**rammar, **u**sage, and **m**echanics (GUM). GUM is a good acronym for proofreading at the sentence level. **[The letters of GUM are boldfaced to help students connect the words to the acronym. The best way to remember an acronym is to use it more than once.]**

3. For the purposes of proofreading only (i.e., not to post to the teacher), **[Notice the in-text definition of "proofreading only."]** make the text completely unfamiliar by printing it in an odd or unusual font. **[Three examples of the same text formatted in three different fonts are provided below to make the instruction explicit.]**

The afternoon and evening courses that she preferred to take were full when she tried to register for them. She didn't want to take an early morning or lunch-time course, so Jennifer signed up for an online writing course. This would be a piece of cake, she told her apartment mates. Everybody knows that online courses are easier than the ones they have to take on campus. She would get through the writing course with just an hour or so of work each week. They didn't even have to meet class at a particular time, leaving students to do the work whenever they want. The registrar's office called it an asynchronous class. Jennifer figured that meant that she didn't have to talk to her teacher unless she had a question. "Not so fast," said Fred, one of Jennifer's friends. He had gotten his first "D" in that class. He gave her his books and warned her that the class had a lot of work in it and that it was harder than she thought to take an online writing course.

(continued)

OWI WRITING EXAMPLE 12.1 (*continued*)

The afternoon and evening courses that she preferred to take were full when she tried to register for them. She didn't want to take an early morning or lunch-time course, so Jennifer signed up for an online writing course. This would be a piece of cake, she told her apartment mates. Everybody knows that online courses are easier than the ones they have to take on campus. She would get through the writing course with just an hour or so of work each week. They didn't even have to meet class at a particular time, leaving students to do the work whenever they want. The registrar's office called it an asynchronous class. Jennifer figured that meant that she didn't have to talk to her teacher unless she had a question. "Not so fast," said Fred, one of Jennifer's friends. He had gotten his first "D" in that class. He gave her his books and warned her that the class had a lot of work in it and that it was harder than she thought to take an online writing course.

The afternoon and evening courses that she preferred to take were full when she tried to register for them. She didn't want to take an early morning or lunch-time course, so Jennifer signed up for an online writing course. This would be a piece of cake, she told her apartment mates. Everybody knows that online courses are easier than the ones they have to take on campus. She would get through the writing course with just an hour or so of work each week. They didn't even have to meet class at a particular time, leaving students to do the work whenever they want. The registrar's office called it an asynchronous class. Jennifer figured that meant that she didn't have to talk to her teacher unless she had a question. "Not so fast," said Fred, one of Jennifer's friends. He had gotten his first "D" in that class. He gave her his books and warned her that the class had a lot of work in it and that it was harder than she thought to take an online writing course.

The different fonts create a mild "cognitive dysfluency"; this phrase means that the new font surprises the brain, which is used to a particular font style and size for reading. This dysfluency can be enough to help you see things in the text that you didn't see before. **[The new term is defined explicitly in-text and the term is repeated afterward. Other explicit language in this lesson includes the use of the imperative: read, print, reread, make.]**

This style of expository writing for developing online lessons for students requires practice and thoughtful revision. Although we can agree with George Orwell that "good writing is like a windowpane," writing with clarity for students and building coherence deliberately are not easy to do. Ernest Hemingway said it best: "There is nothing to writing. All you do is sit down at a [computer] and bleed." Indeed.[1]

SEMANTIC INTEGRITY IN WRITING FOR STUDENTS

Semantic integrity is about having fidelity between what is written and what can be inferred from the writing. In other words, to the greatest degree possible, the inferred meaning should match the intended message: "Semantic integrity is about using language in clear, straightforward, and guiding ways that students can read and interpret sufficiently to take next steps in their writing. When the instructor's text is the instructional voice, it has to ring clearly to be heard and understood" (Hewett 2011, 13). This concept is discussed thoroughly in *The Online Writing Conference: A Guide for Teachers and Tutors* (Hewett 2015).[2] However, it bears repeating here because writing to teach requires a high level of semantic integrity, which matters in all kinds of instructional writing.

When writing to and for students, teachers and tutors should use straightforward language that clearly is directive when giving instructions and nondirective when giving students choices. It is important to avoid using conditional language unless we truly mean that students have a choice and that we do not care which choice they make. For example, a common term that teachers and tutors use when writing to students about their writing is *consider*: "consider dropping this paragraph" or "consider doing more research about XYZ" or "consider rewriting the thesis." Such language is confusing. Does *consider* mean that I should do something or that I must do something? Is it a suggestion that I can ignore or a polite way of telling me what to do? Students always need to know what they are supposed to do and experience from the lesson. Such lessons include writing lessons, assignments, and feedback particularly, but also interpersonal communications.

---

[1] Certainly, many books relevant to style exist, and teachers may have their favorite ones to call upon. Some examples include Nora Bacon's (2012) *The Well-Crafted Sentence: A Writer's Guide to Style*, William Strunk and William Strunk, Jr.'s (2011) *The Elements of Style*, and Joseph M. Williams' (1995) *Style: Toward Clarity and Grace*. Coherence building is not just an issue of style as style typically is understood, and it is crucial to written instructional teaching, however. Therefore, it is important to consult resources that can help to develop stronger coherence in instructional writing.

[2] Much of the following material is adapted from *The Online Writing Conference: A Guide for Teachers and Tutors* and from the accompanying *Instructor's Study Guide*, originally published by Heinemann in 2010 and 2011. These texts are combined into an updated version and published by Bedford/St. Martin's, 2015.

For this reason, I introduce semantic integrity in this chapter and use it throughout Part Three.

The kinds of language discussed in this section can be especially confusing for students who are learning to write in an online course.

WELL-INTENTIONED, BUT POORLY TARGETED COMMENTS Many of the comments students receive on their writing may be about sentence-level concerns even when teachers indicate on the syllabus, assignment, and/or grading rubric that global, content-level concerns are more important for writing and revising. Teachers need to be sure that their feedback and instructions match the provided outcomes and assessment goals.

POORLY MODELED TEXT Students need to understand our expectations at all times. To that end, it is important to model both implicitly and explicitly what we would like to see them doing in their writing. An example of implicit modeling is to avoid using contractions if we do not want students to use contractions in formal writing for us. If we want to make an explicit distinction, we can tell students that we may use contractions when chatting with them through an IM chat feature or in response to their journals, but that we will not use contractions on more formal communications. We then can express that we expect the same levels of formality from them. Another case of explicit modeling is to provide an example or series of examples in instructional text.

For instance, when teaching students about using comparison and contrast as an organizational strategy, it is helpful to demonstrate what such organization looks like, as in the following example.

OWI WRITING EXAMPLE 12.2 Effective Modeling

Writers often look at similarities and/or differences between two items or ideas. Organizing an essay by comparison (similarities) and contrast (differences) works best when two elements are clearly similar or different in an obvious area. It is fairly easy to show where the item is similar or different. The writing becomes more interesting when the writer also demonstrates the unusual or unexpected part of the union of two ideas.

There are at least two patterns for presenting similarities and/or differences. The *block* pattern divides the essay into two primary sections. The first section addresses all of the qualities of one element to be compared or contrasted; the second section addresses the other element and its qualities. The *switch* pattern alternates the discussion of qualities between the two elements, dealing thoroughly with one quality and both elements before moving to the next quality of the two elements.

Both patterns work equally well in short essays, but the switch pattern may be preferable in longer essays because readers can follow the points being made better in a direct comparison or contrast.

Here is an example of what each would look like using the following thesis: *The computer and the human brain operate in similar ways, but the computer will never be as flexible as the brain.*

Block is a divided pattern:

1. Computer
   A. Speed
   B. Path of thought
   C. Number of components
   D. Relative size
   E. Free will
2. Brain
   A. Speed
   B. Path of thought
   C. Number of components
   D. Relative size
   E. Free will
3. Ends with what is unexpected or unusual about the computer and the brain when compared or contrasted.

Switch is an alternating pattern. It makes the point of what is unexpected or unusual about the computer and the brain when compared or contrasted:

1. Speed
   A. Computer
   B. Brain
2. Path of thought
   A. Computer
   B. Brain
3. Number of components
   A. Computer
   B. Brain
4. Relative size
   A. Computer
   B. Brain

(*continued*)

OWI WRITING EXAMPLE 12.2 (*continued*)

  5. Free will

     A. Computer

     B. Brain

  6. Ends with what is unexpected or unusual about the computer and the brain when compared or contrasted.

This outline model gives students an idea of how they might organize their writing and reasons for choosing one style or the other.

JARGON Terminology specific to rhetoric and composition that is not taught as terms important for the course can prove difficult for students. Such terminology includes unfamiliar language about essays and essay development (e.g., rhetoric; position; argument and exposition; thesis sentences, claims, and assertions [and what the differences are among these terms]; topic sentences; content development; organization; and context) and various concerns at the sentence level (e.g., subordinator, interrogatory phrase, introductory clause, appositive, colloquialism, idiom, and cliché). There is nothing wrong with using such terms when they are defined (either explicitly or in context) and used purposefully in the OWC, but it is important to remember that OWI "students have to understand the meaning of these words . . . in application to their own writing without the benefit of the teacher's oral intervention about their writing" (Hewett 2011, 12).[3] We should explicitly teach students how these new or different words apply to their writing while remembering that we are doing this job through writing. For a more in-depth discussion of teacher response/feedback, see Chapter 13.

ABBREVIATIONS AND PERSONAL NOTATION STYLES Especially with regard to feedback on writing, students need to decipher abbreviations and clichéd remarks. In addition to the proverbial "awk" and "frag," which they likely know (N. Sommers 1982), each teacher (and tutor) has his own way of notating an essay, journal, or discussion comment. When these personal ways of responding to student writing are not explained, students may not infer correctly what they are expected to do as a result of them. In other words, are students

---

[3]Also see Nathan (2005), who explains that even in an onsite classroom, American college students are not likely to ask the teacher what a term means (92). If this is true in an onsite setting, it seems even more likely that few online students would risk putting in writing that they do not know what we mean. Jargon provides a coded message that even peers or tutors — if students should ask them — may not be able to unlock to reveal the teacher's intended meaning.

intended to answer a question or interpret a revision action from the words? The instructional text should make the intended response clear.

INEFFECTIVE USES OF INDIRECTION AND POLITENESS LANGUAGE When instructional text is indirect from a linguistic point of view, meaning can be veiled in politeness strategies that do not convey well in written settings. Furthermore, they do not convey in transactional settings like school. Adult students particularly will experience frustration when a requirement to do something is veiled as a question suggesting that students have the choice about what to do. Problem language includes rhetorical questions, indirect suggestions, and conditional language where the intention of getting students to do something different with their writing does not match the interpretation of choice.

Straightforward language is especially important regarding all communications with students — whether written or oral. However, teachers may mistake circumlocution with politeness and politeness with respect. The following section is taken almost verbatim from the Instructor's Study Guide in *The Online Writing Conference: A Guide for Teachers and Tutors* (Hewett 2015, 204–5). Additional examples of linguistically direct and indirect teaching language can be found on pages 117–18 of *The Online Writing Conference*. Teachers interested in learning additional specific feedback strategies that have semantic integrity will want to review those texts.

OWI WRITING EXAMPLE 12.3 Direct and Indirect Language

Here is a way to understand the nature of direct and indirect language as they are described linguistically. The first three examples below use direct language and the fourth example uses indirect language.

1. ***This paragraph needs to be revised.*** This sentence uses direct language to provide information about the writing. It is in the form of a declarative sentence with the function of providing information (form and function match). **Declaratives are helpful sentence forms for teaching online.**

   - *You need to revise this paragraph.*
   - *Your lab report requires six outside sources, and you only have three.*
   - *A case study like this should be developed in chronological (time) order.*

2. ***How will you revise this paragraph?*** This sentence uses direct language to ask a question about the writing. It is in the form of an interrogative with the function of eliciting information (form and function match). **Interrogatives — genuine questions that begin with *what, when, where, who, why,* and *how* — are helpful sentence forms for teaching**

(continued)

OWI WRITING EXAMPLE 12.3 (*continued*)

online. Rhetorical and yes/no closed questions are not helpful (see #4 below).

- *Where can you find three sources that respond to your topic? The first source you use provides a good model.*
- *What is the title of Jacob's article? Who is the publisher?*
- *According to APA style, where should the in-text citation be placed for this quotation?*

3. *Revise this paragraph.* This sentence uses direct language to request or command the writer about the writing. It is in the form of an imperative sentence with the function of commanding (form and function match). **Imperatives are helpful sentence forms within certain contexts for online teaching.**

- *Find three more sources that support the thesis of this lab report.*
- *To brainstorm this idea, write six or seven ways that people can get into trouble when driving with cell phones. Choose the three or four that you think are strongest to write about.*
- *Delete the sentences that don't provide more information about your thesis.*

4. *Shouldn't you revise this paragraph?* or *Does this paragraph need revising?* The first example is in the interrogative form with the function of commanding: form and function do not match. The second example is in the interrogative form with the mixed function of commanding and providing information: form and function do not match. Where form and function do not match, there is a "suggestion," which always provides the potential for mixed messages and for students to ignore the "advice." Rhetorical questions are particularly dangerous because teachers read them as gently pushing students toward an action; students read them as literal and address them as a choice. **Suggestions are not helpful sentence forms** *unless* **they are preceded with the phrase "I suggest that you XYZ" or "I think you should XYZ."**

In line with using linguistically direct language when writing content, assignments, and feedback, it is important to explain carefully, yet briefly, what is happening in the text and how to address it. One of the problems that students have in OWCs is that they realize or learn something is wrong with their essays, yet they may fail to understand what the problem is, why it is problematic, and how to fix it. In other words, when students are working online, they often experience themselves as left to figure out their writing problems on their own. Chapter 13 suggests ways to write feedback that students can interpret and use in their revision and overall writing development.

OWI WRITING EXAMPLE 12.4 Practicing Writing Content

In the same way that teachers norm their grading in a workshop setting, it can be helpful for OWI teachers to get together to practice writing content about rhetoric and composition for online students. The following example content about the components of an essay that argues a position can be shared in an asynchronous or synchronous setting, with teachers revising (1) the content; (2) the phrasing, striving for coherence and semantic integrity; and (3) the presentation, striving for ease of reading and interest level. Teachers can find information about document presentation in both Chapters 13 and 14.

Ask participating teachers, either as individuals or in teaching teams, to revise the material for an OWC. They should present it to the group as a .doc or .docx file so that any formatting will not be lost as it might be in a rich text file. Share the documents in the LMS in a group discussion setting so that they can be downloaded and opened by participants, receive specific comments using the marginal Comments feature of the word processing program, and be saved and uploaded. Use the discussion forum for more general comments about both the content revision process and the participant perceptions of their peer commenting experience.

Arguing a Position

Elements of the Intellectual Argument

- Audience and purpose
- Thesis (assertion)
- Good reasons and logical evidence
- Counterarguments
- Introduction and conclusion
- Documentation

Audience and Purpose

Before you write an intellectual argument, consider your audience and purpose. If your audience is your professor, there is a good chance that she or he knows more about the subject than you do. In that case, the purpose of the argument becomes a test of your ability to form a reasonable thesis and to support and defend it logically and thoroughly. However, even if your professor knows something about your issue, when you conduct a good investigation, you become the subject-area expert and there's a very good chance that your argument will present new materials and ways of thinking about your subject.

(continued)

OWI WRITING EXAMPLE 12.4 (*continued*)

If your audience is broader than your professor alone (possibly including your classmates, peers, or the readers of a newspaper editorial or Internet website), you'll be arguing your position to people who probably know less than you about the issue. Then, you really have the opportunity to influence someone's way of thinking about your issue—the stakes are higher and the writing becomes more exciting.

Thesis (Assertion)

- **Find a topic that interests you.**
- **Choose a topic that will allow you to take a side.** Your position is a *stance* that amounts to an attitude or judgment about some issue.
- **Write an assertion that reveals your position.** An assertion is a statement that often (but not always) includes a modal verb such as *should* or *ought* and asks the writer to make a judgment of fact or of value. Examples of assertions that argue for positions are:

  1. Capital punishment should be abolished because human juries can make mistakes in their decisions.

  2. People who download and "share" music on the Internet are stealing from performing artists.

  3. When children kill other children, as in recent slayings in American public schools, they should be tried as adults.

Notice that each of the above assertions takes a clearly defined position on a controversial issue. The writer's intention can't be mistaken and readers know that a strong argument must follow.

Academic arguments can be written about your college subjects, as well:

  1. Biology or Botany: The health benefits of radiation for food far outweigh the risks.

  2. Psychology: Even though it seems barbaric, electroshock therapy should be used in the fight against emotional illness.

  3. Political Science: America should use its power to stop genocide anywhere in the world.

- **Be certain that your position is arguable.** Your assertion should be consistent with available evidence. You can't build an intellectual argument on opinion alone. Therefore, you must do research to find support for the argument, or claim, that you're making. Then, ask yourself, "Is this a claim that I realistically can ask people to accept?" Likewise, the assertion should present a claim that reasonably can be argued within the space (page) and time (due date) limitations of your assignment.

- **Know what kinds of evidence will be convincing to your audience.** Academic arguments appeal primarily to the intellect — to logic. So, you need reasons for your position and each reason must be supported by evidence that defines, defends, and/or justifies it. Be sure to define special terms for your audience.

Let's use the following assertion as an example: *When children kill other children, as in recent slayings in American public schools, they should be tried as adults.* What reasons can we provide for this assertion? Notice that the claim is qualified by *as in recent slayings in American public schools,* which means that we're not talking about a child who finds her father's handgun and accidentally shoots her best friend. This assertion focuses on purposeful killings, or murder.

Reasons

1. When children make a decision to kill classmates, they are using free will, as adults do.

2. Children who kill their classmates have destroyed the lives of other children and have lost the right to childhood themselves.

3. Children who have killed their classmates should not be in a position to kill again, as they might be if tried as a juvenile and released from custody at age eighteen.

These reasons can be supported by certain kinds of logical, nonemotional evidence that people are likely to find convincing. These kinds of **evidence** are:

1. facts;

2. examples;

3. statistics, percentages, or other numbers;

4. expert testimony from authorities; and

5. narrative stories (anecdotes) from people with experience in the issue.

(continued)

OWI WRITING EXAMPLE 12.4 (*continued*)

Counterarguments

Academic arguments that assert and defend a position need to take into account what people who disagree would say about the argument. The disagreements are called "counterarguments," and your job as a writer is to find the best counterarguments to your position and address them. Ask yourself: *What bias or opinions will my audience have against my assertion or claim?*

Usually, writers address counterarguments after presenting their own reasons. By addressing the opposing point of view, you'll earn your audience's respect and strengthen your logical position.

Two possible counterarguments to the above assertion are:

1. Children who kill, even if the killing appears to be premeditated murder, are not mature enough to have made an adult decision.

2. There is no way to predict whether such children will kill again, so it is better to give them a second chance.

Introduction/Conclusion

Good arguments will present an interesting introduction that tells the reader:

1. what the issue is,

2. why it is controversial (background),

3. why it is important (background), and

4. what your position (assertion) is.

Good arguments also present the reader with an interesting conclusion.

1. The conclusion pulls together the entire argument, summarizing and stressing the main points.

2. It offers you a chance to suggest further consideration of the problem or research that people should do.

3. Sometimes, the conclusion is a good place to ask questions for which you have no answers — this strategy leaves the reader thinking.

Documentation

All arguments written for this college course should have accurate and sufficient documentation. Use your handbook and the course documentation guide (www.documentationguide.edu) to properly document:

1. Internal citations for quoted and paraphrased material and

2. All references used in the paper

13

Providing Readable Instructional Feedback Online

WHAT IS READABLE ONLINE INSTRUCTIONAL FEEDBACK AND WHY IS IT IMPORTANT?

Readable online instructional feedback, also called "response," is developed with students as the audience in mind. Because students need feedback on their writing to have another go at drafting and revision, a writing process that contemporary composition philosophy embraces, teachers need to provide it. Although such response can come from peers and tutors who have been taught useful ways to provide feedback using writing, students benefit most from thoughtful instructor response to their writing. Despite the popularity and value of online peer group response, the feedback from teachers is one thing that students count on as crucial to their learning.

While somewhat true in an onsite setting, in an online setting, instructional feedback represents more than the response to one paper. It becomes a significant, individualized part of the teaching. Feedback becomes the one-on-one interaction between the student and teacher, just as it is in a peer-to-peer or student-to-tutor situation. However, in online settings — particularly fully online OWCs — feedback also plays the larger role of the instructional conference with the requisite give-and-take found in traditional conferences (Hewett, *Online Writing*, 2015). In an online setting, body/face/voice intervention is rare, the occasional phone call notwithstanding; hence, private individual instruction primarily occurs around formal assignments and some informal assignments like journals. Providing accessible, comprehensible (i.e., focused, semantically clear, and potentially helpful) response and feedback that connects with students' own writing needs becomes a challenging responsibility. The goal of this chapter is to provide teachers and tutors with specific ways to render the kind of useful written feedback that constitutes both a writing conference and lesson.

The strategies for feedback presented in this chapter certainly are helpful to students regardless of whether the course occurs online or onsite. However, since the feedback in OWI typically is provided via text even when supplemented by audio/video files, without a face-to-face opportunity for teachers to explain their intentions, online writing students are at great risk of misinterpreting the feedback (Hewett 2004–2005, 2006; see also Freedman and Sperling 1985, regarding feedback more generally).

This chapter does not argue a particular response theory for writing; rather it provides an instructional response style for text-based OWI. Various researchers have articulated useful approaches for responding to student writing whether the writing and instruction occurs onsite or online (see, for example, Straub 2000; Elbow 1993; Anson 1998; N. Sommers 1982; Knoblauch and Brannon 1984; Haswell 1983), and these approaches continue to inform contemporary writing instruction. For the most part, teachers can adapt the feedback strategies recommended in this chapter to their preferred response approaches. However, as the examples demonstrate, this book favors an approach that addresses higher-order, content- and organization-based concerns first and more substantially before addressing lower-order, sentence-level problems in an essay. Additionally, it favors a problem-centered, linguistically direct instructional style in OWI that teaches students what a problem is, why it is a problem, and how to fix it or to avoid it while clearly telling students what they should do through a series of next steps. In an online setting, there is need for intervention in the writing given the lack of interpersonal feedback that students may experience with their teachers. Essay feedback is the major individualized instruction that online writing students receive (Hewett, *Online Writing*, 2015).

In onsite settings, teachers can provide feedback through text, audio and/or video technology, or face-to-face conferences. In hybrid OWI, teachers can provide feedback in all of these media, while in fully online settings, face-to-face conferences are not appropriate. While face-to-face conferences understandably remain a popular venue for talking with onsite students about their writing and assessing it (Beach and Friedrich 2006; Knoblauch and Brannon 1984; Fredrick 2009; Black 1998) — and they are especially valuable for multilingual students (Ferris 2003) — they are too time-consuming to offer for each essay (Bilbro, Iluzada, and Clark 2013). Two other popular approaches are to record one's feedback in a brief (e.g., two to ten minutes) audio or video response. Such feedback enables teachers to drill down into content or sentence-focused specifics because the instructor can point students to particular pages or lines in a text. Some teachers like this type of oral response because they believe it simulates a face-to-face conference scenario or that it makes the feedback more personal (Anson 1997). Others prefer not to type responses given that typing clear feedback can take a lot of time, especially when reading papers also is factored into the equation. Some people, like me, experience some verbosity when recording comments because the unstructured nature of the medium enables one to veer off on this little issue or that side consideration. Given a two-minute oral response, a teacher can speak about 250 words; if typed, those words would equal about a half page of single-spaced text. A longer audio response easily can overwhelm students as it provides a great deal of information for students to digest by themselves. That they must interpret this feedback alone underscores the necessity for thoughtful response in OWI.

Some teachers believe that students uniformly like audio-based commentary because it provides clarity and personalization, an assertion for which research has provided some supportive data albeit with mixed results (see, for example, J. Sommers 2013; Sipple and Sommers 2005; Sipple 2007; Anson 1997). Anecdotally, I have found that students have mixed feelings about the benefits of audio- and text-based response, at times preferring both because they like to hear teachers' voices but want to have written feedback for easy reference as they revise. To date, few have studied audio/visual feedback for student satisfaction in conjunction with writing improvement (see, for example, Warnock 2008; J. Sommers 2013, 2012; Moore and Filling 2012). Some teachers use, but dislike, text-based comments because they are difficult, unclear, and take so long to write (Connors and Lunsford 1993). Indeed, it is likely that most text-based feedback retains confusing features that lead to miscommunication (Haswell 2006; Straub 1996a, 1996b; Scrocco 2012; Ferris 2003; Hewett 2010, 2015) in part because it is difficult to write well. My own sense regarding textual feedback, something I admittedly prefer and do not see becoming extinct, is that the more one practices response using focused, comprehensible writing strategies, the faster one becomes, negating the time-intensity argument to some extent.

HOW CAN WE PROVIDE FEEDBACK WELL ONLINE?

However feedback is provided, there are response elements that all students need from their teachers:

- A personal greeting
- Acknowledgment of their efforts in terms of praise or some positive comment
- A summary of what the writing seems to be about to provide a sense of how a real reader is understanding it
- A sense of how the writing is working globally in terms of content, context, argument strategy, and the like
- To a lesser degree, depending on the stage of the writing, a sense of how the writing is working at the local or sentence level

- A lesson or lessons about how to make some type of revision that will take the paper to the next level of competence
- An action plan or series of next steps

These elements are outlined below in a series of problem-centered approaches that rely on the student's own writing to develop the lessons. They use semantic integrity when the lesson message matches its intention as described in Chapter 12. These elements can be provided to students through an audio/video or written format; in fact, because it is so easy to talk too much and about many different elements of the writing, it seems especially important to use this kind of structure in audio/video response.

Do Not Talk—Teach!

Teaching involves explaining, but it also is a performance: it does something. Teaching instructs through various available strategies. In an asynchronous online setting especially, teaching can look like:

- asking genuine [*wh-* and *how*] questions,
- demonstrating,
- illustrating,
- modeling,
- providing doable tasks with instructions to try them out, and
- explaining. (Hewett, *Online Writing*, 2015, 209)

Given the wide variety of online tools, "teaching can involve drawing [when tools allow], striking out words and substituting others, highlighting, and a variety of other strategies that instructors often don't use" (212). Indeed, teaching asks students to try out the writing they are being given information about. Rather than simply telling students what they did well or poorly, in an online setting, writing readable response means also giving students models for how to address the revision and giving them instruction to do something about the writing. It is worthwhile to remember that "teaching is showing, not just telling. It is doing together—sometimes doing a small piece of writing for the student as a demonstration. It is intervening in the student's writing so that the student can connect the words of the response with the required revisions" (212).

Certainly, some teachers worry that they can give too much information away when they reply to students, a concern about doing the work for students. However, making the reading, writing, and thinking processes as transparent as possible for students can help them to become better critical writers in an online setting. A proactive instructor provides ample examples and clear explanations that model good writing in the essay response itself. Some examples for doing so are found below.

Personalize the Response

Personalizing response in OWI helps students to see themselves as not anonymous in our eyes, but as real people. Getting to know our students takes a different kind of forethought in OWI than it does in a traditional onsite setting. An interpersonal transaction between teacher and student can help students to respond to feedback more positively and proactively. Using the student's name frequently in the response can help. Everyone likes to hear or see his or her own name because it singles him or her out as an individual.

Responding to student writing (especially through writing) is a big job that can take many hours per class. A template that explains common problem areas can be a handy tool that makes the job easier; it can be cut and pasted easily into the feedback document. One problem with using templates to respond to student writing, however, is that it is too easy to present a generalized English lesson that students could read in a common handbook. These lessons often do not transfer, as we know from the problems with skills-and-drills approaches. It is more useful to tailor the information to a student's particular need and content.

For example, here is one sentence from Bob's essay (presented in full in the feedback of OWI Writing Example 13.3): "Imigrants are what help make America be America; by being a multicultural society standing united." Let us pretend that the instructor has a template response for the use of semicolons and inserts it into the written feedback, as shown in response Example 13.1.

OWI WRITING EXAMPLE 13.1 Template Grammar Lesson

You used a semicolon wrongly in this sentence. Semicolons are only used in the following cases:

- When linking two independent clauses into one complete sentence
- When linking two independent clauses where one has a conjunctive adverb or transitional phrase
- When two independent clauses are joined by a coordinating conjunction and the clauses already are punctuated with commas or if the clauses are lengthy
- In a list or series when one of the items contains commas

OWI Writing Example 13.1 is a template grammar lesson that, while correct, lacks helpful characteristics that would enable Bob to do anything with the sentence in revision. For example, at the sentence level, Bob likely does not know what a conjunctive adverb, transitional phrase, or coordinating conjunction is. He may not even be sure about what an independent clause is. Therefore, he likely does not have a good idea of why the semicolon is wrong in his sentence, which makes it hard for him to fix it. If Bob were to eliminate the semicolon, would the sentence then be good? Bob may think so, but a quick glance reveals that Bob has an illogical connection between immigrants and "being a multicultural society standing united" as the sentence currently is written. Most importantly, this sentence in the context of the essay (as the response in OWI Writing Example 13.4 shows) may even be cut from the revision or rewritten when (and if) he writes a clearer thesis to which supportive reasons and examples can be applied.

While it is far from the most important challenge Bob has, possibly he would benefit from a grammar lesson or two. In that case, a more helpful template response, if a template is used at all, would best be developed by individualizing it with Bob's core sentence as an example of the rules.

OWI Writing Example 13.2 provides a personalized grammar lesson in uses of the semicolon — even using the template of prewritten grammar rules — that took me fifteen minutes to write. That is a lot of time for a

---

OWI WRITING EXAMPLE 13.2 Personalized Grammar Lesson

Bob, we have been studying semicolons in class (see notes for Week 7). You used a semicolon wrongly in this sentence: "Imigrants are what help make America be America; by being a multicultural society standing united." Semicolons are only used in the following cases:

- When linking two independent clauses into one complete sentence
  - *Immigrants are what help make America be America; immigrants create a multicultural society where people stand united.*
- When linking two independent clauses where one has a conjunctive adverb or transitional phrase
  - *Immigrants are what help make America be America; because of immigrants, America is a multicultural society.*
- When two independent clauses are joined by a coordinating conjunction and the clauses already are punctuated with commas or when the clauses are lengthy
  - *Immigrants are the people who created America; and immigrants, over the years, have welcomed new immigrants to this country and have created a united multicultural society.*
- In a list or series when one of the items contains commas
  - *Immigrants with various cultural backgrounds, customs, and languages; divergent points of view; and numerous past experiences in political and social situations have created a multicultural, American society.*

(continued)

OWI WRITING EXAMPLE 13.2 *(continued)*

Notice, please, that I corrected the spelling of "immigrants" in these examples. Most important, **notice that each new sentence has different words and a different meaning** because your original sentence cannot use a semicolon as you wrote it.

Reread your sentence. **Decide** whether you want a sentence that uses a semicolon. Then, **rewrite** the sentence to make your meaning clearer.

small potential gain in Bob's writing; yet, without that effort, Bob would not understand the template lesson. Therefore, templates — and any written response that is developed with revision in mind — need to be used with care regarding the overall goals for the student's writing growth. As OWI Writing Example 13.4 reveals, this grammar lesson is not one that I would recommend in Bob's case.

Templates also create problems when the wrong information is copied into a student's document because doing so can lead students to feel like they are not seen as individuals. Therefore, it is important to personalize any templates by making sure that the response has been edited for the student's name, assignment details that might signal a prior response to a different student, and examples particular to the student's own essay.

Personalization through examples from the students' own essays helps to reach students, particularly in asynchronous essay responses. Given the potential for miscommunication when students read instructional text, using examples is a fruitful way to respond directly to students and to keep their reading focused on their own writing. Short lessons use student writing examples and can address a wide variety of global and local concerns in the writing, such as thesis clarification, content development, organization, quotation citation practices, subordination, grammar, usage, and mechanics. These types of lessons are detailed in *The Online Writing Conference: A Guide for Teachers and Tutors* (Hewett 2015).

Use the Four-Step Intervention Process

Formative feedback should include some kind of short lesson for online writing students to enact. In writing lessons with examples for students, a useful way to "teach, not talk" is to provide problem-centered lessons for students with example problems and solutions from their own writing. In the Instructor's Study Guide, an appendix to *The Online Writing Conference: A Guide for Teachers and Tutors*, I identify a four-step intervention process that sets up such a lesson:

1. Identify the problem.
2. Explain why it is a problem.

3. Demonstrate how to address (revise) and avoid the problem.

4. Give the student something to do in revision—a way to change the writing and an instruction to try a revision action. (209)

This four-step "what, why, how, do" process is used in all of the reading-to-learn chapters in Part Two. When I am teaching online through my response to essays, I think: *what, why, how, do.*

These are the four steps of the writing intervention process:

1. *What* is the problem?

2. *Why* is it a problem?

3. *How* can this problem be revised and avoided?

4. *Do* these steps to address the problem.

Because I always use this format with students, they come to expect that I will be teaching them something specific for a revision. If they do not understand the lesson, they know they can connect with me via IM chat or e-mail. When they express that they need to talk or if I believe it would be helpful, I arrange a phone call with them to sort out questions. Changing modalities often can help to reboot the learning.

Fascinatingly, my research suggests that some students do not easily make the move from being told there is a problem in their writing to actually revising it. Such students not only need personalized problem-centered instruction in how to develop their writing but a prompt to try the strategy. Carl Anderson (2000) explains his "have a go" approach for younger children as a way to give them the authority to try something new because he saw a writing conference as both interpersonal and instructional, teaching a specific writing problem for the student to address in revision. Left to their own devices, some college students in online settings are not proactive in reading what the teacher writes and then in following through. Perhaps this trait is connected to the mixed adolegogical traits of OWI students in their connections to learning and to learning online. To prompt action and forward movement, I suggest nudging students to take some kind of action with a clearly directive statement like the one provided to Bob at the end of the template lesson in OWI Writing Example 13.2.

To illustrate more fully how to use a problem-centered approach, response OWI Writing Example 13.3 is contrasted with OWI Writing Example 13.4, which provides written formative feedback from an asynchronous setting that teachers can adapt for a voice-based response. The student, Bob, is the author of the sentence addressed in OWI Writing Examples 13.1 and 13.2.

OWI WRITING EXAMPLE 13.3 Original Feedback Strategy

Overall Comment: How interesting to learn that you and your family have such direct ties to Italy. I hope you're able to maintain connections with family there. You've picked such an important topic, and I agree that we all benefit when we are able to learn from each other.

Thesis/Organization: Your thesis may actually be in the conclusion. Consider that the introduction uses definitions and explanations of what it is to be American that actually can also be applied to people who live in other countries who also love their countries and live in countries with people from different ethnic and racial backgrounds. Your point about not denying immigrants the choice to come and live in America is a good one, which could be supported with the points that these immigrants are just like other Americans who love their country, support family values, etc. The points in the essay would actually do well to support the argument that immigrants benefit, as opposed to detracting from, U.S. culture.

Documentation: With a hot topic argument such as you have chosen, you are wise to support your arguments from outside sources. You also have the right idea to let the reader know when you stop using a paraphrase from an outside source, but you must let the reader know when you begin borrowing. Otherwise, the reader may think that every sentence from the beginning of the paragraph to the citation is taken from the parenthetical source. Don't forget to consistently place the periods after the parenthetical citation and to add a "Works Cited" page.

Style: Paragraph 3, which has the example about the businessman, offers a good example, but using so many short sentences negatively impacts your style. Your reader might not take your ideas seriously if you have a section which sounds choppy as if you cannot write well. Take those sentences and blend them together to make one to two longer sentences. Use subordinators (*while, when, because*) and coordinators (*as well as, but, also*).

Grammar: The essay has some serious spelling problems, but not all of them can be fixed by using Spell Check. Some are problems with homophones. After using Spell Check, read through the essay from the beginning and carefully consider the spellings of these words. You also have subordination problems. The essay has small grammar errors, such as the use of a capital letter (see paragraph 3) where it isn't needed and the failure to italicize a journal title (also in paragraph 3).

Immigrants and Immigration

What is an American? An American is someone who loves thier country and the people in it, and believes in bettering thier own lives as

well as the lives of those around them. [Don't forget to use spell check.]
Does it really matter that these individuals may be of German or Chinese
desent? No, not at all; thier ethnic background has nothing to do with
being American. To say that the majority of people in the United States
have some sort of tie with an ethnic background from a different country
would be a safe asumption. This is what makes our American Culture
unique. [I agree with this point, but consider that you can make this
point about people living in other countries such as China. Are there
other qualities which would make one "American"?] Immigrants bring
to our country strong family structures and strong morals. Foreigners also
help our economy prosper (Julian L. Simon). [I'm not sure how much
of this paragraph is being attributed to Julian Simon. See the note
above.] Imigrants are what help make America be America; by being a
multicultural society standing united. [Review semicolon use; this one
causes a fragmented sentence.]

In todays American society it is not uncommon for their to be families broken up by divorce or other domestic disturbances. [Do you see a
place for an apostrophe in this sentence?] However, immigrants seem to
have much more stronger family values. (Rocky Arcadi) [Is the additional
modifier "more" needed in the previous sentence?] For many immigrants,
family comes first over everything; for many of them family is all they
have. This is especially true of traditional developing societies. Many of
these newcomers have strong traditions and beliefs wich are strict and are
instilled in thier children. By immigrants comming to America with these
type of beliefs and strong traditions it sets good examples for our western
civilization. [This sentence has the error "faulty subordination." See the
note above.] By receiving new cultures to our society it is a chance to
absorb thier rules and respect they have for one another. [After you correct the sentence above, correct this one similarly.] This is ideal to help
restore our family values.

It's been said that "immigration is a threat to our economy." [Don't
use contractions in formal writing.] This statement is so absurd.
Immigration increases purchasing thereby, increases demand for labor.
Immigration not only takes jobs, but also creates them. (Wall Street
Journal) [Read this sentence aloud: "thereby" requires a gerund
(increasing, not increases).] For instance, A man comes to America
from China. [This sentence is a fragment. Can you join it to the next
sentence?] This man opens a small Chinese resteraunt. The resteraunt
makes outstanding buisness. Ten years latter this man owns twelve resteraunts and employees three hundred Americans. Stories like that happen
all the time, wich help our economy. [This section has many spelling
errors.]

(continued)

OWI WRITING EXAMPLE 13.3 (*continued*)

Immigrants are what help America be America. They say that America is just a melting pot. [Who says this? Let your reader know exactly what you mean.] This is what makes our country unique. We have many cultures, many Ideas, and traditions, but all of us have the same dream. That Dream is the American Dream. [Watch capitalization. The previous two sentences have at least one word which doesn't require capitalization.]

The same dream that keeps Americans in America and immigrants to come here. By haveing a variety of cultures helps people understand and learn from each other. [Faulty subordination.] Taking immigration away would hurt this country more than economicly, but, socially also. [This sentence has some comparative words (more than) when it needs a contrastive phrase (not only x, but also y).]

Immigration, I feel is etremly important. Being an Italian American myself, I understand the importance of immigration. My family have traditions and beliefs they teach me, that I'll teach my kids some day. ["Family" is usually thought of as a singular noun, representing one "unit" so your instructor might expect the singular verb "has" here.] Im very proud of background in Italy and America. And no one should be denied the opportunity my parents and I have to be a part of America.

There are many challenges for student readers in essay response OWI Writing Example 13.3. At the least, Bob will have to read the response very closely to catch any formatting cues that indicate the instructor's words versus his. The most obvious formatting cues are the colons after the headings and the use of brackets for the teacher's response. However, the lack of distinguishing features (e.g., colors, highlights, bolded or italicized text) between Bob's writing and the teacher's response embedded in the text can be problematic. One way to address that would be to use the word processing program's marginal Comments feature if Bob does not have any vision impairment that would make reading them difficult and if he is not reading the response through a tablet or android phone, for example.

More important issues include a lack of clear direction in the response. Although the teacher has pleasantly greeted the student, he has not used Bob's name to personalize the response. He has offered feedback in a roughly higher-to-lower order presentation, which is suggestive of an order in which to approach revision. However, the teacher has not taught Bob how to develop the content or repair any problems. There really is no lesson and no use of Bob's own writing to teach. Example problem areas include:

- Asking Bob rhetorical questions or leading questions that reveal lack of semantic integrity. All of the following questions are closed-ended or rhetorical in nature:
  - *Are there other qualities which would make one "American"?*
  - *Do you see a place for an apostrophe in this sentence?*
  - *Is the additional modifier "more" needed in the previous sentence?*
  - *This sentence is a fragment. Can you join it to the next sentence?*
- Telling the student there is faulty subordination without teaching what that is and how to address it in a revision. The same issue occurs when Bob apparently needs a gerund, for example.
- Forgetting to model strong writing by telling Bob not to use contractions in a comment that uses a contraction and using faulty or no punctuation in the comments.
- Failing to include any lesson particular to Bob's most significant writing needs to take this essay into a next step in competency.
- Neglecting to add any kind of action plan or next steps for Bob to work out the revision.

In short, Bob has been left to his own understanding of the feedback, which may be as minimal as his early draft's writing development. In an OWI setting, given the typical lack of interpersonal communication between Bob and his teacher, he is on his own to revise this essay to the best of his abilities. The teacher may believe he has provided Bob with correct and useful feedback, but Bob's ability to fully comprehend the teacher's intentions — to make an accurate cognitive leap between the feedback and his own writing — is minimized by the type of response the teacher has offered and the way that he presented the feedback.

As we easily can see, this essay is highly undeveloped and demonstrates a poor understanding of how to use supporting evidence and sources. Its current thesis also is suspect, as the teacher in OWI Writing Example 13.3 points out by saying, "Consider that the introduction uses definitions and explanations of what it is to be American that actually can also be applied to people who live in other countries who also love their countries and live in countries with people from different ethnic and racial backgrounds." The teacher also rightly stated that the actual thesis might be at the end of the essay ("And no one should be denied the opportunity my parents and I have to be a part of America"). Of course, this essay is riddled with extremely distracting errors. Bob apparently turned it in without so much as a glance, let alone a simple spell check. Nonetheless, aside from asking for that spell check, the teacher does Bob no favor by pointing out errors at this stage.

OWI Writing Example 13.4 demonstrates the strategy I suggest for offering formative feedback in an online setting. My job is much easier than the teacher's job in OWI Writing Example 13.3 because I focus on higher-order concerns alone, leaving out sentence problems better addressed at a later stage of writing. Bob needs the most help with content and organization because without these, there is no essay. Notice that I give him clear guidance on what to do next. He can choose to do it or not. Most students really want to improve their writing, but some will not move forward for a variety of reasons.

In online instruction, there is a need to intervene directly into the writing—possibly more so than in face-to-face settings. Notice that I do not do the work for Bob, I do not tell him how to "fix" his essay, I do not "appropriate" his writing, and I do not leave him floundering with phrases and suggestions that he will not understand. I use appropriate writing-oriented vocabulary at his vocabulary level. There are no rhetorical questions or potentially confusing conditional statements. The response has semantic integrity.

Notice, too, that I use formatting in terms of white space, boldface, italics, underlines, numbers, and highlighting to help Bob see my points. My headings and comments are signaled by boldface. I want to be as clear as possible about what I am asking him to do to improve his writing while not creating the appearance of a coloring book. Such issues of formatting well are presented in depth in Chapter 14.

OWI WRITING EXAMPLE 13.4 Recommended Feedback Strategy

Hi Bob,

Essay Strengths:

I have read your rough essay draft. You seem to feel very strongly that it is a privilege to be an immigrant in America. Your passion about this topic makes me want to read this essay. Because you are so invested in it, I found myself wanting to read more.

Content Development:

My sense of your current thesis comes from your last paragraph. You seem to be saying that:

America should be open to immigrants because of XYZ.

"XYZ," a fill-in-the-blank placeholder, is your primary reason for this statement. Any essay needs a clear thesis, so even if I have not understood your primary position, use this lesson to help you write a clear thesis statement about your position and to provide supporting detail.

Let us pretend that your thesis has to do with the need to open America's borders to immigrants. Such a position needs reasons. Why do you think what you do? What evidence exists for that thinking?

Arguments have particular patterns that readers expect. One pattern is to provide at least one major reason for your thesis per paragraph. Then, in each paragraph, there should be supporting evidence (such as examples, statistics, anecdotes, and authority-based statements). Therefore, paragraph 1 should contain:

Reason 1: Statement of reason. Applicable evidence.

Another paragraph should contain:

Reason 2: Statement of reason. Applicable evidence.

And do this similarly through all of your reasons. Sometimes, there will be more than one paragraph dealing with a particular reason, but the evidence is not helpful if it does not support, justify, explain, or otherwise illustrate a reason for the thesis. If your paragraphs are really short, the chances are that you have not supported your reasons very thoroughly.

Write a clear thesis and well-stated reasons for that thesis in an outline form first. That will make the essay easier to revise.

Source Development and Documentation:

Bob, you will need to check with your handbook on page 245 for guidance on APA style. There also is a video lesson at http://www.usingsources.ourclass. Use this lesson to help you cite sources.

The key to using any kind of documentation — which I see you have tried to do — is to indicate whether the evidence you are providing comes from an authority and precisely what parts of your text come from that authority. For example, you say:

"Immigration increases purchasing thereby, increases demand for labor. Immigration not only takes jobs, but also creates them. (Wall Street Journal)"

It is not clear what information came from the *Wall Street Journal*. One way to address this problem is to introduce the paraphrase and use the title of the article or the author's name:

According to John Brown (2012) of the *Wall Street Journal*, XYZ ("Immigration").

Here, the XYZ represents what exactly is paraphrased (or quoted) from the article. Use the correct author's name and the article title — not the fake one I provided here. Do you see how this process works? If not, ask me for help through our chat feature or use your journal to send questions to me.

Grammar and Mechanics:

It seems clear that this draft is still very rough, Bob. I see that you still need to spell check and proofread. Please do those actions before sending the next draft to me. That way, you will be providing the best draft possible, which will help me to teach you better because I will be able to see what merely is a mistake versus what you do not know how to do.

(continued)

OWI WRITING EXAMPLE 13.4 (*continued*)

Next Steps for Revision:

1. Find your thesis in the current draft. Move the thesis to the beginning of the essay. Usually it is provided in the introduction; often it is the last sentence of an introduction.

2. Locate your reasons and evidence. Number them in the order you want to present them. Develop more reasons if you do not yet have three to four of them.

3. Revise the essay with this thesis and set of reasons.

4. Work on the documentation with the required style.

5. Spell check, proofread, and present your next draft to me in its <u>best possible form</u>. The revision is **DUE March 14.**

Have fun in revising this interesting topic!

Immigrants and Immigration

What is an American? An American is someone who loves thier country and the people in it, and believes in bettering thier own lives as well as the lives of those around them. Does it really matter that these individuals may be of German or Chinese desent? No, not at all; thier ethnic background has nothing to do with being American. To say that the majority of people in the United States have some sort of tie with an ethnic background from a different country would be a safe asumption. **[I think many readers will agree with this statement, Bob.]** This is what makes our American Culture unique. Immigrants bring to our country strong family structures and strong morals. Foreigners also help our economy prosper (Julian L. Simon). Imigrants are what help make America be America; by being a multicultural society standing united.

In todays American society it is not uncommon for their to be families broken up by divorce or other domestic disturbances. However, immigrants seem to have much more stronger family values. (Rocky Arcadi) For many immigrants, family comes first over everything; for many of them family is all they have. This is especially true of traditional developing societies. Many of these newcomers have strong traditions and beliefs wich are strict and are instilled in thier children. By immigrants comming to America with these type of beliefs and strong traditions it sets good examples for our western civilization. By receiving new cultures to our society it is a chance to absorb thier rules and respect they have for one another. This is ideal to help restore our family values.

It's been said that "immigration is a threat to our economy." **[Who made this statement?]** This statement is so absurd. Immigration increases purchasing thereby, increases demand for labor. Immigration not only takes jobs, but also creates them. (Wall Street Journal) For instance,

A man comes to America from China. This man opens a small Chinese resteraunt. The resteraunt makes outstanding buisness. Ten years latter this man owns twelve resteraunts and employees three hundred Americans. Stories like that happen all the time, wich help our economy.

Immigrants are what help America be America. They say that America is just a melting pot. This is what makes our country unique. We have many cultures, many Ideas, and traditions, but all of us have the same dream. That Dream is the American Dream.

The same dream that keeps Americans in America and immigrants to come here. By haveing a variety of cultures helps people understand and learn from each other. Takeing immigration away would hurt this country more than economicly, but, socially also.

Immigration, I feel is etremly important. Being an Italian American myself, I understand the importance of immigration. My family have traditions and beliefs they teach me, that I'll teach my kids some day. Im very proud of background in Italy and America. And no one should be denied the opportunity my parents and I have to be a part of America. [Somewhere in this paragraph, I think, is your essay's thesis — what you want the essay to talk about, Bob. Move that statement or idea to the beginning of your essay as you revise. See my comments above the essay for help.]

TIME AND OWI TEXT-BASED FEEDBACK

OWI Writing Example 13.4 looks like a long response to a student essay, yet it took less than thirty minutes to read the essay and write the response, and it is about equal in length to OWI Writing Example 13.3 given that response's wealth of embedded comments. Thirty minutes, by the way, is about average for me in responding to essays in any medium (except the audio/visual, where I am a little faster). When I used to provide formative feedback by pen on hard copy, I also needed between twenty and thirty minutes per essay, sometimes more. My responses are more complete and comprehensible now that they are structured and typed, not to mention easier to decipher.

Time is a huge issue for OWI instructors — both teachers and tutors — and we are rightly concerned whenever something, including a new response approach, threatens to cause us to expend more time. For example, for teachers who have four classes of twenty students or more per term, thirty minutes per essay response may be more than they can offer, demanding a decrease in what the student is taught through the text-based feedback. It seems important to recognize consciously, though, that such a decrease in teaching is caused directly by the teaching load rather than the text-rich literacy load of OWI.

Writing a problem-centered essay response always will take longer than speaking it, but a text-based response has its own benefits. Written text forces instructors to be targeted and focused in our feedback. We cannot respond to everything in the essay, as research has suggested we should not do. A problem-centered response requires clear examples, and these are easier to produce and articulate in text than through speech. Students can reread this feedback as often as needed, and it forms an individualized lesson that they can take into future writing projects.

There is no panacea for making helpful, cogent written feedback altogether easier and faster. Before we can be good OWI teachers and tutors, as instructors, we first need to know composition theory and pedagogy; understand how students may write and revise; have vocabulary for talking about writing to students; and be flexible, thoughtful writers ourselves. The first key to good online writing instruction is good writing instruction. As teachers and tutors, we need to study, read, and practice to become the best writing instructors we can be. Then, we will be able to see students' core writing challenges more quickly and develop a variety of strategies to help students address revision—all with text. The second key to good OWI is presenting that textual instruction well—with semantic integrity and in a personalized, problem-centered manner.

Even without a magic potion (other than hard work) to make writing feedback easier and faster, there are some helpful strategies for instructional time management. These strategies include the following:

- Practice reading student writing to identify the major problem areas quickly. For example, if the essay is too short for the assignment or has multiple two- to three-sentence paragraphs, the major problem likely is content development as evidenced by brevity and lack of detail. For another example, if there is no clear thesis at the beginning, quickly check the end of the essay to see whether the student has written herself into a thesis. If so, then guidance on how to place the thesis earlier in the essay and how to revise the essay to support the new thesis will be the most important goal.

- Offer each student individualized feedback for one core writing issue using a focused problem-centered lesson. Then, write a lesson that uses text and audio or audio/video to provide a longer tutorial to all students in the class regarding a widespread issue. Such issues often are more general to the entire class, such as addressing the essay assignment's style or presentation issues, but they also might involve common content-level issues. Appendix B provides an example of such a response to the entire class.

- Add a rubric to the response. Some students respond well to rubrics that help them to identify weak and strong writing in their particular essays. An impressionistic rubric can help students to see competencies in terms of developmental levels: needs work, acceptable, and above average (see Appendix B; also see Hewett, *Online Writing*, 2015). Rubrics also can be used for providing grades or other ranges of competency. They are well used online with both written and spoken responses to flesh out a fuller feedback product that has teaching potential.
- Use individualized, personalized templates regarding frequently occurring higher-order and lower-order concerns, but do so cautiously and with respect for the student's likely ability to make the cognitive leap from your examples to her writing.
- Stagger when you collect essays among multiple classes to help with time.

For teachers who still worry about the time it takes to respond to writing in online settings, it may be useful to calculate the actual time differential between your current methods and a problem-centered, personalized response. Time yourself for grading five papers and find the average. How long does it take you to read and respond to the average student's essay using pen and hard copy? How long does it take you to read and respond to the average student's essay using a typed response strategy? Is it longer than thirty minutes? Is the response as thorough as what you can write using typed text? Does the response address all of the areas you want to address? If you find that you are already in the twenty- to thirty-minute range for essay reading and response, give the problem-centered response strategy demonstrated in OWI Writing Example 13.4 a try. At first, it may take you a little longer to think in a different manner about student essays, but you will become faster as you practice. Also, you will learn quickly what the student population in your own institutional setting prefers and needs regarding learning styles, so you can adjust your response depth, type, and amount of feedback as necessary.

As we consider and perfect strategies for teaching students through written feedback, we should keep in mind that, according to Dennis Baron: "reading is in itself an act of rewriting. As our minds process the words we read, we create meanings that a writer may never have intended or even imagined possible." Semantic integrity can help us at least be sure of our intentions in the written instruction, which is a necessary start in helping students read to more accurately infer our instructional meaning.

14

Writing Readable OWI Assignments

WHAT ARE READABLE OWI ASSIGNMENTS AND WHY ARE THEY IMPORTANT?

Readable OWI writing assignments use the qualities of coherence and semantic integrity described in Chapter 12. They are accessible to all students in the class, and they provide clear instruction about what students need to know to succeed in their writing. Additionally, they are constructed for optimal clarity through strong presentation skills.

Providing readable OWI assignments is not as much about *what we ask students to write* as it is about *how we present those assignments to students*. Instructors may have to use predeveloped content unique to the institution or they may have freedom to write their own teaching content about writing practices, such as what constitutes an argument and how to go about writing one. Either way, we teach students to write through what they read in terms of content for discussion/writing and lessons about writing. As writing instructors in online settings, we also are writers. As writers, we are tasked with using clear expository writing and process analysis in developing assignments. Well-written assignments help students to put those resources and lessons into action.

If the written assignment is dense, however, students may not read it well enough to understand the goals and requirements. They may not engage the comprehension themes that Part Two encourages for reading information and content material. If the written assignment is thin and undetailed, students may not have enough detail to understand what to do. Left to their own understanding of the assignment, their writing may go far astray of what the teacher expects—the problem of a mixed or unclear message on the teacher's part. If the written assignment is unreadable due to presentation style, again students will be likely to miss important parts of the assignment. In the online instructional setting, typically there is no synchronous explanation of an assignment, such as writing teachers might provide during onsite class time. Even an explanatory video, which is helpful, may not be viewed in its entirety or be as clear as students need.

These issues are the teacher's responsibility to avoid and, if necessary, to rectify. For instance, the repercussions of unviewed or faulty audio/video assignment explanations can be minimized by an accompanying, clearly written assignment text because the written assignment remains the primary way that online writing students receive their instructions for written work. The goal of this chapter is to assist teachers with providing readable (i.e., focused, semantically clear, and helpful) OWI assignments. We can help students to read the assignment well by writing it clearly in the first place.

To anchor this chapter, here are some useful guidelines for writing and presenting strong assignments that can be used fairly universally. The following general qualities of strong writing assignments reflect contributions from educators nationwide and are equally valuable in onsite and online settings:[1]

1. Do not use intimidating diction, but explain the assignment in straightforward, clear language.

2. Write assignments that encourage complete responses, informed opinions, and thoughtfully supported arguments.

3. Be specific about what you want students to address and how they are to do so if their process matters as well as their content.

4. Provide a reasonable scope for the students' writing level, knowledge, and course expectations.

5. Clearly indicate the levels of generality and specificity needed to succeed in the assignment.

6. Do not assume knowledge — especially cultural or life-based knowledge — that students may not have.

7. Pose one or two — versus numerous — questions that can lead to a coherent response rather than a series of barely connected paragraphs.

8. Use writing topics that do not presuppose the rightness or wrongness of particular points of view.

9. Avoid requiring writing that is too personal or that asks students to reveal too much of their lives.

10. Do not ask student writers to pit themselves against professional writers, but do allow them to model their writing on that of others.

---

[1]These qualities are adapted from a document developed by Muriel Harris of Purdue University's Online Writing Lab and shared on the WCenter Listserv with general permission for everyone to use and adapt as needed. See also Anson (1997); Bardine (1999); and Glover and Brown (2006).

11. Provide students with an audience, purpose, and occasion for their writing context and/or teach them how to do so to contextualize their writing.

12. Be clear about the audience for the writing by not, for example, having contradictory or conflicting audiences. Students may, of course, need to learn to write to primary, secondary, and tertiary audiences in the same essay.

13. Emphasize content over grammar, usage, and mechanics.

14. Teach students how to format to enhance and guide their writing as opposed to placing formatting rules over the writing in importance.

HOW CAN WE WRITE READABLE OWI ASSIGNMENTS?

This section provides a number of strategies for writing readable OWI assignments. Such strategies generally apply to written instructions for any writing course, but in the online setting, where all communications are text-rich, they become more critical for student success.

Be Straightforward

The first principle for these strategies is to be straightforward about what is expected and how to succeed in the assignment. If students do not know the requirements for success, they rightfully will be frustrated and they may have reasonable grounds for complaint if they fail to meet their academic goals.

How do we know whether we have met the mark of sufficient straightforwardness? One way is to ask a student to read and provide feedback prior to assigning the piece. A great place to get that kind of feedback is through the onsite or online writing center/lab (OWL), where students often work as peer tutors. However, professional tutors also can provide another set of eyes (those extra senses that we tell our students about when we ask them to share their writing) for feedback. It is true that everyone needs an editor. Where better to get that help than with a brief visit to the people who are hired to assist our own writing students, many of whom are students themselves?

OWI Writing Example 14.1 demonstrates a discussion (also called a "conference" in some institutions) assignment or prompt. It is less than straightforward in its directions.[2]

---

[2]OWI Writing Examples 14.1 and 14.2 were provided for this book by Professor Andrew J. Cavanaugh (director of writing at University of Maryland University College, a public, primarily online university), and they were altered with his permission.

> **OWI WRITING EXAMPLE 14.1 Nonstraightforward Discussion Prompt**
>
> Please watch the following two short video clips on the Chevy Volt and the Nissan Leaf.
>
> http://cnettv.cnet.com/nissan-leaf-vs-chevy-volt/9742-1_53-50089627 .html?tag=api
>
> http://www.youtube.com/watch?v=wfjzXId4hRc&feature=related
>
> You may want to watch them two or three times each, perhaps even writing down some notes. After watching the videos, please complete the following tasks:
>
> 1. Write ten sentences that compare the Chevy Volt to the Nissan Leaf. Make sure your grammar is correct.
> 2. Write a short outline of how you might organize the writing assignment if you were writing a comparison-contrast essay on the Volt and the Leaf.

The assignment asks students to watch two videos and then do some writing. It is fairly specific about how much to write, but the assignment fails to place this work in the context of what is happening in the class overall, is suggestive rather than directive about the need to watch the videos more than once and to take notes, uses conditional language, and does not provide necessary information like a due date or where to post the assignment.

By the way, the assigned videos do not have transcripts appended for accessibility. Teachers using this assignment would need to create a transcript or choose other videos to make the assignment fully accessible and inclusively available to a wider range of learners.

OWI Writing Example 14.2 is a revision of the assignment that clarifies some of the problems found in the version above. Notice how this new version builds coherence through word repetition and consistency of terminology, which creates a more straightforward prompt.

> **OWI WRITING EXAMPLE 14.2 Straightforward Discussion Prompt**
>
> Conference Exercise: Finding Similarities and Differences
>
> Before completing this exercise, watch Lectures 1 and 2 from Module 3. Use information from those lectures for the following exercise, which is designed to prepare you for an upcoming essay assignment where you will use your skills of comparing and contrasting.

(continued)

OWI WRITING EXAMPLE 14.2 (*continued*)

Watch the following two short video clips on the Chevy Volt and the Nissan Leaf.

http://cnettv.cnet.com/nissan-leaf-vs-chevy-volt/9742-1_53-50089627
.html?tag=api (5:43 minutes)

http://www.youtube.com/watch?v=wfjzXId4hRc&feature=related
(3:32 minutes)

Watch the videos three or more times. Take notes about how the Chevy Volt and the Nissan Leaf are similar and different.

After watching the videos, complete the following tasks and post them to the class conference space under this assignment:

1. Write ten grammatically strong sentences that compare the Chevy Volt to the Nissan Leaf. Use the grammatical rules you learned in Lectures 1 and 2 as well as from Chapter 18 in our handbook.

2. How would you develop a comparison-contrast analysis of the Chevy Volt and the Nissan Leaf? Write a one-page outline of how you would organize such an essay. (Hint: The first video from cnet.com provides a model comparison-contrast analysis.)

Post your response by Tuesday, March 8. Respond to at least two other students' answers by explaining how your outline is similar to or different from theirs. Where your outline is different, indicate how and why you think that difference occurred. Responses are **DUE** by **Thursday, March 10.**

The revised assignment is more complete in terms of what students are to do, which makes it a bit longer. More important, it is contextualized in terms of what students are to learn from doing the work.

Try Out Your Own Writing Assignments

In an online setting where opportunities for additional explanation often are left to chance inquiries on the part of students—and then often provided in writing for them to read—it is best to find out for ourselves precisely what completing our assignments involves. As the teacher, it may not be necessary to complete an entire assignment, but it is useful to read and try out our directions as if we were the intended student audience.

First, let us begin with inclusivity and accessibility:

- Is this assignment fully accessible to all of my students?
- Have I ignored the nature of any common learning styles?

- What additional materials, such as images and video, could I provide to improve accessibility?
- Will anyone need more time to accomplish the tasks given accessibility issues?

Second, if research is required, what does the work actually entail to complete that phase of the assignment?

- Is it clear just where I need to go in the online library to find documents?
- Where (and from whom) can I find help with the library portion of this assignment?
- How long does it take me to find the right kinds of documents for the assignment? How long might it take my students to do the same work?
- Are there particular key words that work better than others? If so, is there any learning-based reason not to share these with students to expedite their work or focus their efforts?
- How many sources have I asked for? Are these too few, enough, or too many given the scope of the assignment?
- Are there sufficient scholarly sources immediately available (e.g., versus magazines or websites) to meet students' needs? Will online students be able to obtain the kinds of sources they need immediately through file transfer or will they need to wait for interlibrary loan? Is there enough time planned in the assignment for such a wait?

We need only ask these questions of our written assignments a few times before learning how to avoid pitfalls during the assignment development itself.

For another example, try engaging the assignment by writing an outline or rough draft using your written instructions. After doing so, ask yourself:

- Is there anything about this assignment that students at this course level may have trouble reading or interpreting?
- How long does this outline or draft process take me?
- Are there any steps in the process that do not make sense, that could be eliminated, that need to be enumerated, or that otherwise require some change on my part?
- Knowing that my expertise is much higher than the students', what does my outline/draft writing tell me about the level of the assignment?
- Am I asking for too much or not enough given the outcomes I want to promote?
- Using my writing experience with this assignment as a gauge, what do I learn about the amount of time it might take students to accomplish it? How would it help them if I share this information regarding time management? If so, how should I provide guidance for estimating time

needed to complete the assignment without putting too firm a number on it and possibly leading students to stop at that time and go no further?

Clearly, having direct experience with our own assignments can provide useful information about what we are asking of online writing students whose tasks are the same as onsite students but who are learning what to do and how to do so primarily by text.

Offer Ample Examples

An important way to write readable assignments is to provide examples of strong and weak writing that should emerge from the assignments themselves. Using the LMS as a place to post such examples eliminates the paper waste of providing hard copies to onsite students and makes it possible to provide many more examples to all students. Teachers can write these models themselves or use examples from student writing—with the student's permission and with the identifying information scrubbed from the texts. When providing models, it is helpful to explain why they are strong or weak examples of writing through marginal comments, embedded comments, and/or a summary statement. If a rubric will be used in the class, using the same rubric for the example can help students to understand the assessment priorities better.

My favorite way to provide a model for students is to write for them at the beginning of the course (Hewett 2010b). Before working in my first computer-supported classroom, I accomplished this exercise as a one-hour chalkboard demonstration. In the online course, this project is our first work together after an introductory icebreaker exercise, and it takes place over the course of one week.

Students provide me with a series of possible topics of interest to them, which gives them a stake in the writing and an impetus to read what I write outside of merely doing an assignment. I choose one of the topics, shape it to make it easy for me to write without too much research, and then I write a rough outline, or "zero draft." That draft, as shown in OWI Writing Example 14.3, demonstrates how free-flowing thinking can lead to ideas for a longer piece of writing.

OWI WRITING EXAMPLE 14.3 Zero Draft of Teacher Writing

Zero Draft

- Cell phones changing our lives/technology changing our lives through communication
- Technology changing human communication

- Books, magazines, blogs, wikis, Google docs
- Computer communication through IM, Skype, video/audio feeds on certain sites like WebEx
- Rotary phone, touchtone phone, cordless phone, cellular phone, smartphone
- ICQ, instant messaging, text messaging (and changing communication rules and standards), Twitter, Facebook
- Letter writing, postcards, one phone in the house (to two or three)
- What has changed? When we talk, how we talk, why we talk, what we talk about, whom we talk with, where we talk

Then, I write a preliminary draft and post both as separate, clearly labeled files for students' review. Allowing sufficient time for online students to sign into the LMS, over the next three or four days, they provide me with feedback using marginal or embedded comments to which I respond, as shown in OWI Writing Example 14.4. Example comments from students typically are thoughtful as they try their hands at critiquing the teacher they hardly know. It is a dialogue and an exercise in trust, so my responses to their comments are honest, yet deeply respectful, as the following examples show. My responses to the comments are presented to them in boldface, italicized text as my standard way to distinguish my words from theirs.

OWI WRITING EXAMPLE 14.4 Student Comments on Teacher Writing

- Depending on the nature of your writing, citations would be necessary for some of the things you've mentioned in your paper, such as direct quotes or statistics to support your claims. Since this essay is used to teach us how to develop our writing from the "zero draft" phase to the "final draft," I would also like to see how some citations would fit into the paper without losing its personality. *I'll look for where sources might be helpful.*
- Since the cell phone has changed how communication is being done, including information about the pros and cons of cell phone usage might give the reader a more well-rounded appreciation for the device. The flow of the material was very easy to follow and engaging. *I'm not sure whether this suggestion would take me off track; I'll think about it.*

(continued)

OWI WRITING EXAMPLE 14.4 (*continued*)

- Also for four pages, there was almost a whole page spent on the initial house telephones. I also believe there should be more statistical information on demographics of who is using the social media technology (texting, video conferencing, Skype), i.e., college students, high school students, or middle aged parents. Also, what social media is being used for, such as work, social planning or entertainment? *I am not writing a long paper, so I have to control how much is said about particular ideas. But I do need to address readers' needs for a balanced essay.*

My next step is to use the Track Changes feature to provide a new draft of the document. Of course, my revision may go through more readings and revisions than the average student's text does in one step of revision, but my tracking of changes demonstrates in ways my words never could what genuinely deep revision looks like. OWI Writing Example 14.5 is one paragraph from the longer example paper that students received. I embedded bracketed comments in the text to demonstrate to students what I was thinking as I revised, and I used underlines to mark the new material. The original tracked changes showed deletions as well.

OWI WRITING EXAMPLE 14.5 Revised Teacher-Writing Paragraph

People often remark that cell phones have changed our lives. They are everywhere, after all, <u>and they are used for many different forms of communication. They are in our pockets or purses at all times.</u> [Rearranged the content to allow for a stronger statement about driving with cell phones.] They are in our hands at dinner and <u>often</u> when driving<u>, triggering a rise of automobile "crashes caused by drivers using cell phones . . . from 636,000 in 2003 to 1.6 million in 2008"</u> (CBSNews, 2010). [Added some factual research to strengthen the logos and ethos.] <u>Now that some</u> cell phone<u>s are</u> waterproof<u>, it is not impossible to find one in the shower and the swimming pool, places once reserved for more private or sports-like activities than talking.</u> [Ah, there are waterproof phones, so I needed to fix that issue.] These <u>mobile</u> phones are so ubiquitous that states have passed laws about holding them while driving, and movie theaters and churches post notices about turning them off <u>to avoid disturbing the event</u>. Cell phones have, indeed, changed our lives. <u>While technology has always affected human communication, it is arguable that the cell phone, as a descendant of the telephone, is one of the most life-changing of technological wonders.</u>

Finally, I provide students with a file that represents a presentation draft ready for others to view. The entire lesson takes me several hours to complete, but these hours are well worth my time. An example of the instructor's own writing process with an explanation of all the work engages students immediately and provides them with a model far more effective than telling students what to do in an expository or list fashion. To make this exercise even more dynamic, one might use such audio/video technology as Camtasia's screen-capture program to show some of the typing in process. The exercise stays with students throughout the course, and it can be referred to in future lessons and feedback to essays as an example. Additionally, it has the added benefit of demonstrating that instructors also are writers who have to think on their feet and risk peer commentary to improve their writing.

Use Redundancy to Help Students Read

Another strategy for writing readable OWI assignments is to build in redundancy. As the CCCC OWI Committee's position statement (2013) and Warnock (2009) suggest, we can provide students with helpful redundancy by placing assignments in the most obvious portals in the LMS. Give students multiple entry points into the documents they most need for reference. For example, always use the "Assignments" portal for assignments and the "Discussion" or "Conferences" feature for shorter, group exercises that require everyone's participation. Then, if students also are going to be discussing their writing in small groups, post the assignment in an appropriate "Group Work" portal as well as in the "Assignments" portal. It is useful to provide a link to the assignment when discussing the assignment at any time in your class notes or other communications to students. Make it as easy to find the assignment as possible. While this redundancy means that if you make any changes to your assignment file, you may need to replace the file in every portal in which you have posted it, the additional few minutes of work will be worthwhile. Providing all students with easy access to the documents they need reduces nuisance e-mails asking where to find such files, decreasing that level of interpersonal contact and creating an opening for more meaningful contact.

PRESENTATION THROUGH FORMATTING AND VISUAL CUES

A final writing strategy for this chapter is about presentation of assignments and other teaching materials. Strong examples for how to visually present teaching materials in readable, comprehensible ways abound in technical communication textbooks (see, for example, Markel 2012) and texts about writing for the Web. For example, Usability.gov provides an excellent web page with insights and examples for strong web-based formatting.[3] These resources are helpful to the digital-era student who is steeped in online communication strategies and who will expect the OWC to look more like digital communications than traditional textbooks or other print-based discourse.

Another resource for presentation methods is a document design method called SPD.[4] The three primary elements of SPD are visual space (i.e., showing relationship among elements by virtue of their distance), visual progression (i.e., sequencing demonstrated through alignment, symbols, and headings), and visual differentiation (i.e., parts indicated through type color, weight, font, and size).

Qualities of strong formatting that engages SPD include the following:

GOOD USE OF WHITE SPACE Leave plenty of white space on any document that students may choose to read online rather than from the printed page. With adequate white space, the reader's eyes will go to the printed text and see it as manageable.

Short, chunky paragraphs are better for online written presentation than the lengthier, scholarship-type paragraphs frequently found in Chapters 1 and 2, for example. The paragraphs in Part Two's example assignments are chunked for student-level readability. Although students do need to learn to read and analyze lengthier text, the instructional text they receive should be more reader friendly given its transactional function of teaching.

Addition of visual components like photographs, drawings, and other imagery can help balance text with white space when developing instructional texts. Such visual elements as text, layout, and concision through spare text and lists may increase the likelihood of people reading a text. Furthermore, headings and subheadings also are known guides for readers, providing outlines of the information presented. Instructional text of any type is best presented with subject headers to keep student readers on track.

THOUGHTFUL USE OF FORMATTING ELEMENTS Use bullets, numbers, boldface, italics, underlining, and such format elements freely, yet thoughtfully. When using bullets, plan the text so that numbers are not also needed; instead, plan your writing to include one or the other and have a reason for your choice. For example, use numbers for lists of elements where order in the list is important. When you need to emphasize something through a font enhancement, choose whether to use boldface, italics, or underlining and then use that style throughout the document. Remember that you not only are teaching students with these elements but also presenting model writing with every

---

[3]http://www.usability.gov/methods/design_site/writing4web.html.
[4]Provided by Professor David Taylor (2013) of University of Maryland University College.

document and instruction you provide. Use of colors and highlights should follow these guidelines as well, keeping accessibility concerns in mind for students with vision challenges.

APPROPRIATE USE OF ICONS AND FORMATTING TOOLS Word processing programs have a number of tools that make our jobs easier. Manually spacing instead of using tabs to paragraph, for example, can lead to nonstandard, sloppy-looking paragraphs. Using the available keys, icons, and shortcuts (e.g., paragraphing tabs, indentations, margins, rulers, tables, charts, and the like) helps in preparing professional-looking documents. All students need such documents for readability and models, but adult students particularly will appreciate a professional-looking text to ensure that their professors know at least as much about writing as they do.

The confidence-building exercise in OWI Writing Example 14.6 demonstrates some of these strong formatting features as ways of communicating clearly to students what they need to learn. Elements of OWI Writing Example 14.6 include modest uses of boldface, italics, numbered lists, and boxed text that call out the key lessons to take away.

OWI WRITING EXAMPLE 14.6 Helpful Use of Formatting

Reading Confidence Builder

In an online writing class, you will find yourself reading more words than in many other college classes. You need to read the syllabus, the teacher's announcements, content lessons about writing, nonfiction and fiction texts to apply to your writing, your writing, peer writing, discussion posts and responses, teacher's feedback, and more. Such helpful formatting practices as shown in OWI Writing Example 14.6 can promote learning.

Your online writing class requires amped-up reading muscles! This exercise will help you to develop those muscles.

Your writing teacher likely will remind you of many of the literacy skills you learned early in your life. Some of these skills are so ingrained in you that you do not realize you do them. As you read the following list, try to remember the first time you became aware of each literacy skill.

1. **Metacognition:** You frequently use your brain to think about what you are reading or thinking.

2. **Schema:** You have a personal set of background knowledge, opinions, and experiences that comprise your unique thinking about the world.

3. **Inference:** You have the ability to take the evidence you find in your reading (or other life experiences), add your schema as a filter, and use them to make educated guesses.

(continued)

OWI WRITING EXAMPLE 14.6 (*continued*)

4. **Questions:** You learned early — before you can remember even — to ask questions about the world; questions represent some of a baby's first communication. You can apply these same questions to your reading before, during, and after you complete it.

5. **Relevance:** You can figure out what is important in what you are reading through a series of context clues and actions like asking questions.

6. **Visualizing:** You can use your imagination, photographs, videos, even music to picture and anchor what you are learning, reading, or writing.

7. **Analyzing:** You can take ideas apart to figure out how they are similar or different, whether one is a cause or an effect, and how or why something happens as it does.

8. **Synthesizing:** You can integrate disparate parts, like the ones you separated in analysis, to pull together new ideas or simply different ones.

These literacy skills all help you to read more fluently and with a greater sense of purpose. When you use them consciously, you can do a better job of reading difficult college-level texts. That is important because sometimes you may struggle with the ideas in the texts or even with giving yourself the necessary time to read them well.

Here are a few more ideas for amping up your reading skill muscles:

Read aloud to reinforce the ideas you are learning. Reading aloud forces us to pay attention to individual words and sentences and how they fit into the whole essay. When you read for context, you make use of all the literacy skills listed above.

In addition, reading silently uses only your vision — one of five senses. Reading aloud uses your vision, hearing, and speech — three of the five senses. (When we read to someone else, by the way, we include their hearing, which increases the number of senses focused on the reading.)

To become more comfortable with reading aloud, **listen to an audio** of your teacher reading. If your teacher does not read to you, listen to an audio of a professional reader for a books on tape presentation. After you have listened, **read something in an exaggerated voice and tone.** Be silly or angry or funny. The idea is to get rid of any possible nervousness about reading aloud and hearing yourself read. You can record your voice and listen to it, but if that thought causes more anxiety, skip this step for now. After you have exaggerated the reading, **read it again** by settling into a reasonable pace, tone of voice, and inflection. This time, **pay attention to what you are reading** and not to your own voice. This way, you can take in the content and learn from reading aloud.

Especially for learning new ideas and understanding new content, **plan to
reread frequently.** The best readers do not "get it" in just one reading. What
do others tell us about rereading?

"When you reread a classic you do not see more in the book than you did
before; you see more in you than was there before." Clifton Fadiman
"'Tell me what you read and I'll tell you who you are' is true enough, but I'd
know you better if you told me what you reread." François Mauriac
"To read a book for the first time is to make an acquaintance with a new
friend; to read it for a second time is to meet an old one." Chinese Saying

How do these quoted thoughts reflect (or fail to reflect) your own experiences
of rereading? Write a brief journal entry about this exercise and your responses
to having completed it.

One rereading strategy is:

1. **Skim** the material the first time looking for major context clues and
   textual signals like headings, subheadings, bolded words or phrases,
   and definitions.

2. **Read** the entire piece more carefully using a pen/pencil to annotate
   and a highlighter to underscore key words and content.

3. **Write** a few notes about the article in your book or notebook or on the
   physical article when you have finished reading it.

4. **Put** it away.

5. **Read** again the next day with a focus on what you deemed important
   (using annotations and highlights) the previous day.

All of these reading strategies also work for studying content and for
understanding it well enough to use it in your own writing.

The examples selected thus far in Parts Two and Three of this book
are used to suggest strong formatting of assignments. The following three
examples (OWI Writing Examples 14.7, 14.8, and 14.9) illustrate different
ways to format explanatory material and instructional directions, which are
common to composition assignments. Use of white space, bullets and numbering, highlighting, boldface, and the like make assignments more readable documents. Given that OWI students may read their assignments from
screens of various sizes, distinguishing the most crucial parts of the text is
important.

In OWI Writing Example 14.7, the text shows a small part of a longer assignment explanation. It is presented in short, chunky paragraphs that leave white space for an uncrowded look. The teacher uses boldface to emphasize the assignment number (3) and type (arguing a position). Bold font along with all capital letters also emphasize due dates. It is common knowledge among digital communicators that using all capital letters can be perceived as shouting, but in the case of an assignment, such capped words — used with discretion — can stress important points. To further emphasize due dates, the teacher highlights the text. Done indiscriminately, the text would become unreadable, but done prudently and in a standardized way that students can learn to expect from all written assignments, the added emphasis becomes something students' eyes may seek out. Finally, the teacher underlines key vocabulary particular to the assignment that likely connects to other writing lessons essential to completing this assignment.

OWI WRITING EXAMPLE 14.7 Formatting with White Space, Highlights, and Underlined Text

Assignment for Essay 3:
Arguing a Position

Proposal for Peer Response DUE 3/22 (Posted to Conference <u>AND</u> Study Group)

Preliminary Draft DUE 3/31 (Posted to Workbook <u>AND</u> Study Group)

Presentation Draft DUE 4/12 (Posted to Assignments)

Goals for the arguing a position essay:

In our texts and in our writing, we have started to look at the <u>evidence</u> people present for and against their views (e.g., <u>examples</u>, <u>statistics</u>, <u>anecdotes</u>, <u>authority</u>, and <u>testimony</u>). We are discussing their <u>ethos</u> in terms of their <u>goodwill</u> for their audience, their <u>good sense</u>, and their demonstrated knowledge of the subject. Additionally, we have begun the most important work of all: looking at the <u>biases</u> and <u>agendas</u> of writers and speakers about these issues. Their <u>language choices</u> tend to reveal their <u>opinions</u>.

One of our major goals this term is to <u>earn informed opinions</u> through this kind of careful reading, discussion, and scrutiny of the issues. The act of <u>writing</u> both helps us to think through the issues and to present arguments about them. In this essay, you should back up or <u>support</u> your <u>earned opinions</u> with ample evidence. You also will use <u>counterarguments</u>.

In OWI Writing Example 14.8, the text is from a literature review assignment. This part of the assignment is presented as a common outline with numbered primary text and lettered secondary text. The outline works to suggest a chronological (numbered) process for collecting and using peer-reviewed articles in a literature review. When this text is accompanied by content that teaches students what a literature review does and models how such a review might look, then the chronological process provides students with sufficient guidance to develop a rough draft for which the teacher can provide formative feedback. In addition to the outline format, the teacher uses boldface, sparse underlining, and fully capitalized words. In the online environment, some of these words could be shown in another color for added emphasis. The emphasized number of necessary resources, APA citation requirements, and due dates at the end of the outline provide redundancy to material that would be in the completed assignment and, likely, the syllabus as well.

OWI WRITING EXAMPLE 14.8 Formatting with Outline and Bolded Text

Suggested Writing Process

1. Collect your sources. Find about 30–40 peer-reviewed academic articles related to your topic. **Narrow these to 15–20 total useable sources.**

2. Sort through the sources initially by skimming and scanning, which are reading skills that you have in your repertoire. <u>DO NOT</u> read all of these articles because many of them will not address your topic fully. Carefully read <u>only</u> the truly relevant material!

3. Read, summarize, and evaluate the **15–20 scholarly research articles** that remain, taking notes as you did for Assignments 1–3. Record:

    a. Bibliographic information

    b. The article's primary points and/or research questions

    c. The research methods

    d. Its findings

    e. Its conclusions

    f. Your perception of where the article fits conceptually in terms of the potential organization (chronology, advancements, geography, research questions, or other themes)

4. Arrange the articles in the organizational categories/scheme you choose. Some articles will fit in more than one category.

(*continued*)

OWI WRITING EXAMPLE 14.8 (*continued*)

5. As you summarize and provide the information from the articles, also compare and contrast them with others in the same category.

6. Use transitions to connect the various articles as you would when writing a story or narrative. An endless list of articles with no clear connection among them is boring and it does not fit the requirements for this assignment.

7. **The final paper should be 12–15 double-spaced pages in the body with a separate title page and a separate references section/pages (14–17 pages total).**

8. Follow **APA manuscript guidelines.**

OWI Writing Example 14.9 illustrates the use of a table that develops a sample outline for students. The table separates the *what* of the document set and thesis question from the example text that students might write using their own topics. This piece of a written assignment provides a model outline that students can follow in terms of content and organization. Such a model can help students to articulate their early findings in preparation for drafting the essay. This example simply uses boldface within the table.

OWI WRITING EXAMPLE 14.9 Formatting with Outline, Table, and Boldface Text[5]

Sample Outline	
Document Set to Review:	"Changing Times — The Origins of the Modern Civil Rights Movement, 1954–1956"
My Thesis Question:	What are the origins of the modern civil rights movement?
I Will Look For:	**Origins** of modern civil rights movement during this time.
I Found:	**Origin 1:** Brown v. Board of Education (1954) — provided legal basis of the modern civil rights movement

[5]Example provided by Professor David Taylor of University of Maryland University College.

Origin 2: Brave individuals took a stand (Rosa Parks, Little Rock Nine, Freedom Riders) and inspired others

Origin 3: Individual actions led to mass actions and direct actions (Montgomery Bus Boycott, March on Washington)

Origin 4: Mass media coverage of actions raised national awareness and momentum

15

OWI Writing Strategies for Interpersonal Communication

WHAT ARE OWI WRITING STRATEGIES FOR INTERPERSONAL COMMUNICATION AND WHY ARE THEY IMPORTANT?

Interpersonal communication always matters in an educational setting, but it seems so much more crucial in an online environment where most of the talk is conducted textually. When the body/face/voice connections of traditional teaching settings are removed, educators and students need to rely on other means of communicating important messages — those that deal directly with the learning and those outside of it.

Interpersonal communication is provided online through a variety of digital media. In the LMS, teachers communicate through returned writing responses, as discussed in Chapter 13, journals, discussion boards, class messages, IM chat, and even through grades. Some LMSs incorporate e-mail and audio/video technology like Skype. At times, teachers move outside the LMS for texting, tweeting, Facebook or other social media, and — perhaps too rarely — the phone. Some of these media are synchronous, which carry the immediate possibility of correcting miscommunication, while other media are asynchronous, which open new potential to consider the message and tone prior to communicating.

With all of these communication media available, it may seem odd that teachers express discomfort with the lack of body/face/voice connections; yet, long before online education brought a new set of challenges, teachers and students already were experiencing in-person miscommunication.

In the digital setting, new opportunities to rethink and revise our communications exist. In a speech, Sherry Turkle (2012) says:

> Human relationships are rich and they're messy and they're demanding. And we clean them up with technology. Texting, e-mail, posting, all of these things

let us present the self as we want to be. We get to edit, and that means we get to delete, and that means we get to retouch, the face, the voice, the flesh, the body—not too little, not too much, just right.

Her thought is apt in that technology does, indeed, give us a chance to clear up misunderstandings before they happen—if we actually look over the written text before clicking or touching the Send icon. Unfortunately, all too often, instructors and students fail to proofread before sending a message, leading to multiple opportunities for miscommunication.

Although technology does allow us to revise, edit, and rethink our digitally supported communications, the reality is that we fail frequently to edit our communications or we read the intended student audience in ways that may not lead to the desired interaction. Thoughtful communication can take a great deal of time, in fact, and adds to the already heavy literacy load of OWI. Nonetheless, lack of time or desire to make the effort necessary for strong communications are not good reasons to give interpersonal communication short shrift. Poor communication may result in student dissatisfaction, loss of learning, and even decreased retention—already problematic considerations in OWI.

Speaking of the Millennials, Erik Qualman says, "You're talking about a younger generation, Generation Y, whose interpersonal communication skills are different from Generation X. The younger generation is more comfortable saying something through a digital mechanism than even face to face." Indeed, social networking and a habit of texting rather than talking has led some students to be oddly free with what they say through digital technology, sometimes leading to embarrassing or awkward moments. Students can be notoriously poor communicators in an online environment. Many seem to be more comfortable with online interactions than face-to-face ones, but that comfort level does not equal a sophisticated sense of how to interact appropriately in different settings. Given the primarily transactional nature of a college course—despite the composition field's intentional goals of developing more personal relationships—student communications often are written simply to say what is on their minds rather than to interact in any rhetorically or interpersonally nuanced ways. Students may not recognize a need for formality when they are talking to teachers through text. Register—untaught and unknown to some—can be blurred online where typically incomplete sentences suggest blunt tones. Indeed, in informal social settings, there is an anything-goes tendency to digital communication that leads even our state and national leaders to say odd and inappropriate things that may cost them their careers and reputations.

Teachers' communications need to be models of appropriate, intentional interaction and formality levels that, if also taught explicitly, students may choose to follow. The goal of this chapter is to assist teachers with providing meaningful and appropriate interpersonal communication with students in an online setting.

HOW CAN WE WRITE (AND TEACH) READABLE INTERPERSONAL COMMUNICATION?

There are many opportunities to communicate with students interpersonally in any OWC. Each of these opportunities requires us to be especially thoughtful about what and how we say things. Similarly each gives us a time for explicitly and implicitly teaching students similar ways of interacting.

Demonstrate How and When to Communicate

In an OWC, we must make sure that students know how, when, and through what medium to communicate with us.

Most OWCs take place through an LMS, which will have a variety of public and private communication venues. Public venues typically include announcement pages, class discussion/conference portals, and folders for assignments and written instruction modules. Private venues typically include an LMS-based e-mail system, private chat venue, workbook and/or journal space for private discussion or interaction with the teacher, and an assignment posting portal where messages can be included with a posted file/assignment.

We need to teach students early about the expected uses of different communication venues. For example, they need to know that the announcement page will be updated regularly—perhaps once a week or even more often depending on the teacher's typical habits—and that they should look for class messages there every time they log into the LMS. Although some LMSs are integrating explanatory features or triggering updates for everyone to read, teachers should take the lead in explaining that the announcement page contains critical assignment and teaching messages. One colleague uploads weekly, short, spontaneous, and unedited videos—without editing out hesitations ("um") and mistakes—videos to remind students of what was accomplished during the week and to preview the next week's work. These communications become a standard medium through which the teacher can converse with students.

Each of the available or regularly used public and private communication venues can be defined and explained to students in a simple table like Table 15.1.

It helps to indicate when students should use particular venues and when they might expect to hear from us, too. To that end, teachers should decide how often they need to check the LMS and when they will do the primary work of responding to student e-mails and other messages. Students need to know that their instructors are not on call 24/7, but also they need to know how to ensure they can reach us if and when an urgent need arises.

While Table 15.1 does not consider every possible type of communication venue (e.g., writing spaces like wikis and blogs), it covers a wide variety

TABLE 15.1 Table of LMS Communication Venues

Communication Venue	Private or Public	Purpose	When to Communicate	When to Expect Teacher's Response
Announcement page in LMS	Public to class	Formal updates about course/entire class concerns	Review for additions or changes every time you log in to course	Posted by teacher but not interactive for questions or response
Syllabus in LMS	Public to class	Formally describes course and writing requirements	Review regularly to stay current in course	Posted by teacher but not interactive for questions or response
Discussion/ conference portal in LMS	Public to class	Formal guided discussions or responses to teacher's prompts	Until the discussion is formally completed; abide by due dates	Several times per week
Peer/small group discussions in LMS	Public only to particular peer group and teacher	Formal guided discussions within small groups; peer response about writing	Until the discussion is formally completed and in response to peer feedback/questions; abide by due dates	Rarely; teacher will check in to the group but may not provide response if guidance seems unnecessary
Writing modules in LMS	Public to class	Formal distribution center for instruction about writing	Review per the syllabus or when an announcement or assignment indicates	Posted by teacher but not interactive for questions or response
Assignment files in LMS	Public to class	Formally explains writing and other assignments	Review regularly to stay current in course	Posted by teacher but not interactive for questions or response

(continued)

229

TABLE 15.1 Table of LMS Communication Venues *(continued)*

Communication Venue	Private or Public	Purpose	When to Communicate	When to Expect Teacher's Response
Assignments folder in LMS	Private to teacher and student	Post formal assignments and formal comments regarding them	As instructed by due dates	Within _____ days after posting
Audio/video interaction media in LMS (when available)	Public to class	Formal teaching venue or information chat venue	As assigned or as needed	Immediately when online in the LMS
E-mail in LMS	Private to recipients	Private, formal communication of various natures	As needed	Within _____ hours/days after posting
Workbook or journal folder in LMS	Private to teacher and student	Post journal or informal assignments and informal comments regarding them	As instructed by due dates or as needed	Within _____ days after posting
IM chat in LMS	Private to recipients	Brief, informal interactions to meet specific needs	As needed or by prior arrangement	Immediately when online in the LMS

(continued)

TABLE 15.1 Table of LMS Communication Venues *(continued)*

Communication Venue	Private or Public	Purpose	When to Communicate	When to Expect Teacher's Response
Class chat space in LMS	Public to class and teacher	Informal "coffee break" or "water cooler" for off-topic connections	As needed, desired, or by prior arrangement	Immediately when online in the LMS
Telephone	Private to callers	Informal voice interactions to respond to problems or teach individually	As needed or by prior arrangement via e-mail or chat	Within a reasonable time frame available to both callers
E-mail outside LMS — if allowed or encouraged	Private to recipients	Private, formal communication of various natures	As needed	Within ____ days after posting
IM, Skype, Facebook messages — if allowed or encouraged	Private to recipients	Brief, informal interactions to meet specific needs	As needed	Within ____ days after posting

of the media students might use to communicate in the course. Realistically, the fewer venues we offer and expect students to use with us, the better. Many students struggle with the various portals of an LMS; it may seem more complex than it is because it has an educational purpose. The LMS also might seem more foreign to adult students than a similar universal communication platform might be in a workplace setting because the educational function places these students in a learner status as opposed to worker status.

Therefore, we should resist adding those venues enumerated in the final row of this table. There should be a good access-based or instructional purpose—such as allowing audio/video interaction and recording not available in the LMS and crucial to the course itself—before asking students to engage yet another medium and one that is outside the LMS. Before asking students to set up new accounts with even free software like Twitter, it is helpful to consider that students may not be as interested in an extended classroom community as writing instructors are, as Chapter 3 indicates. It behooves us to remember that we and the students have business, social, and personal lives outside the writing course, and many of us would prefer not to be on call twenty-four hours a day as these media seem to require.

Table 15.1 also provides information about using the telephone. While its use is up to individual teachers, a voice call often can cut through the overwhelming amount of text needed to communicate and correct misunderstandings. Using the telephone does not require downloading yet another technology; its use generally is comfortable and familiar. Some OWI teachers do not have an institutional onsite office, which means that they must use a personal telephone. Teachers may not want to give out telephone numbers, which is an understandable boundary. In these cases, it is reasonable to ask students for a number to call them; although the caller's number may be revealed on the student's phone, this strategy sets an expectation of who is to make the call and who is to be the recipient. Using an appointment for a telephone call is respectful of both parties' time, and it provides a model for students to follow.

Finally, levels of formality also have been indicated in the table. We should recall that the student-teacher relationship in most cases is a functional—not friendship—relationship. To that end, while composition teachers retain the right to determine what their students should call them (e.g., Dr., Professor, Mr./Mrs./Ms., or first name), there should be an appropriate level of formality to remind students of the difference in status. For example, in online classes, "Dr. Hewett" seems more formal than I would like in this text-based setting, but encouraging students to use my first name feels falsely leading, as if our relationship was equal. It is not equal for two reasons: I have things I can teach them about writing, which is the only reason we are connected, and I am charged with providing grades at the end of the term. Our relationship is transactional. Therefore, I typically refer to myself as "Dr. H." Even that choice seems somewhat affected, but it is my personal compromise (see Warnock 2009, for a similar discussion). While not all readers will agree with me on this point, we may agree that teachers should account carefully for our choices of register and tone so as to encourage students to be their own best communicators and to have some level of assurance that they are not making poor choices in how they talk with us.

Consider Tone in Synchronous Settings

As with all writing by teachers in OWI, being straightforward and having semantic integrity are primary needs. The message to be communicated should be well considered to mitigate the need for follow-up communications about the topic of concern. While tone always is important when communicating with students, it is especially crucial to having a written message accepted or rejected on an affective level. A kind tone can help to offset a necessarily difficult message to deliver or one that will be disappointing to hear.

IM chat offers a unique opportunity to examine how we use tone synchronously in OWI. For example, in a synchronous IM chat, we might need to tell a student that a proposed topic will not be acceptable. Tone is differently conveyed by OWI Writing Example 15.1, an example of two different IM chat message responses to a student's desired topic.

OWI WRITING EXAMPLE 15.1 Two Teacher IM Chat Responses

Student: So, I wanted to do the paper on live-birth abortion.

Teacher Response 1: NO. I told the class to avoid that kind of controversial issue. Didn't you read the assignment?

Teacher Response 2: I'm afraid that won't work. It's too controversial for our assignment, and the issues go too deep for any one person to argue well in just three weeks of research and writing. Let's chat a little more to find another topic.

Both responses firmly convey the message that the topic must be changed, but the first response carries an angry tone conveyed through the capital letters of the "no" and the closed-ended question that can sound sarcastic to the now embarrassed or frustrated student. The second response conveys a little sympathy while it offers a reason beyond rule following and an offer for the teacher's assistance in refocusing. Perhaps somewhat oddly for IM chat, the second response uses complete sentences. Because this is an instruction-based chat, complete sentences help to convey the teacher's entire message and, if the chat is archived, to make the message clearer and more comprehensible for the student to reread later outside the immediate context of the chat.

Because of the tradition of drop-in conferences during onsite office hours, teachers need to decide how to provide similar access to their online students. Initiating IM chat through the LMS is one way to offer access to all students. IM chat has characteristics that can stimulate an engaging talk or work session with students. It has the nature of voice, uses turn-taking conventions, is nearly synchronous in terms of possible interaction speed, yet it can be responded to at the speaker's convenience. Speakers typically communicate in short, spontaneous exchanges that may be comprehensible only to the two people talking (Hewett and Hewett 2008, 457).

How teachers should use IM chat in teaching writing depends on the particular context of the chat. Outside of drop-in chats initiated by students, teachers can use IM chat proactively. For example, in many LMS configurations, students automatically have an IM presence when they sign in to the LMS; although there always is the possibility of disturbing the student, a brief and informal connection through the chat feature may help to set a friendly and caring overall tone for current and future interactions. I make it a habit to check in with each student via IM chat at least once early in the term. I just say hi and introduce myself, wait for a response if I can, and ask how the course is going. Surprisingly, for students who attend a fully online university, I often have been told that I am the first teacher to connect that way. My experience has been that after we have chatted, students are more forthcoming about asking me questions, which is a desirable trait in my OWCs.

IM chat can be used more formally, too. It is a fine tool for brainstorming ideas and focusing on specific writing concerns, which makes it a favorite of writing tutors who want to try to replicate an in-person setting. In a tutorial setting or a peer exchange, students may appreciate informality whereas when the teacher is involved, they may get more clarity about their writing from a more formal message and tone. When students have a problem and we are using IM to help, we may need to measure our words more carefully and construct more complete sentences, as in the teacher's second response in OWI Writing Example 15.1.

As a rule, teachers always should be polite and use the level of register expected from the students. If we want to be informal with chat, we can do so, but a statement that clarifies the difference between a less formal and more formal exchange can be helpful: "I'm a bit more informal here on chat than in e-mail because we are having such an immediate communication, and I know we can quickly correct any misunderstandings." That having been said, students probably benefit if we smoothly shift to a more formal register to explain something clearly for them.

Concerns about tone shift with the available media. A communication through audio/video, class chat space, and the telephone are like IM chat in that formality and register levels may vary according to the message that we want to convey and the need for clear communications. However, other media—often asynchronous—may require different tone. A syllabus or assignment requires an informational, explanatory tone, yet it also carries a directive and commanding tone of setting the behavior, habits, rules, and expectations of the course. Students rely on high degrees of semantic integrity for such communications. Similarly, the tone of written communications to all students in the class through the discussion/conference portal or to a smaller peer group will vary with the message—friendly agreement, gentle prodding, thoughtful modeling, or decisive statement about how well the expectations are being met. Very often, teachers need to mix instruction with encouragement and explanation with redirection.

Consider Tone in Asynchronous Settings

Allowing angry, frustrated, or disrespectful tones to creep into a message can be highly detrimental to the kinds of relationships that OWI teachers want to build with students. The asynchronous medium of e-mail provides an opportunity to look at tone and message-based issues more completely.

While being respectful and kind, an e-mail requires high attention to semantic integrity, clarity, and the formality that demonstrates the transactional nature of a teacher-to-student interaction. Whereas synchronous IM chat sometimes is recorded and phone interactions rarely are, asynchronous e-mail by nature has a long shelf life and easily is passed among students and to one's peers and administrators. What has been communicated through e-mail may be used both for or against the participants when a dispute arises. E-mail requires particularly thoughtful communication from teachers.

OWI WRITING EXAMPLE 15.2 Example Student E-Mail[1]

Hi, Professor Jones,

I am going out of town tomorrow. My company wants me to go to Tallahassee, Florida, for a seminar. I won't be back until next Wednesday. I don't know if I'll have Internet access while I'm gone. I hope that's okay.

Chloe

---

[1]OWI Writing Examples 15.2 through 15.11 are adapted from communication training provided to the author by Professor Andrew Cavanaugh of University of Maryland University College.

In the e-mail of OWI Writing Example 15.2, a student has given short notice about her expected absence from a course. Today's students may have different reasons for not being in class or for needing the professor. A student's work responsibilities and family needs may cause us to hear from her in an on-the-fly type of message such as this one. Moreover, the asynchronicity of e-mail—often necessary in OWI—means that the student sender does not need to engage in an immediate discussion about the issue. The message therefore appears to absolve the individual of responsibility for changing the situation. By the time the e-mail reaches the recipient, the issue may be a done deal, not resolvable to the recipient's needs or requests. In this way, asynchronous messages can frustrate the teacher as receiver by not allowing for immediate resolution. Conversely, it can enable needed breathing space between receipt and response, to the benefit of one or both parties.

This simple e-mail communication in OWI Writing Example 15.2 presents a message that is ripe for problems. It is short, as many e-mail messages are, states the student's problem without complete detail, and ends with "I hope that's okay," which seals the student's expectation that her absence from coursework is not up for any kind of discussion. It leaves the teacher few options because it is not as if he can talk the student out of going on a work trip, for example. Therefore, he is left to determine how to respond with respect to the course goals and rules.

How the teacher responds will set the stage for the student (1) understanding the expectations for her work while she is on a business trip, (2) knowing when to communicate with the professor, and (3) situating herself in the course as a fully participating student.

OWI WRITING EXAMPLE 15.3 Abrupt Teacher E-mail Response

Chloe,

You are expected to have access to the class wherever you are. You should have access to the Internet in Florida even if it is in a coffee shop. I expect you to contribute to class discussion while you are away. You will have points deducted from your class participation grade for missing our conference postings this week.

Professor Jones

In OWI Writing Example 15.3, the teacher has indicated that the OWC is an anywhere/anytime experience in which students always should be full participants regardless of their circumstances. This message is provided as a formal and inflexible position with sanctions for the absence. Flexibility actually is not the issue here, and bending course rules should be determined by each instructor in accordance with his or her institution's guidance. However, the lack of empathy for Chloe's situation is extremely off-putting and could affect her attitude to the point of dropping the course. Access also must be considered here — not as an issue of disability but of an adult student's need to prioritize workplace and school responsibilities, which may result in lack of Internet access. Often, both can be accommodated, limiting a need for choosing one over the other. In this case, the teacher can make a similar point with a different, friendlier tone while maintaining formality.

OWI WRITING EXAMPLE 15.4 Friendly Teacher E-Mail Response

Hi, Chloe,

Thank you for the update. I appreciate your telling me.

We have a conference answer due on Monday. You should see whether a local coffee shop or hotel lobby might provide Internet access. If you get access, you can post your answer to that exercise. However, if you don't have Internet access, I can be a little flexible. If you post the answer by 11:00 PM EDT on Wednesday, I can give you some credit for your contribution.

Please let me know if such situations arise in the future. I understand that you might have had a spontaneous request from your company to travel. If you know of any other traveling plans that might interfere with your Internet access, let me know as soon as possible, please. When I have this information earlier, I may be able to help you in determining class priorities for your absence.

Best regards,

Professor Jones [or preferred name]

The response in OWI Writing Example 15.4 is much improved in tone and completeness of message. It also is more work as, by now, readers will recognize that communicating well through text can require more time to choose words carefully (even if first spoken using speech recognition software) and to edit the text for nuance. In this example, the teacher has decided when he will stick with the rules and when he will be flexible. When flexibility is not possible, a more firm yet still kind message can be given, as shown in OWI Writing Example 15.5.

> **OWI WRITING EXAMPLE 15.5 Friendly, yet Firm Teacher E-Mail Response**
>
> Unfortunately, the responses to this particular conference are extremely time-bound because of the next paper's due date. For that reason, if you cannot comment, I cannot give you credit for that discussion. However, please remember that I am available by e-mail if you need to check in about your writing while you are out of town.

Conversely, students also may write e-mails that reveal inflexibility and negative emotions that can frustrate teachers. OWI Writing Example 15.6 provides a student's e-mail with a frustrated message; its tone blames the teacher.

> **OWI WRITING EXAMPLE 15.6 Student Confusion E-Mail Message**
>
> Hi, Professor Jones,
>
> I am totally confused. I have no idea how to post my answer to your conference questions. I also think the class is very confused. I have taken many classes on this LMS, and yours if the first one I have had trouble with.
>
> Joe

As humans, we are usually fairly certain that someone else is responsible for our problems. In the OWI setting, it very well may be us, the teachers, who are to blame. It just as easily could be the student. Asynchronous media lend themselves all too easily to playing the blame game. Returning blame to the student is unhelpful and certainly harmful to a clean teacher-student relationship. Good relations demand that instructors demonstrate maturity by choosing not to take such a blaming response personally.

Unfortunately, OWI Writing Example 15.7 is extreme in its high-toned and heady attitude. It may devastate a student who took a rare risk in asking a question in the online setting, while also leading to disciplinary action by the professor's supervisor if the student complains.

> **OWI WRITING EXAMPLE 15.7 High-Toned Teacher E-Mail Response**
>
> Dear Joe,
>
> I really have no idea why you are having trouble with the course. The conferences are simple, and they are explained in the syllabus. You must simply post a response. It might help if you told me what else in the course is confusing you.

Please don't compare me to other instructors on this LMS. I don't know what other courses you might have taken, but I can assure you that I am well qualified to teach this course and have done it many times with great student satisfaction. If you would focus and do the work, you will learn much from this experience.

Sincerely,

Professor Jones

OWI Writing Example 15.8 provides a more reasonable response to student frustration and enables the student to take control of his learning by (1) trying again with the given instructions; (2) determining whether a more immediate, synchronous interaction would be helpful; and (3) giving the student an alternative help venue should Joe feel uncomfortable using the teacher's time for this problem. Finally, notice how formatting works in this example. Shorter paragraph chunks with increased white space, as well as enumerating the steps to resolve a problem, may seem simultaneously friendlier and clearer.

OWI WRITING EXAMPLE 15.8 Reasonable Teacher E-Mail Response

Dear Joe,

Thank you for your message. I am sorry that you are having difficulties with these issues in the class. Even experienced students can find the technology to be frustrating at times.

In posting an answer to the conference, please follow these directions:

1. XYZ
2. XYZ
3. XYZ

If this doesn't work, try calling 410-555-5000, so the Help Desk consultant can help you. If you want, I'm happy to set up a phone call with you to walk through the problem together.

Please let me know what other features in the class might be confusing to you, and please encourage your classmates to check in with me, too. I want all of you to experience success in this course.

Sincerely,

Professor Jones

A student's defensiveness about his writing can arise in any composition course. Onsite teachers are well acquainted with students who stand outside the classroom door after class because they want to be heard regarding a poor grade or misunderstood essay. In an online setting, such negative feelings may emerge in an e-mail. Online communicators—especially students who are inexperienced in education-focused online communications—may be susceptible to pressing Send without a careful review of an e-mail with an angry tone. The student's defensiveness can lead to a teacher's offensive position; together, these emotions can do genuine harm to the student-teacher relationship, as OWI Writing Examples 15.9 and 15.10 reveal.

OWI WRITING EXAMPLE 15.9 Defensive Student E-Mail

Professor Jones,

Let me take this opportunity to assure you I am a responsible, 50-year-old man and that I take my education seriously. Furthermore, I have taken over 30 credits at this university successfully. Moreover, I maintain a very responsible position as a manager at XYZ Corporation.

With this in mind, I am highly insulted by your criticisms of my paper. I spent a significant amount of time drafting, writing, and refining the paper. I write very often for my job. My colleagues and my boss find my writing to be very polished and professional. To have my essay thoroughly demolished, marked, and demeaned by you was certainly surprising, not to say shattering.

Go ahead and vent back at me if you want. I look forward to your response.

Lee

In this example, Lee seems quite ready to take on Professor Jones in his e-mail, and his deepest message—that of feeling demeaned and shattered—is almost hidden by his angry words. The response shown in OWI Writing Example 15.10 is almost unbelievable, yet it is all too real.

OWI WRITING EXAMPLE 15.10 Brusque Teacher E-Mail Response

Lee,

I suppose you didn't like my comments, but I also am a responsible, mature instructor who has taught at both at this university and at other institutions for over 15 years. I know what I'm talking about when I respond to your essay, having done this for many writing students before you.

I commented on your paper objectively, systematically, and sensitively. However, whatever your writing skills are, this particular paper was poor.

You defined the problem incomprehensively, you developed the solution inadequately, and you concluded the paper confusingly.

If you read my comments and follow the assignments carefully when writing papers for this class, you will have a better experience. I look forward to stronger writing from you in future assignments.

Dr. Jones

From top to bottom, OWI Writing Example 15.10 fails the written interpersonal communication test. Lee is greeted brusquely whereas we know from previous examples that Professor Jones usually greets a student more formally. He mocks the student by mirroring his language in the first paragraph. Then, he abuses the student about his writing abilities. Professor Jones, who signs his name differently here presumably to intimate his anger and higher status as a Ph.D., finishes the e-mail with a statement that puts the entire problem back in the student's hands. How many students might drop the class if they received this e-mail?

OWI WRITING EXAMPLE 15.11 Nuanced Teacher E-Mail Response

Dear Lee,

Thank you for your message. I am sorry that the comments on your paper did not turn out the way you expected. I thought the problem you chose to discuss for the paper was fascinating and hoped I had conveyed that message.

In my feedback, I talked about the second paragraph and its need for more development. I wrote a lesson that I hoped would help you build content to this interesting draft. I also suggested some specific examples to support the point. You are free to use those or others in your revision. In addition, I mentioned some run-on sentences and pronoun-antecedent agreement problems. Finally, I gave you a series of next steps to help you with revision.

Are there were any specific points I made in my response that you disagree with? Knowing that would help me greatly in assessing the situation.

I can see that you are not happy with this response to your paper. Would you like to talk about it in an IM chat or phone conference? If so, please be ready to let me know what points concern you the most. I won't argue the grade since this essay is revisable for a new grade, but I will listen carefully and discuss your concerns.

Sincerely,

Professor Jones

OWI Writing Example 15.11 provides a much more nuanced communication that is respectful of the student's needs while supporting the original feedback to the student's writing.

Finally, since we actually must teach each student through our online feedback to their writing, when students do not understand the lessons being taught, they may need additional interaction. It is up to OWI instructors to maintain professionalism and provide both implicit and explicit communication models with their tone and message. That next communication should use professional communication strategies that steer clear of unhelpful, sarcastic, or personal statements.

Teach through Modeling

The class or small group discussion/conference also requires online writing instructors to use strong written communication skills. Typically, this written discussion uses the medium of a discussion board in the LMS. These discussions are venues for large or small group formal talk about a prompted topic, and they are designed to replicate the kinds of face-to-face conversations teachers hope for in onsite classes (Warnock 2009). In fact, teachers often consider these online discussions to be low-stakes writing opportunities because they provide additional opportunities to write and support one's thinking (72).

In fully face-to-face courses, discussion may be required but its quality and quantity are difficult to measure when the talk is oral. In some OWCs (both hybrid and fully online), written discussions are required each week with guidelines for how many posts a student must make, how long to make each post, and how many responses students must offer to each other. Online, the class and group discussion venue is considered to be a primary teaching opportunity as well as a key means for students to talk together asynchronously as, presumably, they would orally in an onsite classroom (Warnock 2009, 68); students have the opportunity to develop fluent reading and writing through these discussions. Online discussions are archived, public, graded, and, from an interpersonal communication perspective, higher stakes for students than we might want to admit. And if the students attend to the interactive design and interpersonal communication of a threaded discussion board post, they know the writing has some high stakes.

More so than IM chat or e-mail communications, online discussions cross genres between writing to teach about a relevant topic and interpersonal communication with students. Hence, all of our writing-to-teach skills are brought to bear. One thing that makes these discussions so delicate for teachers is that students often are reluctant to participate. It is difficult for them to hold a course-based discussion asynchronously because that is not the way people normally do it. Students normally talk in a somewhat spontaneous, free-flow manner in class when they talk at all. While it is true that many students text often and fluently using their phones, the one-to-one nature of most social texting does not transfer to the text-based, education-focused group discussion. Additionally, they may be afraid of offending their peers, being flamed in response to a perceived criticism, or bringing down the teacher's criticism. As Chapter 3 explains about reading, we do not always do a good job of teaching students how to critique what they read and the text's underlying thinking; when that text is from a peer, politeness conventions challenge the students even more.

The success of asynchronous discussions depends on students coming into the LMS at particular times during the week to post their own thoughts through writing and to respond to their peers and teacher's posts. The conversations teachers hope for are interactive, philosophically open to the class, thoughtfully metacognitive, and filled with writing (Warnock 2009, 69). Sometimes, what they get are halfhearted, back-scratching, noncontextual comments. Warnock (2009) suggests providing a generative guide for questioning and consciously enacted role-play in order to avoid such discussions (73–74).

Here, we focus on three ways that teachers can communicate with their students in support of class and small group discussions: using writing prompts, writing model responses, and providing clear initial guidance.

USING WRITING PROMPTS Typically, writing teachers take on the responsibility of providing the prompt for a new discussion. Ideally this prompt will be connected to reading students are doing, enabling them to read more critically. Part Two provides a number of reading exercises that would make useful prompts. OWI Writing Example 15.12 is a sample discussion post that asks students to engage in a small group discussion (although a full-class discussion certainly could be developed) regarding an essay chosen simply to address the reading comprehension theme of visualization.

OWI WRITING EXAMPLE 15.12 Discussion Post for an Assigned Article

Using the discussion board, talk to your small group about "The Lottery" by Chris Abani, keeping the comprehension theme of visualization in mind. Share your thinking by describing some of the images it has brought to mind. Consider when you read the article the first and second times through. What kinds of mental images emerged? What kinds of other images came to mind? Were they still images (e.g., paintings, photographs, or drawings), action images (e.g., movie or TV scenes), sounds (e.g., songs or MTV/YouTube videos), or real-life memories?

In your discussion board, write what you feel comfortable talking about knowing that your writing is public to your small group and teacher.

(continued)

OWI WRITING EXAMPLE 15.12 (*continued*)

After your discussion session, write a 250- to 300-word, single-spaced journal response regarding visualization and how it can help when reading college texts. How can you take this skill and make it more your own, using it consciously in your current college term's work?

As you write, use one or more of the Visualizing Thinking Stems we reviewed. Post your journal response to the appropriate assignment by the given due date.

As this example shows, a prompt can be connected usefully to a reading, and it should provide ideas to jump-start the written discussion. Merely telling students to write about an article will not lead to fruitful discussion. In OWI Writing Example 15.12, questions are used to get the writing started. The discussion itself, which can be synchronous given available technology, enables students to share their thinking and to consider what they may want to say in the connected journal entry, which is the final product of this particular exercise. A variation on this prompt would be to ask students to directly cite the text when they refer to it, which enables them to practice an important writing skill in a conscious manner. It also helps to ask students to cite each other in their posts (Warnock 2009); doing so teaches them that they legitimately can make use of their peers' ideas by giving them credit for having written them.

The manner of sharing their thoughts on a reading such as this one involves students carefully considering what they are comfortable with writing. Knowing what to say, when to say it, and understanding the consequences of having said something publicly to peers and/or teachers also is a literacy skill they need to learn, and they can learn it partially through the teacher's writing prompts.

WRITING MODEL RESPONSES Moderating a discussion is a way to encourage student responses. Warnock (2009) provides a number of useful discussion moderation examples. Prior to discussion moderation, however, teachers can set an example for students to follow in a conscious manner. Offering model responses to a prompt helps students respond with more certainty—especially if their writing course includes overt instruction in reading online discussions or in reading metacognitively. Sometimes, we need to provide such models more than once. OWI Writing Example 15.13 is a response to a discussion post that might emerge from the discussion assignment of OWI Writing Example 15.12.

> **OWI WRITING EXAMPLE 15.13** Teacher's Model Response to Discussion Prompt
>
> When I read Chris Abani's essay "The Lottery," I was immediately reminded of a short story also called "The Lottery" by Shirley Jackson. In Jackson's story, the people of a town annually held a lottery to stone one citizen as a superstitious way of securing good crops for the next year. Everyone was made to participate so that no one could leave the town and report its crimes; even the defector would be guilty and responsible for the town's crimes. That's how I knew the townspeople understood they were doing wrong. In reading Abani's essay, I thought of the stoning from Jackson's story. I visualized the people holding and casting stones, also a Biblical image. When the narrator described the cornered man, who realized he was doomed and going to be killed, I still thought of the stoning. However, when the narrator described the tire around the victim's neck and the gasoline being poured on the man, I suddenly knew that a match would be lit and the man would be burned to death: Abani said: "This singular action and the man's pleas for mercy resigned, he sobbed softly, mumbling inaudibly, but he didn't move as the young man emptied the contents of the can onto him." I could smell the burning tire and the man's horrible death cries rang in my ears. When the narrator was made complicit in the burning by having to spit on the victim, I recalled another image — that of several children in a photograph of the Vietnam conflict era. They were running from, yet burning with, napalm that the South Vietnamese had mistakenly dropped on an innocent village. These mental images all connected for me, leading me to feel, smell, see, and hear the horror of people who are victims of the larger group's self-righteous behavior.

Along with this sample post, teachers could provide students with two additional model types. OWI Writing Example 15.14 illustrates a use of boldface and brackets within the text to explicate how the teacher was responding directly to the prompt. Such metacomments implicitly teach students how to develop their own posts as responses to the prompt and to each other.

> **OWI WRITING EXAMPLE 15.14** Teacher's Model Response to Discussion Post with Metacomments
>
> When I read Chris Abani's essay "The Lottery," I was immediately reminded of a short story also called "The Lottery" by Shirley Jackson. **[Here I am using my schema to connect with this essay. Also, I introduced both pieces through titles and authors, as we are learning to do with every reading in**

(continued)

OWI WRITING EXAMPLE 15.14 (*continued*)

the class.] In Jackson's story, the people of a town annually held a lottery to stone one citizen as a superstitious way of securing good crops for the next year. Everyone was made to participate so that no one could leave the town and report its crimes; even the defector would be guilty and responsible for the town's crimes. That's how I knew the townspeople understood they were doing wrong. **[I inferred from the story that people knew they were guilty, which is a way of using my critical reading skills.]** In reading Abani's essay, I thought of the stoning from Jackson's story. I visualized the people holding and casting stones, also a Biblical image. **[I am beginning to address the core of the prompt, which asks me to visualize the events from this essay.]**

OWI Writing Example 15.15 offers a second, even more explicit model of a response to the example discussion post. This example gives students an idea of how to respond to each other and how we, as teachers, might respond to them.

OWI WRITING EXAMPLE 15.15 Model Student and Teacher Responsive Discussion Posts

Student Response: I didn't visualize the things you saw. Now I remember reading Jackson's "The Lottery." I thought I had seen something with that title in the past. I was thinking about the way the mob in Abani's essay just judged that man without a trial or a jury. The elder who tried to stop the mob didn't succeed, but I wonder why he didn't try harder. When I read about him, I visualized a mob in a Simpson's cartoon — isn't there a mob scene in almost every show? And the one person who would try to talk down the mob, I saw him as the Dr. Hibbert character — older, wiser, and totally ineffectual.

Teacher Response: I like the way you both are thinking here and describing what Abani's essay has brought to your minds. Personally, I was shocked at the image of the children running from the napalm because it made me think of the victim (thief?) in Abani's story as amazing because he didn't run like people often do when in danger. How did he get the courage to just accept his fate? Good responses!

These models — especially when provided and explained explicitly and overtly — provide a sense of the kind of critical discussion responses that writing teachers hope for from their students.

PROVIDING CLEAR INITIAL GUIDANCE Finally, students will benefit from clear guidance about what is expected of them and us regarding the class discussions. Because of the frequent need to grade such participation, students need to know all of the parameters that might affect their work. OWI Writing Example 15.16 demonstrates such guidance to which the instructor can refer students throughout the semester.

OWI WRITING EXAMPLE 15.16 Additional Guidance for Discussion Board Posts

Here is some additional guidance about writing discussion board posts. A sample Discussion Board post is provided in the Course Documents.

- Your posts need to show critical thought and should integrate knowledge gained from the readings and virtual classroom. That means you can <u>and should</u> cite from sources as you explain your thinking.

- Initial posts in response to the prompt should be between 250 and 400 words. Secondary posts that further explain your thinking or that respond to your peers or me should range between 200 to 250 words. That said, usually I won't count your words. I just know that it takes time (shown by length) to develop a reasonable and thoughtful response to the prompts I give you. I will be able to recognize a "long enough" response by its detail, depth, and overall quality.

- Use APA style in-text citations as we are doing for all of our writing in this course. <u>You must cite your sources including words you use from your peers' or my comments.</u> You do not have to use sources outside of the readings; however, provide a References list if you do.

- It may help to type your post first in a stand-alone word processing program like Microsoft Word or Works and then copy the text into the discussion board. This process can help to avoid the frustration of losing your draft if the LMS freezes.

- Respond to each other's posts. Build a discussion thread, which means some back-and-forth commenting. The response posts need to show the same critical thinking as the primary posts. When you comment as part of a thread, directly refer your classmates to other posts or threads that support your position, politely challenge each other's thinking, and try to develop the thinking more fully.

- Provide context for your comments. We all have different schemas, experiences in different workplaces, and varying school backgrounds. Remember that we need to explain our comments to each other; do not assume a shared background.

(continued)

OWI WRITING EXAMPLE 15.16 (*continued*)

- What you write here can become fodder for your formal papers, and it may be connected to work for an informal journal entry. If you use ideas raised by a classmate, cite the classmate like you would another published piece: (Jones, 2015, Abani Discussion).
- All of our discussion posts are DUE for my review by 11:00 PM EDT on Wednesday of each week.

BE A THOUGHTFUL COMMUNICATOR

George Bernard Shaw once said, "The single biggest problem in communication is the illusion that it has taken place." In an online instructional setting, that illusion can remain up until grades are given and student feedback is solicited. We need to practice our interpersonal communication strategies until they are a solid part of our online education work. Some additional tips toward that end include the following:

- Remember that semantic integrity—especially the quality of being straightforward—and coherence and formatting strategies remain crucial to writing interpersonal communication that works in an OWC environment.
- Be respectful of the work students do, but also respect your own efforts. This mutual respect enables you to hold a boundary when necessary and to yield ground when possible and potentially helpful to the student or to your relationship with the student.
- When time is not crucial to resolving a problem, encourage students to write back with more details of their needs or questions. For example, provide them with your questions about the interaction to let them know where they were not yet clear. Ask them to use their reading strategies of metacognition and finding relevance, for example, to develop a message that conveys what you need to know.
- When writing, be as clear as possible about future plans and especially about any changes that seem needed to the class. Adult learners particularly may be frustrated at changes even when they are conveyed in a timely way and support student needs. You may find it helpful to listen to them if such a frustration arises and consider the solutions they raise.
- Explain the types of interpersonal communication you expect from students early and repeat this explanation whenever needed. Give students explicit models for what you require while implicitly modeling clear and coherent written messages every day.

- Tell students when you are providing them with a model for interpersonal communication. It may be useful to offer a video with example communications at the beginning of the term.
- Open up the issue of interpersonal communication as part of the course's explicit writing subject matter. Doing so can help students to keep their communication metacognitively and reflectively in mind.
- Make the lessons about interpersonal communication interesting by providing a quote as a discussion or journal prompt. For example, the following quoted statements can be used for teaching and thinking with OWI students through interpersonal communication strategies:
  - "The most important thing in communication is hearing what isn't said." Peter Drucker
  - "E-mail, instant messaging, and cell phones give us fabulous communication ability, but because we live and work in our own little worlds, that communication is totally disorganized." Marilyn vos Savant
  - "Communication leads to community, that is, to understanding, intimacy and mutual valuing." Rollo May
  - "I'm a great believer that any tool that enhances communication has profound effects in terms of how people can learn from each other, and how they can achieve the kind of freedoms that they're interested in." Bill Gates
  - "To effectively communicate, we must realize that we are all different in the way we perceive the world and use this understanding as a guide to our communication with others." Tony Robbins
  - "Self-expression must pass into communication for its fulfillment." Pearl S. Buck
  - "Communication works for those who work at it." John Powell

APPENDIX **A**

Additional Resources for Teaching Reading Comprehension Themes

QUOTES FOR ENGAGING READING COMPREHENSION THEMES

Metacognition

Quotes about thinking metacognitively:

- "Style used to be an interaction between the human soul and tools that were limiting. In the digital era, it will have to come from the soul alone." Jaron Lanier
- "The digital camera is a great invention because it allows us to reminisce. Instantly." Demetri Martin
- "What's insidious about the fear of what others will say is that you rarely hear them say it. You imagine what they'd say. You imagine they care that much about you. The fragility of our own egos gets the better of us." Jeff Jarvis, *Public Parts: How Sharing in the Digital Age Is Revolutionizing Life, Business, and Society* (Simon & Schuster, 2011)

Quotes about reading metacognitively:

- "I was reading the dictionary. I thought it was a poem about everything." Steven Wright
- "Reading furnishes the mind only with materials of knowledge; it is thinking that makes what we read ours." John Locke
- "I am a dreamer of words, of written words. I think I am reading; a word stops me. I leave the page. The syllables of the word begin to move around. Stressed accents begin to invert. The word abandons its meaning like an overload which is too heavy and prevents dreaming. Then words take on other meanings as if they had the right to be young. And the

words wander away, looking in the nooks and crannies of vocabulary for new company, bad company." Gaston Bachelard

- "A book is the only place in which you can examine a fragile thought without breaking it, or explore an explosive idea without fear it will go off in your face. It is one of the few havens remaining where a man's mind can get both provocation and privacy." Edward P. Morgan
- "Nothing is worth reading that does not require an alert mind." Charles Dudley Warner
- "I like intellectual reading. It's to my mind what fiber is to my body." Grey Livingston
- "Writing has nothing to do with communication between person and person, only with communication between different parts of a person's mind." Rebecca West
- "The ability to read awoke inside me some long dormant craving to be mentally alive." Malcolm, X, *The Autobiography of Malcolm X* (Grove Press, 1965)

Schema

Quotes about schema as worldview:

- "I'm a bit of a caveman—I don't go out into the digital space very often. I lie facedown on the grass and count how many bugs I can find." Dave Matthews
- "My ears won't fool me. Even when I do a [musical] session on digital, we still warm it up somewhere in the process, in mastering or mixing, running the signal through some tubes somewhere." Steve Cropper

Quotes about reading and the influences of our schema:

- "Lovers of print are simply confusing the plate for the food." Douglas Adams
- "No matter how busy you may think you are, you must find time for reading, or surrender yourself to self-chosen ignorance." Confucius
- "I divide all readers into two classes; those who read to remember and those who read to forget." William Lyon Phelps
- "The time to read is any time: no apparatus, no appointment of time and place, is necessary. It is the only art which can be practised [*sic*] at any hour of the day or night, whenever the time and inclination comes, that is your time for reading; in joy or sorrow, health or illness." Holbrook Jackson
- "Children are made readers on the laps of their parents." Emilie Buchwald
- "Reading aloud with children is known to be the single most important activity for building the knowledge and skills they will eventually require for learning to read." Marilyn Jager Adams

Inference

Quotes about inference as worldview:

- "I want to be part of the resurgence of things that are tangible, beautiful and soulful, rather than just give in to the digital age. But when I talk to people about this they just say, 'Yeah, I know what you mean,' and stare at their mobiles." Jack White
- "My own experience is use the tools that are out there. Use the digital world. But never lose sight of the need to reach out and talk to other people who don't share your view. Listen to them and see if you can find a way to compromise." Colin Powell
- "More and more, job listings are exclusively available online and as technology evolves nearly every occupation now requires a basic level of digital literacy with web navigation, e-mail access and participation in social media." Michael K. Powell
- "Further, the next generation of terrorists will grow up in a digital world, with ever more powerful and easy-to-use hacking tools at their disposal." Dorothy Denning

Quotes about reading and the influences of inference:

- "The digital revolution is far more significant than the invention of writing or even of printing." Douglas Engelbart
- "There are answers that cover the short, medium and long term. Everyone needs to realise [sic] that the thing the internet is good at is copying files, especially text files, between different locations. It is not a bug that needs cured, it doesn't need fixed, it's what makes the internet work. More people are reading more words from more screens every day. It's not going to be long before the majority of text people read is in a digital format." Cory Doctorow
- "Having your book turned into a movie is like seeing your oxen turned into bouillon cubes." John le Carré
- "Never judge a book by its movie." J. W. Eagan

Questioning

Quotes about thinking with questions:

- "I've seen a study in the last year that digital sound actually induces stress in the listener." T Bone Burnett
- "One of the things that I've been doing recently in my scientific research is to ask this question: Is the universe actually capable of performing things like digital computations?" Seth Lloyd
- "And what better way to reinvent the form than to toss virtually 99% of everything that's been done with it and start with a brand-new canvas,

reinvent it from the ground up? Digital comics gave me the opportunity to do that, and producing things digitally gave me the opportunity to do that." Scott McCloud

Quotes about reading with questions:

- "Though schools are looking to computers as a way to increase literacy, we have no hard proof that the digital revolution has increased reading. What is certain, however, is that more people are writing, and they are writing more than ever." Dennis Baron
- "What is reading, but silent conversation?" Charles Lamb
- "If you resist reading what you disagree with, how will you ever acquire deeper insights into what you believe? The things most worth reading are precisely those that challenge our convictions." Unknown

Finding the Relevance

Quotes about thinking for relevance:

- "Not since the steam engine has any invention disrupted business models like the Internet. Whole industries including music distribution, yellow-pages directories, landline telephones, and fax machines have been radically reordered by the digital revolution." John Sununu
- "No matter how great we get with digital formats of instrumentation, nothing really quite duplicates the real thing." Michael Bolton
- "Digital reading will completely take over. It's lightweight and it's fantastic for sharing. Over time it will take over." Bill Gates

Quotes about reading for relevance:

- "As with other technologies that facilitated textual production, the computer is giving both writers and readers the opportunity to produce and consume massive amounts of text." Dennis Baron, professor of English and linguistics at the University of Illinois, in *A Better Pencil: Readers, Writers, and the Digital Revolution* (Oxford, 2009)
- "Books had instant replay long before televised sports." Bern Williams
- "We are too civil to books. For a few golden sentences we will turn over and actually read a volume of four or five hundred pages." Ralph Waldo Emerson

Visualizing

Quotes about thinking with vision (visualizing):

- "I like having the digital camera on my smart phone, but I also like having a dedicated camera for when I want to take real pictures." Jeff Bezos

- "I enjoy doing digital work. I enjoy sculpting digitally. I've had my digital sculptures on covers of the top digital magazines." Rick Baker
- "How can I impress strangers with the gem-like flame of my literary passion if it's a digital slate I'm carrying around, trying not to get it all thumbprinty?" James Wolcott
- "In traditional schools, you're penalized for making a mistake. But that won't work in the new information culture, in the digital world we live in today." Daniel Greenberg
- "Soon it's all going to be digital anyway. It's all going to be saved on a little coin somewhere." Richard Donner
- "Design, in its broadest sense, is the enabler of the digital era—it's a process that creates order out of chaos, that renders technology usable to business. Design means being good, not just looking good." Clement Mok
- "When you look at a city, it's like reading the hopes, aspirations and pride of everyone who built it." Hugh Newell Jacobsen
- "Of all of our inventions for mass communication, pictures still speak the most universally understood language." Walt Disney

Quotes about reading with vision (visualizing):

- "Paper should be edible, nutritious. Inks used for printing or writing should have delicious flavors. Magazines or newspapers read at breakfast should be eaten for lunch. Instead of throwing one's mail in the wastebasket, it should be saved for the dinner guests." John Cage, *M: Writings '67–'72*
- "A great book should leave you with many experiences, and slightly exhausted. You should live several lives while reading it." William Styron
- "Often while reading a book one feels that the author would have preferred to paint rather than write; one can sense the pleasure he derives from describing a landscape or a person, as if he were painting what he is saying, because deep in his heart he would have preferred to use brushes and colors." Pablo Picasso
- "After three days without reading, talk becomes flavorless." Chinese proverb
- "Lord! When you sell a man a book you don't sell just twelve ounces of paper and ink and glue—you sell him a whole new life. Love and friendship and humour and ships at sea by night—there's all heaven and earth in a book, a real book." Christopher Morley
- "He fed his spirit with the bread of books." Edwin Markham
- "Bread of flour is good; but there is bread, sweet as honey, if we would eat it, in a good book." John Ruskin

Analyzing

Quotes about thinking using analysis:

- "It's all about sound. It's that simple. Wireless is wireless, and it's digital. Hopefully somewhere along the line somebody will add more ones to the zeros. When digital first started, I swear I could hear the gap between the ones and the zeros." Eddie Van Halen
- "Digital downloading of music has affected us all in adverse ways." Wynonna Judd
- "Digital media has destroyed much of the magic and mystery of the medium." John Dyer
- "Working in the digital domain, you're using approximations of things; the actual sound wave never enters the equation. You deal with sections of it, and you're able to do so much more by just reducing the information to a finite amount." Sean Booth
- "Digital for storage and quickness. Analog for fatness and warmth." Adrian Belew

Quotes about reading using analysis:

- "Reading makes a full man, meditation a profound man, discourse a clear man." Benjamin Franklin
- "Reading maketh a full man; conference a ready man; and writing an exact man." Francis Bacon, Sr.
- "To choose a good book, look in an inquisitor's prohibited list." John Aikin
- "Books can be dangerous. The best ones should be labeled 'This could change your life.'" Helen Exley

Synthesizing

Quotes about thinking using synthesis:

- "Many people see technology as the problem behind the so-called digital divide. Others see it as the solution. Technology is neither. It must operate in conjunction with business, economic, political, and social system." Carly Fiorina
- "It's not about revenues: The fundamental economics in digital business is scale and margins. The top line has become the bottom line." Yuri Milner
- "Digital imaging allows both groups to rise above the limitations of mess and clutter and mechanics, and apply our talents to creating images limited only by our imaginations." Buffy Sainte-Marie

- "I think that the balance needs to be restored, and I would note that in the camp in which I am in, one finds libraries, universities, the Internet industry, the manufacturers of digital media, and consumers." Rick Boucher
- "The Internet is not just one thing, it's a collection of things — of numerous communications networks that all speak the same digital language." Jim Clark

Quotes about reading using synthesis:

- "Coming to understand a painting or a symphony in an unfamiliar style, to recognize the work of an artist or school, to see or hear in new ways, is as cognitive an achievement as learning to read or write or add." Nelson Goodman
- "The wise man reads both books and life itself." Lin Yutang
- "It often requires more courage to read some books than it does to fight a battle." Sutton Elbert Griggs

MORE THINKING STEMS FOR ENGAGING READING COMPREHENSION THEMES

Note: Thinking stems for Questioning can be found in Chapter 7 and for Relevance in Chapter 8.

Metacognition Thinking Stems

- I'm thinking _____.
- I'm noticing _____.
- I'm wondering _____.
- I'm seeing _____.
- I'm feeling _____.
- I'm considering _____.

- I'm contemplating _____.
- I'm meditating _____.
- I'm pondering _____.
- I've been thinking about _____ and noticing that _____. This is a new thought because _____.

Schema Thinking Stems

- That reminds me of _____.
- I'm remembering _____.
- I have a connection to _____.
- I have a schema for _____.
- I can relate to _____.

- When I read _____ the first time, I thought _____, but now that I'm reading it again, I think _____.
- I'm reading _____ through a filter of _____, which is different from my teacher/peers because _____.

Inference Thinking Stems

- My guess is _____.
- Maybe _____.
- Perhaps _____.
- This could mean _____.
- It could be that _____.
- From what I know about _____ and what I'm reading, I predict _____ will happen.
- The evidence says _____ and I know _____, so I infer _____.

Visualizing Thinking Stems

- I'm picturing _____.
- I can imagine that _____.
- I can feel (see, smell, taste, touch, hear) _____.
- My mental images include _____.
- When I read _____, I pictured _____, and/but the reality differed _____.
- When I heard _____, I saw _____ in my mind.

Analyzing Thinking Stems

- _____ and _____ are similar in _____ ways.
- The differences are _____.
- Because of _____, _____ happened.
- _____ happens when _____ occurs.
- I'm taking it apart to consider _____.
- When I read _____, I thought _____. But this new idea changes _____.

Synthesizing Thinking Stems

- Now I understand why _____.
- I'm changing my mind about _____.
- I used to think _____, but now I think _____.
- My new thinking is _____.
- When I put _____ and _____ together, I begin to think _____.
- When I read _____, I realized the connections between _____ and _____. Now I'm thinking _____.

APPENDIX **B**

Integrating Reading Comprehension Themes in the First-Year Writing Course

EXAMPLE ASSIGNMENTS FOR A FIRST-YEAR WRITING COURSE

The following example assignments have been created to help OWI teachers understand how reading comprehension themes can be introduced into an extant writing assignment without requiring significantly more work than already has been built into the assignment. For instance, one reading comprehension exercise might be substituted for an already existing writing/discussion exercise per essay assignment. Improving students' reading skills and giving them conscious practice enables them to address the reading connected to the writing—in whatever manner the teacher presents a writing assignment—more fully. Similarly, reading comprehension themes can be introduced into all writing assignments as background material for the writing and as explanation for how to connect reading to researched writing in particular. Teachers can adopt any of the comprehension themes outlined in Part Two and adapt the provided example exercises as desired.

These two example assignments introduce and build on the master skill of summarizing, which is linked here to the comprehension theme of *questioning* a reading. Essay 1 uses asking questions to help students write a summary, and it adapts material from the questioning exercise in Chapter 7.

Essay 2 demonstrates a scaffolded teaching approach; it uses and builds on asking questions and writing a summary to teach students the reading comprehension theme of *synthesis*, which also is a writing strategy. In other words, Essay 2 contrasts a known reading and writing skill (summarizing via questioning) to teach a second reading and writing skill (synthesis), and it adapts material from the synthesis exercise in Chapter 11. All of these reading and writing skills would be engaged in future essay assignments depending on the stated course outcomes.

These assignments are presented with straightforward language and clearly labeled parts that model what students should see in every assignment:

- Set of due dates
- Brief explanation of the point of the essay
- Background material about the skills being taught
- A "try this" section that includes reading, thinking, and sometimes pre-writing and/or an instructional example with a due date for the student's action
- Formal assignment parameters

These parts can be broken into separate documents or provided as an entire document. Whatever teachers choose, I recommend posting the assignment into at least two parts of the LMS—in spaces where students intuitively will look for it. Wherever offering redundancy enables students to find the assignment, they have a better chance of reading it in full and understanding its scope.

Finally, I have done these assignments myself as a way of testing what I am asking of students, learning how long it might take them to do the work (I always double to triple my time for novice writers), and revising any parts that are not clear, doable, or necessary to the assignment's desired outcomes. These are teaching strategies recommended in Part Three.

Assignment for Essay 1: Writing an Article Summary

Preliminary Draft <u>DUE 2/14</u> (Published to "Discussion Posts" for peer response)
Presentation Draft <u>DUE 2/28</u> (Published to "Assignments" for teacher response)
Project value: 10% of total grade

The **summary essay** (Essay 1) asks you to present information from a source objectively and concisely. The summary/synthesis essay (Essay 2) asks you to read the source actively and critically and to identify the source's main idea and relevant supporting points by asking questions and summarizing before synthesizing. As such, it asks you to develop a particular angle about the source that would be appropriate for the audience. The source materials presented in these two assignments are all you will need to complete your first two essay assignments.

Background:
This first essay is an article summary. This assignment will connect directly to Essay 2, so you will want to really give this assignment a good effort.

A summary, as described in chapter 1 of *Reading and Writing across the Curriculum*, is a <u>brief, complete, and objective explanation</u> of the contents and point of view of an article or essay. A good summary is clear, coherent, and accurate.

The ability to write an effective summary is one of the more important writing skills a writer can possess. You need to be able to summarize before you can be successful at most of the other kinds of writing that will be demanded of you. A summary, like a paraphrase, is a rewrite of an original passage <u>in your own words</u>, but the summary will be significantly shorter than the original, and it will give a broad overview of the material. Summaries can cover any kind of original material, from a paragraph to an entire article or book.

You must be able to summarize to answer questions such as "What was the movie about?" "How did the game go?" and "What did I miss in class today?" Your questioner doesn't want to know every line and action in the movie, every play in the game, or every word from class. The questioner wants you to select the important details and recap them. Similarly, when you summarize a reading you need to be able to find the important data and then present it as clearly and concisely as possible.

Politicians and corporations employ people to read every newspaper and newsmagazine and summarize relevant stories and articles. Moviemakers ask scriptwriters to pitch summaries of their films. The more concise the summary the better, yet if any major details are omitted the purpose of the summary is lost — its readers will be uninformed on key aspects of the news and may make embarrassing errors as a result. The summaries that you write in college are as important to your academic career as these summaries are to these politicians and business people, and accuracy and concision are just as important, too.

There are various <u>purposes</u> for summaries. They are used frequently in academic writing to describe an article before:

1. critiquing it,
2. showing relationships,
3. applying theoretical perspectives,
4. reporting research,
5. overviewing literary works,
6. summarizing evidence and opposing arguments, and/or
7. demonstrating understanding in testing situations.

A summary helps you to comprehend what you've read and to explain to someone else the point of an article or essay. The <u>audience</u> for a summary may be a fellow student, a scholar, or a more general public. It's important to understand your audience so that the summary is aptly written with that reader or set of readers in mind. (For essays 1 and 2, your audience will be your classmates and me; for essays 3 and 4, the audience will shift—watch how your writing needs to shift, too!)

Your interpretation of an article will be influenced by your own personal and professional background—your frame of reference (also called a schema). For example, an article about the building of the largest mall in North America would be read and summarized differently by someone who is an architect than it would be by someone whose father's local book business was shattered by the opening of a mall's major book seller. However, as much as possible, the summary should objectively represent the article or essay—not showing the bias or agenda of the summary author.

Note that summaries are brief, which makes them different from paraphrases (which are nearly as long as the original piece). They may include a quotation from the original, but typically only when the original language is especially important to the reader's understanding.

Obviously, you cannot write a good summary of a source that you do not understand. One way to write a solid summary is to ask questions of what you are reading. Asking questions is a reading comprehension theme that you learned way back in elementary school and have been practicing in your classes ever since. Questioning strategies go beyond simply asking the wh- (what, where, when, why, and who) and how questions. They instead try to get at the heart of the matter even when there is no clear truth or definite answer. Your answers to those questions will help you to develop a summary such as that of my example below.

Try this (DUE: 2/7 Post to Journal):
Read the following short article, which is a case study from a university web page.

Notice the use of boldface questions as they appear in brackets [ ], which I always use to symbolize my thinking as opposed to an author's thinking about something. In these brackets, the questions are intended to probe the author's assumptions. For me, they indicate incomplete definitions, explanations, and reasoning in the article as it is written.

Read this article. Below, I summarize it in about 150 words. My primary strategy is to use my questions to learn what the author is saying.

> Animals are also used in case studies. One area of psychology that uses primate case studies is the field of language acquisition. **[What is language acquisition?]** Researchers debate whether language is something unique to humans, or if it appears in lower animals also. **[How are researchers defining "language"? What are the reasons for assuming that language can be unique to humans? What are the reasons for assuming that lower animals don't have language? In fact, what is a "lower animal"?]** If a psychologist could show that a non-human animal uses language like humans, it would demonstrate that

language is not a unique feature of humans. [**This statement assumes that it's possible to demonstrate a non-human animal using human-like language. Does that indicate that animal-to-animal language isn't considered language? What would make this a valid assumption?**]

Dr. Sue Savage-Rumbaugh at the Language Research Center (LRC) at Georgia State University is working with a collection of chimpanzees and bonobos on the question of whether non-human primates can acquire language. [**What's a bonobo?**] One such bonobo is Kanzi.

Kanzi was born in 1980 and was raised in an English language environment. [**We need a lot more information here. My dog has been raised in an English-language environment. What does it mean to have been raised here?**] His mother was a research subject in language training studies. [**How was she a research subject? What kinds of activities did she undergo in language research?**] He spent all of his time with her during her training. When Kanzi was two years old, his mother was sent to a different primate center to breed. It was at this point that the researchers at the LRC discovered that Kanzi could understand their language. It seemed that he had acquired language much the same way a human child does—by being exposed to it throughout infancy and early childhood. [**There are lots of assumptions here, too. Kanzi spent time with his mother—did his mother teach him language or did he get it through osmosis from the researchers? What kinds of exposure did Kanzi have to language? Did his mother learn to speak the language or recognize it in some other way? Was Kanzi ever videotaped with his mother when researchers weren't around using human language?**]

Kanzi could use a picture board to point to the correct symbol when the experimenters said the name of an item. [**Why are symbols considered evidence of language? Is this a common assumption about language?**] New symbols were added to his picture board, but he was not trained in their meaning. Instead, researchers used the new words in conversation. [**What is the implication here?**] Kanzi can point to the symbol or the real object when he hears the word. In addition, he can "tell" his human companions what he wants to do by pointing to the symbols on his picture board. [**"Tell" is placed in quotes. Why? How do the researchers know that Kanzi's act of pointing to the board means that he wants something?**]

Dr. Savage-Rumbaugh interprets Kanzi's behavior as evidence that non-human primates can understand and acquire human language. [**What does it mean that she "interprets" the behavior as evidence? Are there other ways she should consider thinking about the behavior?**] She believes this demonstrates that language is not a unique capability of humans. [**Again, what is the definition of "language" being used here?**] Other psychologists disagree with her findings and believe that Kanzi has been trained, much like a circus animal. They do not believe that he creates or understands new word combinations, which is the crucial aspect of human language acquisition. [**Ah, here is information the case needed to give earlier. Is there a bias in this definition about language acquisition that can't be addressed by what we know from this case?**

Has Kanzi been asked to create word combinations that could be considered sentences? How is a circus animal like or different from Kanzi?] http://www.nvcc.edu/home/elanthier/methods/case-study-samples.htm

You can see that there are many questions I have about this case as it is written. As an interested and discerning reader, I want and need to know much more before I can come to any conclusion about who I think is more right in this case. My questions lead me to what I can summarize about this article. Here is my summary:

> In this article, which is a case study by Elizabeth Lanthier written in 2002 about language acquisition, the primary question is whether a bonobo (a type of chimpanzee) named Kanzi has the ability to acquire human language. Dr. Sue Savage-Rumbaugh works with Kanzi at the Language Research Center (LRC) at Georgia State University. She believes that he has acquired some English language abilities because he recognizes certain words that he never was taught directly. Kanzi also can point to pictures to "ask" for what he wants. His mother had been taught these words, and he may have learned them the same way as human children: from "infancy and early childhood" exposure. Dr. Savage-Rumbaugh thinks that Kanzi's language abilities are like those of human children. Some scientists do not agree with her and ask whether Kanzi can produce original word combinations. The questions about whether chimpanzees can acquire human language are not answered in this case study.
>
> Lanthier, Elizabeth. "Case Study 2." Case Study Samples. 2002. Web. http://www.nvcc.edu/home/elanthier/methods/case-study-samples.htm

Notice that the summary:

- is built on the questions I asked of the article,
- tries to answer questions based only on the article and NOT on my opinion,
- uses names and places to help readers connect the article with the summary, and
- is much shorter than the article (156 words as opposed to 368 in the original).

Exercise:

- Read Chapters 1 and 3 of *Reading and Writing across the Curriculum*; they provide good information about writing a summary. The demonstration summaries are helpful, as are the discussions of where a thesis goes, how a summary is written, and how summaries are organized. Please pay careful attention to these chapters; highlight important information to which you'll want to return.
- Write a brief journal entry that outlines what you have learned about summaries from your readings and my example (above). Indicate any areas in the Essay 1 assignment that you think will be challenging for you

and why. Ask questions that you would like me to answer. **Post this entry in the LMS Journal space by 2/7.**

Essay 1 Assignment:
Preliminary Draft <u>DUE 2/14</u> (Published to "Discussion Posts" for peer response)
Presentation Draft <u>DUE 2/28</u> (Published to "Assignments" for teacher response)

- Read the articles featured in chapter 14 of *Reading and Writing across the Curriculum*. This chapter's theme is "Has the Jury Reached a Verdict?"
- Choose one essay to summarize; it should be either an expository or an argumentative essay, not a narrative essay. The essay you choose to summarize will be included as <u>part of</u> your Essay 2 assignment. As you read the essay, mimic my questioning strategy. You can write your questions directly in your book, on a separate sheet of paper, or using your computer's word processer.
- This essay has three paragraphs plus a reference citation.
  - **Paragraph 1:** Write a brief summary of the article's main idea and its most important main points. For context, this paragraph should include the author, article title, and date of publication. Provide the place of publication if possible. Paragraph one should be from 200 to 300 words depending on the length of the article you have selected.
  - **Paragraph 2:** Write a discussion of the author's point of view, bias, and possible agenda. For example, the author of "Case Study 2" uses the third-person point of view and attempts to be unbiased toward either position. How do we know she does that? Give examples from the article. However, she only provides a brief amount of material about the scientists that disagree with Dr. Savage-Rumbaugh. Is there a possible agenda in that choice? What does the author seem to want to do? Use the evidence of the article itself and cite (quote) from the article to show readers what you think is happening. Whether the article was published in a scholarly journal or website as opposed to a general magazine or blog also provides more information about the piece in terms of reliability and the writer's authority.
  - **Paragraph 3:** Write a thoughtful opinion as to this article's potential value for understanding the issue under consideration. In other words, if you were writing about the bonobos case study, I would not care whether you think bonobos can acquire human language; instead, I would want to know whether you think there is enough believable information in this article to help you learn and understand the issue. What else would you need to know? Hint: Return to the questions you wrote when reading the article.

This question is actually a starting point for Essay 2, but we are beginning to <u>critique</u> here because your conscious thinking may help you to be exceptionally objective in paragraphs 1 and 2. Remember: Your opinion about the issue in general is NOT what the summary requires. First, you must EARN your opinion by reading deeply, discussing, and thinking broadly about it.

- **Citation:** <u>Write an MLA bibliographic citation</u> for the article at the end of the article.

- **Time Management:** Reading, questioning, and writing a solid preliminary draft should take no less than 2½ to 4 hours. Don't worry if it takes you longer; give this essay the time it needs. Revising and providing a presentation draft after receiving and giving peer feedback should take another 2 to 4 hours depending on how thorough you were with the preliminary draft.

- **Presentation:** Double space and write two full pages. Your name should be at the top of the first page. Save your file with essay number, whether it's a preliminary or presentation draft, and your last name, for example, I would save may essay as Essay1_Preliminary_Hewett. Use your word processing program to number the pages (Insert → Page numbers → Top of Page).

- **Refer to the article using the present tense because we are using MLA style.**

- **Carefully proofread.** Use the proofreading skills that we have been practicing in discussion groups. Reread aloud and listen for complete sentences, comma usage that clarifies meaning rather than confuses it, and common punctuation errors, such as capitalization where it doesn't belong or questions without question marks. Periods and commas belong inside quotes.

- **ALWAYS spell-check your document.** Spelling errors are so annoying that they can keep the reader from understanding (or wanting to understand) your message. (Do you wear dirty athletic shoes to the prom? Do you leave a piece of broccoli between your teeth if you have the chance to see it and remove it?)

Assignment for Essay 2:
Writing a Synthesis of Three Articles

Preliminary Draft <u>DUE 3/7</u> (Published to "Discussion Posts" for peer response)

Presentation Draft <u>DUE 3/21</u> (Published to "Assignments" for teacher response)

Project value: 20% of total grade

The **summary essay assignment** (Essay 1) asked you to present information from one source objectively and concisely. This synthesis essay assignment

(Essay 2) asks you to read three sources actively and critically and to identify their main ideas and relevant supporting points by asking questions and summarizing before synthesizing. As such, it asks you to develop a particular angle about the source that would be appropriate for the audience.

Background:

In Essay 1, you used the reading comprehension theme of <u>questioning</u> to help you write a summary. In this essay, you will use those skills, but you will add the reading comprehension theme of <u>synthesis</u> to write a <u>summary and synthesis that connects and allows you to critique the ideas in the articles.</u>

<u>Synthesis and summary are related yet different writing skills.</u> Students sometimes mix up the skills of synthesizing and summarizing. Teachers can see this confusion in writing where we ask students to use research to support their claims. Not only do many students provide often poor summaries of what an author has said, but they also may fail to use sources to support new ideas. One way to avoid this problem is to look at the task first from the perspective of reading rather than writing. <u>Good writers first understand what they read.</u>

Let us look at the nature of summary and synthesis as different ways of writing about what you read.

We know that a summary is a <u>brief, complete, and objective explanation</u> of the contents and point of view of an article or essay. A good summary is clear, coherent, and accurate.

Synthesis, on the other hand, combines ideas from various sources to build or form new information and ways of thinking. Synthesis is about combination. When things are combined, they become something new. All of nature uses synthesis, and you will hear about this high-level occurrence in nearly all of your college courses.

Let us look at a few examples of synthesis (adapted from the OWI synthesizing exercise in chapter 11). [**These exercises can be creatively presented using text, images, and/or audio. Audio can be self-recorded, as with the nursery rhyme "There Was an Old Lady" mentioned below. Any of these can be downloaded from the Web depending on fair-use copyright laws.**]

- Red, blue, and yellow are the primary colors. All colors come from red, blue, and yellow. When combined, they create different colors. Red + blue = purple. Blue + yellow = green. Yellow + red = orange. Combine any shade of these colors and new colors emerge. Each is a synthesis of the original colors.

- A synthesizer is a musical instrument that either generates entirely new sounds or imitates the sounds of other instruments. Although it generally has the shape of a keyboard, which suggests piano or organ sounds, a synthesizer is really a source of many instrumental sounds. This one instrument not only creates sounds, but it also combines a variety of sounds to create new timbres and instrumental harmonies through electronic technologies.

- Synthetic fabrics are combinations of different types of chemically produced fibers that have properties (e.g., waterproofing or softness) that are different from natural fibers like cotton, wool, and silk. A variety of different synthetic fabrics can be made by combining the chemicals with the natural fibers (e.g., nylon, acrylic, polyester, Kevlar, and spandex). Women's jeans manufacturers currently combine denim with spandex to create a more moveable, pliable pair of jeans, for example.
- Children's songs and rhymes can demonstrate synthesis. Two examples are "The House That Jack Built" and "There Was an Old Lady."[1] Read "There Was an Old Lady," and look at how it combines actions (what the old lady swallowed) to come to an unexpected (or expected!) end:

> There was an old lady who swallowed a fly
> I don't know why she swallowed a fly—perhaps she'll die!
> There was an old lady who swallowed a spider,
> That wriggled and wiggled and tickled inside her;
> She swallowed the spider to catch the fly;
> I don't know why she swallowed a fly—perhaps she'll die!
> There was an old lady who swallowed a bird;
> How absurd to swallow a bird.
> She swallowed the bird to catch the spider,
> She swallowed the spider to catch the fly;
> I don't know why she swallowed a fly—perhaps she'll die!
> There was an old lady who swallowed a cat;
> Fancy that to swallow a cat!
> She swallowed the cat to catch the bird,
> She swallowed the bird to catch the spider,
> She swallowed the spider to catch the fly;
> I don't know why she swallowed a fly—perhaps she'll die!
> There was an old lady who swallowed a dog;
> What a hog, to swallow a dog;
> She swallowed the dog to catch the cat,
> She swallowed the cat to catch the bird,
> She swallowed the bird to catch the spider,
> She swallowed the spider to catch the fly;
> I don't know why she swallowed a fly—perhaps she'll die!
> There was an old lady who swallowed a cow,
> I don't know how she swallowed a cow;
> She swallowed the cow to catch the dog,

---

[1] See McGregor (2007, 108–9).

She swallowed the dog to catch the cat,
She swallowed the cat to catch the bird,
She swallowed the bird to catch the spider,
She swallowed the spider to catch the fly;
I don't know why she swallowed a fly—perhaps she'll die!
There was an old lady who swallowed a horse . . .
She's dead, of course!

Try this (DUE: 3/1 Posted to Peer Group):
This exercise is intended to teach the differences between summary and synthesis and to provide practice in both skills. While synthesis typically involves reading more than one text, for the purposes of an example, I work with one text alone. The following example text, "American Idol Worship" by Thomas de Zengotita, provides a way to demonstrate the difference between reading to summarize a text and reading to synthesize and find new ideas. The core exercise directly follows the text. **[OWI Instructors: See Chapter 11 for the full text of Thomas de Zengotita's "American Idol Worship."]**

Exercise:

1. Read the text and find the thesis and supporting details. Ask questions of the text as you did for Essay 1. Write them down somewhere.

2. Write a sample summary of the text's main points. Remember that summarizing requires not only condensing the text but also judging for importance and organizing for comprehension of the importance. Your extant (current) knowledge or personal schema (background) helps make this level of reading possible. Completing a summary is the first part of this exercise.

3. The second part of this exercise is synthesis. Here are some stem sentences to help you synthesize the text yourself. A stem sentence provides a blank for you to fill in; it helps with learning a new reading and writing skill because the stem sentence provides a particular focus for your thinking.

   a. As _____ says, "_____," which is why _____.

   b. People seem to crave the chance to show off their talents even when they don't have any talent. _____ suggests that is because _____.

   c. _____ believes that _____. However, he/she is wrong because _____.

4. Use the blank part of the stem sentences for your use of the original text, as shown by underlines. Be sure to use quotation marks if you use the direct, exact words from the text. The rest of the writing you do

represents your own thinking. When the stem sentences are completed and you have written sentences before and after them for context, these sentences represent a <u>synthesis</u> of another person's thinking with your own—leading to entirely new thinking and expression of those thoughts. These stem sentences can help you begin to work with the text more originally.

5. **Post your summaries and synthesis responses by 3/1 to your peer group**, so you can see and comment on how your classmates are trying out the skills of summary and synthesis. In your responses to peers, download their files, write directly in them using brackets [ ] or the Comments feature of Microsoft Word to tell your peers what you think about the summary and the point you learn from their synthesis. Add your name to the end of the file name when saving the document, and upload it to the LMS for them to see. **Complete this work by 3/5.**

[Provide students with an example summary and synthesis using stem sentences, as shown in the synthesis exercise in Chapter 11, pages 163–67.]

Essay 2 Assignment:
Preliminary Draft <u>DUE 3/7</u> (Published to "Discussion Posts" for peer response)
Presentation Draft <u>DUE 3/21</u> (Published to "Assignments" for teacher response)

- Reread three of the articles featured in Chapter 14 of *Reading and Writing across the Curriculum*. Recall that this chapter's theme is "Has the Jury Reached a Verdict?" As you read the articles, mimic my questioning strategy and the one you practiced for Essay 1. You can write your questions directly in your book, on a separate sheet of paper, or using your computer's word processor.
- Summarize the three articles in at least <u>three different paragraphs</u>. One of these summaries should be your revised summary from Essay 1.
- Next, find the main ideas in each article.
  - Where are the ideas similar among these three articles? Where are they different? Your job is to make a connection among the three articles by finding a significant similarity or difference or some area in which their themes cross over.
  - Write between <u>three to five paragraphs</u> (after the summary paragraphs) to discuss these similarities and/or differences. Your goal is to synthesize the articles using the authors' words and your original thinking about whether they are similar and/or different. The result will be new thinking (new because it came from you) about them.
  - Remember that the kinds of questions you can ask about these articles include the author's point of view, bias, and possible agenda. What

does the author seem to want to accomplish through the article? Who is the audience (reader) for whom the article is written? Use the evidence of the article itself and cite (quote) from the article to show readers what you think is happening. Whether the article was published in a scholarly journal or on a website as opposed to a general magazine or blog also provides more information about the piece in terms of reliability and the writer's authority.

- Your writing should include a thoughtful opinion as to each article's potential value for understanding the issue under consideration. Remember that the goal of a synthesis is to combine the thinking in these three articles to reveal your fresh perspective about what the authors themselves are saying. Is there sufficient (enough) believable information? Have the authors' missed any necessary information? What do you learn about the topic from your reading and synthesis of the articles?

- The stem sentences shown below can help you to write synthetically about these three articles. Use them any way you want; you can even change their wording and use them more than once. Notice that it is okay to use first person (I) in this essay, but it also is good to use third person (Smith states, "_____.") as needed.

  Synthesizing Thinking Stems
  — Now I understand why _____.
  — I'm changing my mind about _____.
  — I used to think _____, but now I think _____.
  — My new thinking is _____.
  — When I put _____ and _____ together, I begin to think _____.
  — When I read _____, I realized the connections between _____ and _____. Now I'm thinking _____.

- Next, when you have a strong preliminary draft, write an introductory paragraph that states the purpose of the essay (by this time in your writing process, you will have a good idea of your purpose). Then, write a concluding paragraph that pulls all the ideas together, summarizing your main points.

- Write an MLA bibliographic citation at the end of your essay.

- **Quotations and Paraphrase:** When you quote from the articles (use the exact words of the author) or paraphrase (use your own words about what the author is saying), you must provide the page number and author's name. Use the two strategies below as models:

  - Smith explains that "_____" (433). ["433" is the page number]
  - I used to think _____, but now I understand _____ because _____ (Smith 433; Jones 400). [this example shows that you got your ideas from two of the three authors]

- **Time Management:** Reading, questioning, summarizing, synthesizing ideas, and writing a solid preliminary draft should take no less than 4 to 8 hours. Don't worry if it takes you longer; give this essay the time it needs. Because there are no tests to study for in this class, all of your writing becomes the evidence of your developing thinking and skills, and it is where your course time primarily will be used. Revising and providing a presentation draft after receiving and giving peer feedback should take another 4 to 8 hours depending on how thorough you were with the preliminary draft.
- **Presentation:** Double space and write as many pages as you need to complete the assignment. Your name should be at the top of the first page. Save your file with essay number, whether it's a preliminary or presentation draft, and your last name; for example, I would save my essay as Essay2_Preliminary_Hewett. Use your word processing program to number the pages (Insert → Page Number → Top of Page).
- **Refer to the article using the present tense because we are using MLA style.**
- **Carefully proofread.** Use the proofreading skills that we have been practicing in discussion groups. Reread aloud and listen for complete sentences, comma usage that clarifies meaning rather than confuses it, and common punctuation errors, such as capitalization where it doesn't belong or questions without question marks. Periods and commas belong inside quote marks except when page numbers are indicated [**Thomas states that, "People should think about their agendas before they speak" (55)**].
- **ALWAYS spell-check your document.**

EXAMPLE RESPONSE TO THE WHOLE CLASS

Hi everyone! I've finished reviewing all the essays that were turned in. To do so, I used an assessment rubric that you can find under "Course Content." Here are a few things everyone needs to know. You don't need to respond to this discussion post unless you want to.

Rubric

The rubric is organized by the essay's *content, form* (organization), and then *style and correctness*. Those are my priorities in that order. If your content is poor, the rest doesn't matter much because your organization and style will likely change in revision. If your content is great, then I look closely at the rest. Does that make sense? In essence, I'm checking for the higher-order concerns of content and organization before I worry about style and sentence structure. That will help you to make the most of your revisions.

I tried to give each of you a brief lesson on an important issue for revision and a manageable number of things to work on in revision. In no case did I address every single issue in the essay. You'll need to use your handbook, peers, and the university's Online Writing Lab for additional help if you're concerned. You can also send me a message and we can arrange an individual IM chat or phone call. My goal was to help you address your major issues and to acknowledge your strengths as you draft.

If you see that I've given an example that uses "XYZ," consider XYZ to be a placeholder or a fill-in-the-blank for what you need to write.

Use and Documentation of Sources

Using my example essay about kindness, notice that you need to cite pages from which you paraphrase and quote. Without the citations, you are plagiarizing whether you mean to or not.

When you introduce an article for the first time, try following my example as a model if you find you need more than one sentence to introduce it. Such an introduction usually can be done in a single sentence and can be easier for readers to follow. If you have some of the context for the article, use that, too.

When referring to the author, use the full name the first time. After that, use only the last name. It isn't necessary to use Mr. or Ms.

I know that some of you are having APA/MLA confusions, and I'll write another lesson for you soon. However, for now, here is a simple rule to remember:

If you are using MLA, the verbs relative to the paraphrase and quotation will use present tense verbs. For example: *As Amy Brown says after the Civil War: "John Brown's body lies a moldering in the grave."*

If you are using APA, the verbs relative to the paraphrase and quotation will use past tense verbs. For example: *As Amy Brown said after the Civil War: "John Brown's body lies a moldering in the grave."*

So, if I tell you to change your verb tense regarding APA or MLA, refer back to this example, please.

For this assignment, cite your source article twice in the bibliographic references — once in MLA and again in APA. This part of the assignment gives you practice in both forms. Half the essays I read for the last assignment flubbed the bibliographic references. Here's the deal: You didn't get the source article from the place where it was first published. You got it from our textbook. Therefore, the text has to be what you cite. For MLA, go to your handbook page 622 and look up "work in an anthology." For APA, go to your handbook page 720 and look up "article or chapter in an edited book." Also, use my kindness essay as a model for how to write the bibliographic references.

Your handbook guides are written with the idea that you can figure out how to look up other common issues. For example, your textbook has two editors and not one. But where you'll find the example for work in an anthology isn't the same place that you'll find works by two editors. So, you'll have to check that out in another part of the guide. How you cite the two editors will differ from MLA to APA, too. Just do a little bit of detective work. You'll need this skill for your academic work in other classes anyway.

Style and Correctness

Transitional sentences are important for providing coherence as writers change ideas and paragraphs. Return to my track changed version of my kindness essay presentation draft for an example of how I provided connections among the articles and between paragraphs. Use this as an example of how to "glue" together your points. Your handbook also will help you if you look up "transitions."

Commas are always used after introductory clauses. Although I'll likely address this issue again, please begin changing your writing to accommodate it now. Here are some examples from your essays:

> If I had not found the lady who the money belonged to, I know in my heart that I would have brought the money back into the store and left it with the manager at the store in case anyone came in looking for it.
>
> In the above example sentence, the underlined section is an introductory (or subordinate) clause. Look up those terms in your handbook. Since such a clause does not stand by itself as a complete sentence, it needs a comma to join it to an independent clause. [**Notice that I just wrote two sentences with introductory clauses as examples!**]

If you have a tendency to confuse the use of *that* and *which*, look them up in your handbook. The issue is restrictive and nonrestrictive clauses.

The assignment says that you need to put a period or a comma inside your quotation marks. That's true EXCEPT for when the quote marks are followed by a parenthetical page citation. In that case, the period goes outside the quote marks. [e.g., Jane Doe says, "X, Y, and Z" (49).]

I'll highlight this issue again, but please try to break the habit of saying, "I feel XYZ"; replace it with "I **think** XYZ" or "I **believe** XYZ." The reason is that in college (academic) writing, no one really cares what you *feel* about an issue. Readers do care what you *think* and *believe* and why, however.

Presentation of Draft

Write your own original title for your essay. Neither "Essay 1" nor the assignment's title will work. Write a title that reflects the ideas that you're actually writing about.

Appropriate formatting of the essay includes such details as using tabs to indent a paragraph (rather than tapping the space bar five times) and using a hard page return to separate the body of the text from the bibliography. If you use Microsoft Word or any other common word processing program, you can learn how to find and use these tools through the Help guide. Please learn to use them!

On a similar note, please use the program's assigned function to insert page numbers in each document.

I've seen a few really good peer reviews. Keep up that strong work! As for the more dashed-off reviews, well, you and I both know if you wrote one — take good care of each other as readers and be generous. Please make sure everyone gets at least two reviews. If you can find the extra time, write an extra review for someone who doesn't have any.

I think those are all of my notes from reading your pieces. **I'll look for your Presentation drafts in the Assignments folder on Monday (due Sunday night by 11:59 PM).** Find Essay Assignment 1 and upload the document there; <u>do not paste in the essay</u>. When I grade those essays, I won't go into the kind of detail I did for your preliminary drafts, but I will tell you about (1) strengths you'll want to repeat in future essays and (2) weaknesses that you'll want to both fix (possibly for the portfolio) and avoid.

Have a great day!

ESSAY 1 ASSESSMENT RUBRIC

Student Name: _____

	Competency	Fails to Meet Competency √−	Meets Competency √	Exceeds Competency √+
Content (Fluency)	• Essay has an appropriate original title. • Essay meets requirements: subject, organization, and length (approximately 4–5 body pages). • Essay presents a clear thesis about a moral dilemma. • Introduction discusses the background, or reasons, for the problem: why this issue is a problem, why people disagree about the problem, and the main points the essay will discuss. • The essay body summarizes two articles in relation to the main issue. • Relevant support from articles includes facts, figures, examples, and quotations. • Conclusion paragraph summarizes the major points of the author's position through an appraisal of moral behavior.			
Organization (Form)	• Essay is unified in that it summarizes and discusses two articles or essays related to the moral dilemma. • Paragraphs address the assignment's requirements.			
Style & Expression	• Writing is clear and precise. • Sentence meaning is clear. • Sentence structures generally are correct.			
Grammar & Mechanics (Correctness)	• Essay is substantially free of major errors in grammar, spelling, punctuation, and mechanics and completely free of distracting errors. • Essay introduces and explains, paraphrases and quotes correctly and completely. • Essay uses MLA or APA guidelines for in-text citation. • Essay uses both MLA and APA guidelines for the cited article at end of summary.			

Comments:

References

Abani, Chris. 2012. "The Lottery." In *The Writer's Presence: A Pool of Readings* (7th ed.), edited by Donald McQuade and Robert Atwan, 25–27. Boston: Bedford/St. Martin's.

Adler-Kassner, Linda, and Estrem, Heidi. 2007. "Reading Practices in the Writing Classroom." *Writing Program Administration* 31 (1/2): 35–47.

Alexander, Jonathan. 2006. *Digital Youth: Emerging Literacies on the World Wide Web.* Kresskill, NJ: Hampton Press.

Allen, I. Elaine, and Seaman, Jeff. 2011. *Going the Distance: Online Education in the United States, 2011.* Babson Survey Research Group. http://www.onlinelearning survey.com/reports/goingthedistance.pdf.

Allen, I. Elaine, Seaman, Jeff, Lederman, Doug, and Jaschik, Scott. 2012. *Conflicted: Faculty and Online Education, 2012.* Babson Survey Research Group, *Inside Higher Ed,* and Quahog Research Group. http://www.insidehighered.com/sites/default /server_files/files/IHE-BSRG-Conflict.pdf.

Anderson, Carl. 2000. *How's It Going?: A Practical Guide to Conferring with Student Writers.* Portsmouth, NH: Heinemann.

Anson, Chris M. 1997. "In Our Own Voices: Using Recorded Commentary to Respond to Writing." *New Directions for Teaching and Learning* 69 (Spring): 105–13.

———. 1998. "Reflective Reading: Developing Thoughtful Ways to Respond to Students' Writing." In *Key Works on Teacher Response: An Anthology*, edited by R. Straub, 361–82. Portsmouth, NH: Heinemann/Boynton Cook Publishers.

Anson, Chris M., and Robert A. Schwegler. 2012. "Tracking the Mind's Eye: A New Technology for Researching Twenty-First-Century Writing and Reading Processes." *College Composition and Communication* 64 (1): 151–71.

AT&T. 2013. "Two Things at Once: It's Not Complicated" (TV commercial). http:// www.youtube.com/watch?v=usfGA6I1Hos.

Bardine, B. A. 1999. "Students' Perceptions of Written Teacher Comments: What Do They Say About How We Respond to Them?" *High School Journal* 82 (4): 239.

Bartholomae, David, and Anthony Petrosky. 2002. *Ways of Reading: An Anthology for Writers* (6th ed.). Boston: Bedford/St. Martin's.

Beach, Richard, and Tom Friedrich. 2006. "Response to Writing." In *Handbook of Writing Research*, edited by Charles A. MacArthur, S. Graham, and J. Fitzgerald, 222–34. New York: Guilford.

Belfer, Karen, and Ron Wakkary. 2005. "Team Assessment Guidelines: A Case Study of Collaborative Learning in Design." In *Assessing Online Learning*, edited by Patricia Comeaux, 34–53. Bolton, MA: Ankar Publishing.

Berrett, Dan. 2012. "Freshman Composition Is Not Teaching Key Skills in Analysis, Researchers Argue." *The Chronicle of Higher Education*, March 21. http://chronicle .com/article/Freshman-Composition-Is-Not/131278/.

Bilbro, J., C. Iluzada, and D. E. Clark. 2013. "Responding Effectively to Composition Students: Comparing Student Perceptions of Written and Audio Feedback." *Journal on Excellence in College Teaching* 24 (1): 47–83.

Birch, Barbara M. 2008. *English L2 Reading: Getting to the Bottom* (2nd ed.). New York: Routledge.

Black, Laurel Johnson. 1998. *Between Talk and Teaching: Reconsidering the Writing Conference.* Logan: Utah State University Press.

Blair, Kristine. 2015. "Teaching Multimodal Assignments in OWI Contexts." In Hewett and DePew, 2015.

Breuch, Lee-Ann Kastner. 2015. "Faculty Preparation for OWI." In Hewett and DePew, 2015.

Britton, Bruce K., and Sami Gülgöz. 1991. "Using Kintsch's Computational Model to Improve Instructional Text: Effects of Repairing Inference Calls on Recall and Cognitive Structures." *Journal of Educational Psychology* 83 (3): 329–45.

Bruffee, Kenneth A. 1984. "Collaborative Learning and the 'Conversation of Mankind.'" *College English* 46 (November): 635–53.

———. 1993. *Collaborative Learning: Higher Education, Interdependence, and the Authority of Knowledge* (2nd ed.). Baltimore: Johns Hopkins University Press.

Bunn, Michael. 2013. Motivation and Connection: Teaching Reading (and Writing) in the Composition Classroom. *College Composition and Communication* 63 (3): 496–516.

Burgstahler, Sherryl, and Rebecca Cory, eds. 2008. *Universal Design in Higher Education: From Principles to Practice.* Cambridge, MA: Harvard Educational Press.

Burnett, Bruce, and Alan Roberts. 2005. "Online Collaborative Assessment: Unpacking Process and Product." In *Assessing Online Learning*, edited by Patricia Comeaux, 55–71. Bolton, MA: Ankar Publishing.

Byerly, Greg, Jason Holmes, David Robins, Yin Zang, and Athena Salaba. 2006. "The 'Eyes' Have It—Eye-Tracking and Usability Study of SchoolRooms." *SchoolRooms* 1 (1). http://www.imakenews.com/sirsisr/e_article000666600.cfm?x =b8nT8bl,b60LLntw,w.

Cleary, Michelle Navarre. 2013. "Flowing and Freestyling: Learning from Adult Students about Process Knowledge Transfer." *College Composition & Communication* 64 (4): 661–87.

College Board. (2004). "Writing: A Ticket to Work . . . or a Ticket Out. A Survey of Business Leaders." Report of the National Commission on Writing for America's Families, Schools, and Colleges. http://www.collegeboard.com/prod_downloads /writingcom/writing-ticket-to-work.pdf.

Conference on College Composition and Communication (CCCC). 2009. *CCCC Statement on Second Language Writing and Writers.* http://www.ncte.org/cccc /resources/positions/secondlangwriting.

CCCC Committee for Effective Practices in Online Writing Instruction. 2013. *A Position Statement of Principles and Example Effective Practices for Online Writing Instruction.* http://www.ncte.org/cccc/resources/positions/owiprinciples.

CCCC OWI Committee for Effective Practices in Online Writing Instruction. 2011. *The State of the Art of OWI.* http://www.ncte.org/library/NCTEFiles/Groups /CCCC/Committees/OWI_State-of-Art_Report_April_2011.pdf.

CCCC Committee for Principles and Standards for the Postsecondary Teaching of Writing. 1989. *Statement of Principles and Standards for the Postsecondary Teaching of Writing.* http://www.ncte.org/cccc/resources/positions/postsecondary writing.

Connors, R. J., and A. Lunsford. 1993. "Teachers' Rhetorical Comments on Student Papers." *College Composition and Communication* 44 (2): 200–23. doi:10.2307/358839.

Council of Writing Program Administrators, National Council of Teachers of English, and the National Writing Project. 2011. *Framework for Success in Postsecondary Writing.* http://wpacouncil.org/framework.

Davidson, Cathy N. 2012. *Now You See It: How the Brain Science of Attention Will Transform the Way We Live, Work, and Learn.* New York: Penguin.

DePew, Kevin Eric. 2015. "Preparing for the Rhetoricity of OWI Technologies." In Hewett and DePew, 2015.

Dunn, Patricia. 1995. *Learning Re-Abled: The Learning Disability Controversy and Composition Studies.* Portsmouth, NH: Heinemann.

Elbow, Peter. 1993. "Ranking, Evaluating, and Liking: Sorting Out Three Forms of Judgment." *College English* 55 (2): 187. doi:10.2307/378503.

Ferris, Dana. 2003. *Response to Student Writing: Implications for Second Language Students.* Mahwah, NJ: Erlbaum.

Fleischer, Cathy. 2010. *Reading & Writing & Teens: A Parent's Guide to Adolescent Literacy.* Champaign, IL: NCTE.

Fredrick, Terri. 2009. "Rethinking Evaluation: Using Computer Reviewing Tools to Talk with Students about Their Writing." In *Writing and the iGeneration: Composition in the Computer-Mediated Classroom*, edited by G. Carter and M. A. Clayton, 121–40. Southlake, TX: Fountainhead.

Freedman, Sarah, and Melanie Sperling. 1985. "Written Language Acquisition: The Role of Response and the Writing Conference." In *Acquisition of Written Language: Response and Revision*, edited by S. Freeman, 106–30. Norwood, NJ: Ablex.

Glover, C., and E. Brown. 2006. "Written Feedback for Students: Too Much, Too Detailed, or Too Incomprehensible to Be Effective?" *Bioscience Education E-Journal* 7 (3). http://www.bioscience.heacademy.ac.uk/journal/vol7/beej-7-3.aspx.

Gos, Michael. 2015. "Nontraditional Student Access to OWI." In Hewett and DePew, 2015.

Green, Katie R., Tershia Pinder-Grover, and Joanna Mirecki Millunchick. 2012. "Impact of Screencast Technology: Connecting the Perception of Usefulness and the Reality of Performance." *Journal of Engineering Education* 101 (4): 717–37.

Griffin, June, and Deborah Minter. 2013. "The Rise of the Online Writing Classroom: Reflecting on the Material Conditions of College Composition Teaching." *College Composition and Communication* 65 (1): 140–61.

Haas, Christina. 1996. *Writing Technology: Studies on the Materiality of Literacy.* Mahwah, NJ: Erlbaum.

Haswell, Richard. 1983. "Minimal Marking." *College English* 45 (6): 600–4. doi:10.2307/377147.

———. 2006. "The Complexities of Responding to Student Writing; or, Looking for Shortcuts via the Road of Excess." *Across the Disciplines: A Journal of Language, Learning, and Academic Writing* 3. http://wac.colostate.edu/atd/articles/haswell2006.cfm.

Henning, Teresa. 2012. "Writing Professor as Adult Learner: An Autoethnography of Online Professional Development." *Journal of Asynchronous Learning Networks* 16 (2): 9–26.

Hewett, Beth L. 2004–2005. "Asynchronous Online Instructional Commentary: A Study of Student Revision." *Readerly/Writerly Texts: Essays in Literary, Composition, and Pedagogical Theory* (Double Issue) 11 & 12 (1 & 2): 47–67.

———. 2006. "Synchronous Online Conference-Cased Instruction: A Study of Whiteboard Interactions and Student Writing." *Computers and Composition* 23 (1): 4–31.

———. 2010. "From Topic to Presentation: Making Choices to Develop Your Writing." In *Writing Spaces: Readings on Writing*, Volume 1. edited by Charles Lowe and Pavel Zemliansky, 59–81. West Lafayette, IN: Parlor Press.

———. 2011. *Instructor's Study Guide for the Online Writing Conference: A Guide for Teachers and Tutors*. Portsmouth, NH: Heinemann.

———. 2015. *The Online Writing Conference: A Guide for Teachers and Tutors*. Boston, MA: Bedford/St. Martin's.

———. 2015. "Grounding Principles of OWI." In Hewett and DePew, 2015.

Hewett, Beth L., and Kevin DePew, eds. 2015. *Foundational Practices in Online Writing Instruction*. Perspectives on Writing. Fort Collins, CO: The WAC Clearinghouse and Parlor Press. Available at http://wac.colostate.edu/books/owi/.

Hewett, Beth L., and Christa Ehmann. 2004. *Preparing Educators for Online Writing Instruction: Principles and Processes*. Urbana, IL: NCTE.

Hewett, Beth L., and Russell J. Hewett. 2008. "IM Talking about Workplace Literacy." In *Handbook of Research on Virtual Workplaces and the New Nature of Business Practices*, edited by Kirk St. Amant and Pavel Zemliansky, 455–72. New York: Information Science Reference.

Hewett, Beth L., and Charlotte Robidoux. 2010. *Collaborative Writing in Virtual Workplaces: Computer-Mediated Communication Technologies and Tools*. Hershey, PA: IGI Global.

Hirvela, Alan. 2005. "Computer-Based Reading and Writing Across the Curriculum: Two Case Studies of L2 Writers." *Computers and Composition* 22: 337–56.

Horning, Alice S. 1978. "The Connection of Writing to Reading: A Gloss on the Gospel of Mina Shaughnessy." *College English* 40 (3): 264–68.

Howard, Jennifer. 2012. "The Digital World Demands a New Mode of Reading." *The Chronicle of Higher Education*, August 5. http://chronicle.com/article/The-Digital-World-Demands-a/133289/.

Howard, Rebecca Moore. 2001. "Collaborative Pedagogy." In *A Guide to Composition Pedagogies*, edited by Gary Tate, Amy Rupiper, and Kurt Schick, 54–70. New York: Oxford University Press.

Howard, Rebecca Moore, Tricia Serviss, and Tanya K. Rodrigue. 2010. "Writing from Sources, Writing from Sentences." *Writing Program Administrators* 2 (2): 177–92. doi:10.1558/wap.v2i2.177.

Jacobs, Frederic, and Stephen P. Hundley. 2010. *Understanding and Supporting Adult Learners: A Guide for Colleges and Universities*. San Francisco: Jossey-Bass.

Johnson, David W., Johnson, Roger T., and Holubec, Edythe Johnson. 1993. *Circles of Learning: Cooperation in the Classroom*. Edina, MN: Interaction Book Company.

Jukes, Ian, Ted McCain, and Lee Crockett. 2010. *Understanding the Digital Generation: Teaching and Learning in the New Digital Landscape*. Kelowna, British Columbia: 21st Century Fluency Project.

Kinneavy, James. 1971. *A Theory of Discourse*. New York: Norton.

Kintsch, Walter, and T. A. van Dijk. 1978. "Toward a Model of Text Comprehension and Production." *Psychological Review* 85: 363–94.

Knoblauch, Cy H., and Lillian Brannon. 1984. "Responding to Texts: Facilitating Revision in the Writing Workshop." In *Key Works on Teacher Response: An Anthology*, edited by R. Straub, 296–327. Portsmouth, NH: Heinemann/Boynton Cook.

Knowles, Malcolm S., Elwood F. Holton III, and Richard A. Swanson. 1998. *The Adult Learner: The Definitive Classic in Adult Education and Human Resource Development* (5th ed.). Houston, TX: Gulf Publishing.

Kuo, Chia-Ling, Hongbo Song, Renee Smith, and Teresa Franklin. 2007. "A Comparative Study of the Effectiveness of an Online and Face-to-Face Technology Applications Course in Teacher Education." *International Journal of Technology in Teaching and Learning* 3 (2): 85–94.

Kuo, Yu-Chun, Andrew E. Walker, Brian R. Belland, and Kerstin E. E. Schroder. 2013. "A Predictive Study of Student Satisfaction in Online Education Programs." *The International Review of Research in Open and Distance Learning* 14 (1). http://www.irrodl.org/index.php/irrodl/article/view/1338/2416.

Lang, James. 2012. "The Benefits of Making It Harder to Learn." *The Chronicle of Higher Education*, June 3. http://chronicle.com/article/The-Benefits-of-Making-It/132056/.

Landergan, Katherine. (January 29, 2013). "Harvard Professors Write Clear Collaboration Policies for New Semester After Cheating Scandal." *Boston.com*. http://www.boston.com/yourcampus/news/harvard/2013/01/harvard_professors_write_clear_collaboration_policies_for_new_semester.html

Levine, Arthur, and Diane R. Dean. 2012. *Generation on a Tightrope: A Portrait of Today's College Student*. San Francisco: Jossey-Bass.

Lewis, Lesle, and Peg Alden. 2007. "What We Can Learn about Writing Blocks from College Students with Output Problems, Strong Writing Skills, and Attentional Difficulties." *Journal of Teaching Writing* 23 (1): 115–46. http://journals.iupui.edu/index.php/teachingwriting/article/view/1360/1309.

Lunsford, Andrea A., and Lisa Ede. 2012. *Writing Together: Collaboration in Theory and Practice*. Boston: Bedford/St. Martin's.

Maclellan, Effie. 1997. "Reading to Learn." *Studies in Higher Education* 22 (3): 277–88.

Markel, Mike. 2012. *Technical Communication* (10th ed.). Boston: Bedford/St. Martin's.

Marshak, Robert. 1983. "What's Between Pedagogy and Andragogy? *Training and Development Journal* (October): 80–81.

Mayo, Lori. 2000. "Making the Connection: Reading and Writing Together." *English Journal* (March): 74–77.

McGregor, Tanny. 2007. *Comprehension Connections: Bridges to Strategic Reading*. Portsmouth, NH: Heinemann.

Medina, John. 2008. *Brain Rules: 12 Principles for Surviving and Thriving at Work, Home, and School*. Seattle, WA: Pear Press.

Miller-Cochran, Susan. 2015. "Multilingual Writers and OWI." In Hewett and DePew, 2015.

Moffett, James. 1983. *Teaching the Universe of Discourse*. Portsmouth, NH: Boynton-Cook.

Moore, N., & M. Filling. 2012. "iFeedback: Using Video Technology for Improving Student Writing." *Journal of College Literacy and Learning* 38: 3–14.

Nathan, Rebekah. 2005. *My Freshman Year: What a Professor Learned by Becoming a Student.* Ithaca, NY: Cornell University Press.

Oswal, Sushil. 2015. "Physical and Learning Disabilities in OWI." In Hewett and DePew, 2015.

Oswal, Sushil, and Beth L. Hewett. 2013. "Accessibility Challenges for Visually Impaired Students and Their Online Writing Instructors." In *Rhetorical Accessibility: At the Intersection of Technical Education and Disability Studies,* edited by Lisa Meloncon, 135–55. Amityville, NY: Baywood.

Prensky, Marc. 2001. "Digital Natives, Digital Immigrants." *On the Horizon* 9 (5). Accessed May 29, 2007. www.marcprensky.com/writing/Prensky%20-%20Digital%20Natives,%20Digital%20Immigrants%20-%20Part1.pdf.

Pusser, Brian, et al. 2007. *Returning to Learning: Adults' Success in College Is Key to America's Future.* Lumina Foundation for Education. New Agenda Series. http://www.luminafoundation.org/publications/ReturntolearningApril2007.pdf.

Rodrigo, Rochelle. 2015. "OWI on the Go." In Hewett and DePew, 2015.

Rose, Mike. 2012. "The Missing Element in Student Success. *Inside Higher Ed,* September 7. http://www.insidehighered.com/advice/2012/09/07/advice-using-classroom-teaching-enhance-student-success-essay.

Rosin, Hanna. 2013. "The Touch-Screen Generation." http://www.theatlantic.com/magazine/archive/2013/04/the-touch-screen-generation/309250/?single_page=true.

Ross-Gordon, Jovita M. 2011. "Research on Adult Learners: Supporting the Needs of a Student Population That Is No Longer Nontraditional." *Peer Review* 13 (1). http://www.aacu.org/peerreview/pr-wi11/prwi11_rossgordon.cfm.

Salvatori, Mariolina Rizzi, and Patricia Donahue. 2012. "What Is College English? Stories about Reading: Appearance, Disappearance, Morphing, and Revival." *College English* 75 (2): 199–217.

Sapp, David Alan, and James Simon. 2005. "Comparing Grades in Online and Face-to-Face Writing Courses: Interpersonal Accountability and Institutional Commitment." *Computers and Composition* 22: 471–89.

Scrocco, D. L. A. 2012. "Do You Care to Add Something? Articulating the Student Interlocutor's Voice in Writing Response Dialogue." *Teaching English in the Two-Year College* 39 (3): 274–92.

Selfe, Cynthia L., and Gail E. Hawisher, eds. 2007. *Gaming Lives in the Twenty-First Century: Literate Connections.* New York: Palgrave Macmillan.

Sipple, S. 2007. Ideas in Practice: Developmental Writers' Attitudes toward Audio and Written Feedback." *Journal of Developmental Education* 30 (3): 22–31.

Sipple, S., and J. Sommers. 2005. *Research on Student Preferences. A Heterotopic Space: Digitized Audio Commentary and Student Revisions.* Accessed April 24, 2013. http://www.users.muohio.edu/sommerjd/research.htm.

Small, Gary, and Gigi Vorgan. 2008. *iBrain: Surviving the Technological Alteration of the Modern Mind.* New York: HarperCollins.

Smith, Michael, and Jeffrey D. Wilhelm. 2002. *Reading Don't Fix No Chevys: Literacy in the Lives of Young Men.* Portsmouth, NH: Heinemann.

Sommers, Jeff. 2012. "Response Rethought . . . Again: Exploring Recorded Comments and the Teacher-Student Bond." *Journal of Writing Assessment* 5 (1). http://www.journalofwritingassessment.org/article.php?article=59.

———. 2013. "Response 2.0: Commentary on Student Writing for the New Millennium." *Journal of College Literacy and Learning* 39: 21–37.

Sommers, Nancy. 1982. "Responding to Student Writing." *College Composition and Communication* 2: 148. doi:10.2307/357622.

Spiegelman, Candace. 1998. "Habits of Mind: Historical Configurations of Textual Ownership in Peer Writing Groups." *College Composition and Communication* 49 (2): 234–55.

———. 2000. *Across Property Lines: Textual Ownership in Writing Groups.* Carbondale: Southern Illinois University Press.

Stapleton, James L., H. Joseph Wen, Dave Starrett, and Michelle Kilburn. 2007. "Generational Differences in Using Online Learning Systems." *Human Systems Management* 26: 99–109.

Straub, R. 1996a. "Teacher Response as Conversation: More Than Casual Talk, an Exploration." *Rhetoric Review* 14 (2): 374–98. doi:10.2307/465862.

———. 1996b. "The Concept of Control in Teacher Response: Defining the Varieties of 'Directive' and 'Facilitative' Commentary." *College Composition and Communication* 47 (2): 223–51.

———. 2000. *The Practice of Response: Strategies for Commenting on Student Writing.* Cresskill, NJ: Hampton.

Street, Hannah. 2010. "Factors Influencing a Learner's Decision to Drop-Out or Persist in Higher Education Distance Learning. *Online Journal of Distance Learning Administration* XIII (IV). http://www.westga.edu/~distance/ojdla/winter134/street134.html.

Thurlow, Crispin, and Susan McKay. 2003. "Profiling 'New' Communication Technologies in Adolescence." *Journal of Language and Social Psychology* 22 (94). doi:10.1177/0261927X02250060.

Turkle, Sherry. 2012. "Connected but Alone?" Transcript. http://www.ted.com/talks/sherry_turkle_alone_together/transcript?language=en.

U.S. Department of Education, National Center for Education Statistics. 2013. *The Condition of Education 2013* (NCES 2013-037), Institutional Retention and Graduation Rates for Undergraduate Students. http://nces.ed.gov/pubs2013/2013037.pdf.

Warnock, Scott. 2008. "Responding to Student Writing with Audio-Visual Feedback." In *Writing and the iGeneration: Composition in the Computer-Mediated Classroom,* edited by Terry Carter and Maria A. Clayton, 201–27. Southlake, TX: Fountainhead.

———. 2009. *Teaching Writing Online: How & Why.* Urbana-Champaign, IL: NCTE.

———. 2015. "Teaching an OWI Course." In Hewett and DePew, 2015.

Warnock, Scott, Kenneth Bingham, Dan Driscoll, Jennifer Fromal, and Nicholas Rouse. 2012. "Early Participation in Asynchronous Writing Environments and Course Success." *Journal of Asynchronous Learning Networks* 16 (1): 35–47.

Wisconsin Educational Communications Board. n.d. *Into the Book.* Wisconsin Public Television and the Agency for Instructional Technology. http://reading.ecb.org/teacher/questioning/index.html.

Wolf, Maryanne. 2007. *Proust and the Squid: The Story and Science of the Reading Brain.* New York: HarperCollins.

Wolfe, Joanna. 2010. *Team Writing: A Guide to Working in Groups.* Boston: Bedford/St. Martin's.

Wolfe, Tom. 2012. "Hooking Up." In *The Writer's Presence: A Pool of Readings* (7th ed.), edited by Donald McQuade and Robert Atwan, 617–25. Boston: Bedford/St. Martin's.

Xu, Di, and Shanna Smith Jaggars. 2013. "Adaptability to Online Learning: Differences across Types of Students and Academic Subject Areas." CCRC Working Paper No. 54. Teacher's College Columbia University.

Yoon, Sung-Eui, Enrico Gobbetti, David Kasik, and Dinesh Manocha. 2008. *Real-Time Massive Model Rendering.* San Rafael, CA: Morgan & Claypool.

Zengotita, Thomas de. 2013. "American Idol Worship." In *40 Model Essays: A Portable Anthology* (2nd ed.), edited by Jane E. Aaron and Ellen Kuhl Repetto, 134–36. Boston: Bedford/St. Martin's.

Vygotsky, Lev. 1962. *Thought and Language.* Boston: MIT Press.

Index